That Workshop Book

That Workshop Book

SAMANTHA BENNETT ★ foreword by Cris Tovani
illustrations by Anna Loring

HEINEMANN   Portsmouth, NH

Heinemann
361 Hanover Street
Portsmouth, NH 03801–3912
www.heinemann.com

Offices and agents throughout the world

The author and publisher wish to thank those who have generously given permission to reprint borrowed material:

Figure 2.2: "Barred Owl" from *Smithsonian Handbooks: Birds of North America—Western Region* by Fred J. Alsop III. Copyright © 2001 DK Publishing. Reprinted by permission of DK Publishing. All rights reserved. www.dk.com

Cover image from *Changing Place: A Kid's View of Shelter Living* by Margie Chalofsky, Glen Finland, and Judy Wallace. Copyright © 1992. Reprinted with permission from Gryphon House, P.O. Box 207, Beltsville, MD 20704-0207. (800) 638-0928, www.ghbooks.com.

Cover image from *The Best Part of Me: Children Talk About Their Bodies in Pictures and Words* by Wendy Ewald and M. Tingley. Copyright © 2002. Published by Little, Brown Books for Young Readers. Reprinted with permission of Hachette Book Group, USA.

Library of Congress Cataloging-in-Publication Data
Bennett, Samantha.
    That workshop book : new systems and structures for classrooms that read, write, and think / Samantha Bennett ; foreword by Cris Tovani ; illustrations by Anna Loring.
        p. cm.
    Includes index.
    ISBN-13: 978-0-325-01192-9
    ISBN-10: 0-325-01192-3
    1. Language arts. 2. English language—Composition and exercises—Study and teaching. 3. Lesson planning. I. Loring, Anna. II. Title.
    LB1576.B46 2007
    372.6—dc22   2007027312

Editor: Harvey Daniels
Production editor: Sonja S. Chapman
Cover design: Monte Mead
Interior design: Cat & Mouse
Cover and interior illustrations: Anna Loring
Compositor: Tom Allen
Manufacturing: Steve Bernier

Printed in the United States of America on acid-free paper
18 17 16 15   VP   7 8 9 10

For making me laugh.
For keeping me grounded.
For cheering me on.
For being what matters most.
For you.

About the Illustrator

Anna Loring is an artist and art teacher at the Rocky Mountain School of Expeditionary Learning in Denver, Colorado. She specializes in printmaking, painting, illustration, collage, and basically, making everything she touches more interesting and beautiful. She used drawing and collage for the illustrations in this book and added a little paint, pastel, and lots of love for the cover image.

Contents

Listen in on a readers workshop and read work produced in a writers workshop as students read and write to uncover answers to the question "What makes a bird a bird?"

Systems, Structures, Rituals, and Routines Highlighted:

- ★ Building Classroom Community
- ★ Writing Folders and Writing Files
- ★ Portfolio Assessment
- ★ Conferring

Listen in on book groups in a readers workshop and read work produced in a writers workshop as students read, write, and talk to understand the complex reasons families become homeless, the support they need, and how students can show empathy.

Systems, Structures, Rituals, and Routines Highlighted:

- ★ Doing Your Own Assignments
- ★ Academic Journals
- ★ Anchor Charts
- ★ Using a Mentor Text for Writer's Craft and Product Design
- ★ Book Groups

★ CHAPTER FOUR ★

Jen's Readers 77

Listen in on a readers workshop designed to help make the invisible processes of reading comprehension more visible in students' reader's notebooks.

Systems, Structures, Rituals, and Routines Highlighted:

- ★ Reader's Notebooks
- ★ Portfolio Assessment
- ★ Conferring
- ★ Read-Aloud Time

★ CHAPTER FIVE ★

Ali's Writers 109

Listen in on a writers workshop as students read, write, look, think, confer, relook, rethink, and revise their writing about their best body parts.

Systems, Structures, Rituals, and Routines Highlighted:

- ★ Using a Mentor Text for Writer's Craft and Project Design
- ★ Teacher Write-Aloud
- ★ Anchor Charts
- ★ Conferring
- ★ Peer Feedback

★ CHAPTER SIX ★

Josh's Memorialists 139

Listen in on a humanities workshop as students participate in a Socratic seminar to try to deepen their thinking about justice, revenge, and the politics of memory in order to design a memorial for the Sand Creek Massacre.

Systems, Structures, Rituals, and Routines Highlighted:

★ Doing Your Own Assignments
★ Using a Real-World Model/Mentor Text for Writer's Craft and Project Design
★ Using an Academic Journal to Track Changes in Student Thinking Over Time
★ Socratic Seminar
★ Criteria Lists and Rubrics

★ CHAPTER SEVEN ★

Jenn's Citizens 173

Listen in on a humanities workshop as small groups discuss the Fourth Amendment of the Constitution and write to both build and demonstrate understanding about the question "How can I access power in our democracy?"

Systems, Structures, Rituals, and Routines Highlighted:

★ Small-Group Discussions
★ Teacher Think-Aloud
★ Writing to Build Understanding
★ Writing to Demonstrate Understanding

★ CHAPTER EIGHT ★

Take Flight 205

Foreword

Before reading this book, I was pretty sure that I knew how to plan for and meet the needs of most of my students. I was relatively confident that I had *it* figured out. When asked to read the manuscript of *That Workshop Book* by Sam Bennett, I didn't anticipate how blown away I'd be by the thinking it held. I was struck by how much I didn't know. I expected to read each chapter and nod my head and say, "Yep, I do that," and "Yes, that is something I've done for years." Instead, I wrote margin notes, recorded ideas to try on Monday, and became once again hopeful that I could inspire my second hour of struggling readers. I jotted down questions about planning and final products—I couldn't wait to talk to colleagues about the ideas I had read. I was struck by how much I still had to learn. Oddly, it was comforting. Knowing that I wasn't there yet felt invigorating. I had been challenged to dive back in and do better. But this time, I didn't feel alone. In this book, I had found a coach.

Good instructional coaching is about support. Often the unsung heroes, coaches have the opportunity to leave their mark on the world with every person they train, inspire, and mentor. They help teachers shake off the dust, pull up their bootstraps, and have another go. After twenty-three years of experience, I've learned that athletics and teaching have a lot in common. Wasn't it Yogi Berra who said, "If you don't know where you are headed, you might not get there"? Was he talking about baseball or unit design? In athletics, the best players have coaches who inspire, instruct, and encourage. It makes sense that teachers should have good coaching as well.

A good coach pushes but not too hard. She listens but not with an agenda, serving as a sounding board and mirror. She builds confidence and is a partner in fearless risk taking by showing and not just telling. Yes, I'm lucky. I get to work alongside Sam on a regular basis. However, readers of this book are lucky, too, because inside they will find Sam's words resonating with passion and joyful teaching. You, too, can have Sam as your coach by simply opening up this book.

That Workshop Book will surely be a groundbreaking text. Innovation and best practices permeate the pages. You'll hear Sam's voice naming thinking and nudging instructional change. She'll make you want to investigate your teaching beliefs and notice how they are reflected in your instructional practice. Sam's coaching packs a powerful punch, always refocusing us back upon authentic learning and real-world instruction. For teachers who feel alone with the challenges they face, this is the book for you. For instructional coaches who are stuck and unsure where to lead, this book will show the way. It will help you work through the tricky parts, negotiate the roadblocks, and think through to the future.

I need this book and I think you will, too.

—Cris Tovani

Acknowledgments

My friend Leanna and I were sitting on the beach in Mexico (that is a funny story in itself, but I'll save it for next time), and the topic of writing the acknowledgments for this book came up. Here is a script of our conversation:

L: Make it short and sweet. Five to ten people, tops.

S: Are you crazy? I may never get the chance to do this again. I want to thank my dead dog for licking my face the first three days of my first year of teaching, when all I could do was sob for hours on end.

L: No way. If you try to thank everybody, you'll forget somebody and you'll feel horrible. It's like trying to have a big wedding.

S: I've never been the kind of person to invite ten people to a private beach ceremony. I'm going big.

L: OK, but you're going to forget someone.

S: I've got an idea, . . . trust me. It'll work. I'll cover all the bases, but I have so many people to thank! I'm going back . . . waaaaaaaaaay back. [See the end for my brilliant plan.]

End of script. Beginning of acknowledgments.

First, thanks to the Queen of Unconditional Love, my mom, Sharon Lundgren, who has been telling anyone who would listen (sorry to the clerks at King Soopers) that her daughter has been reading since she was three months old and is now writing a book. Since I was in your belly, you've been filling my ears with wonderful words from books and even wonderfuller words of love and encouragement. You taught me to honor my teachers—a core belief that still guides my thoughts and actions every day. Thank you. I love you.

Thanks to my editor, El Diablo, otherwise known as the incomparable Harvey Daniels. There was never a more perfect foil for my bluster.

When I was late with the first chapter and wrote, "I need some more time. I figured out a way to make it not so dry and preachy," you responded with, "No rush on the sermon. 'Juiceless and preachy!', I can read the reviews now!" What more could a first-time author ask for? Truly Smokey, you are my hero. Thanks for the fun and the funny. Maybe we can even meet someday?

Thanks to Cris Tovani, the Dorothy to my Toto. Spending the past six years in your classroom has been a master seminar on how to honor student thinking and save students' lives through literacy. Thank you for leading by example. Your influence is visible on every page of this book.

Thank you to my teaching partners throughout the years. Each of you has made my brain grow bigger, my heart grow stronger, and my spirit grow more courageous:

★ Colleen O'Brien, since we were sixteen years old, I have been in awe of your leadership, your deep concern for others, and your passion to act on that concern and squeeze in one more good deed each day. Thank you for the periodic reality checks and reminders to focus on what matters most. Your service to others and dedication to giving children access to power inspires me daily. I promise I will go door-to-door when the time comes. Governor 2010?

★ Reny Sieck, you taught me to ask students to do important things and make sure they were performing, literally. Our laughter still rings in my ears.

★ Jud Kempson, you were the first to open my eyes to professional, collegial learning. From the Diversity Study Group, to *Best Practice*, to *In the Middle*, all of this began with you (and Therese, Tony, Nicolle, Daisy, and Terry, too). I love you and miss you every day.

★ Vicki Casella, you set the bar high and I learned to jump higher because you expected me to. You were the first to ask me to share my thinking with other teachers and you always gave me more responsibility than I could handle and said, "Handle it." Your example has greatly influenced my life. I love you.

★ Marjorie Larner, you taught me how to really listen and to label what I heard. You, too, are on each page of this book.

★ Brooke O'Drobinak, I miss our weekly commute, discussing and debating the state of education and how to help schools be great places for children and adults by helping teachers one-by-one. Thank you for being the zookeeper when I was the elephant in the room and for your lifelong friendship. Your insight, love, and careful attention have had a profound influence on my beliefs and practice.

★ Beth Dorman, your brilliance and visionary leadership are a constant source of light on the horizon for students and teachers. Thank you for your attention to rigorous thinking and for taking the time to make me a better writer.

★ Leanna Harris (Yin), you make me slow down, look, listen, and learn. You broaden my perspective and show me shades of gray and you are (almost) always right. I feel so lucky and so honored to have been your partner and so happy that we are married to the same man. Over humus or sand, you make me a better adult.

Thanks to my colleagues at the Public Education and Business Coalition Think Tank Extraordinaire. When you hang around with people who are writing books, you start to think you can do it too. To the teacher–researcher–staff developer–reader-writer-thinker–Brilliant Ones of the PEBC who started all the amazingness, and have continued through three generations of research and writing—Ellin Oliver Keene, Susan Zimmermann, Steph Harvey, Anne Goudvis, Cris Tovani, Debbie Miller, Marjorie Larner, Chryse Hutchins, Lori Conrad, and Dianne Sweeney—your reach is far, wide, and incredibly powerful. Suzanne Plaut, thanks for the original spark and belief that I had something to share. Rosann Ward, thanks for the leadership and the constant offers of support. Judy Hendricks, thanks for everything. Current PEBC Teachers and Staff Developers—keep writing!

Thanks to my favorite teachers from childhood who showered me with love above all else: Joy Powell and Peg Lindenmeyer. Until my junior year of high school, I was going to be the millionaire CEO of some sort of business. Because of the best high school social studies teachers in the world—Jim Bond, Ed Ellis, and Eric Coble—I decided to be a teacher instead. Thanks.

Leadership is a tricky business. There are three school leaders for whom I would do anything, no questions asked (OK, maybe just a few): Lynette Porteous, Dianne Talarico, and Jim McDermott. Thank you for putting students first, honoring teachers, and being the chief learners in your schools and districts.

Thank you to my RMSEL colleagues. You make me jump out of bed every day with a smile on my face and a spring in my step. I feel so fortunate to work alongside the smartest, most dedicated, most talented learners on the planet. Thank you for growing the school of our dreams each day.

Thank you to the teachers who allowed me to shine a bright light on their practice:

* ★ Peter Thulson, my favorite poet on the planet, you were the first to tell me that I could actually write. Thank you for your influence on my teaching, my limericks, and my life. What I want more than anything is to read your book next. Get writing.

* ★ Katie Shenk—beauty, hilarity, and brilliance in one amazing package. Will you marry me? Any day I need to be inspired, I just step into your room and soak it all in. Thank you for being a constant model of endless possibilities for children.

* ★ Jen Wood, thank you for being a role model of perfection in our midst, for staying up late to share one more brilliant quote from your students, for recommending inappropriate books, and for reminding me that the shoes make the outfit.

* ★ Ali Morgan, thank you for your attention to making beautiful things, for inspiring your colleagues, for taking the risk to join us, for forgiving me when I push too hard or make no sense, and for the countless hours thinking about how to help your students learn more, do more, and be more.

* ★ Josh Feiger, as my former student and one of my favorite teachers in the world, you have a huge chunk of my heart. Thank you for *always* being right and advocating for students above all else. You helped me get unstuck at each phase of this book—thank you for being my teacher. Does this get me any points?

* ★ Jenn Brauner, I truly couldn't be more proud or more awed by your work with adolescents. Thank you for your dedication to depth, excellence, and creating better adults.

If I could capture the moon, I would give it to my favorite art teacher–illustrator, Anna Loring. Everything you touch explodes with sparkling light. Thank you for bringing the Teaching Fairy to life (twice), for translating the essence of childhood and learning-filled classrooms to each chapter illustration, and for your daily work helping children create beautiful, breathtaking art. All I can say is, "What the . . . ?" LBJ has a cute little dimpled grin on his face, I'm sure.

To the incredible teachers I planned to write about but ran out of room: Colleen O'Brien, Katey Edson, Judy Racine, Laurie Wretling, Sarah Bayer, Steve Jenkins, Maggie Smiley, Anne Thulson, Jeff Cazier, Angie Zehner, and Cris Tovani. Thank you for helping students think hard, do the work, and be invested in this wonderful world every day. I am so thankful for your thinking and leadership.

Thank you to the brilliant minds at Expeditionary Learning Schools, especially Gretchen Morgan, Scott Dolquist, Ron Berger, and Greg Farrell. I hope this book is a tribute to your vision.

Thank you to my CFG: Heidi Barker, Linda Erickson, Stevi Quate, Deana Sands, and Nancy Shanklin. Our conversations have filled me with the energy to teach, to help, and to keep advocating for students and teachers. Thank you for reading drafts and helping me think it all through.

Thank you to Susan Tamulonis and Elizabeth Spruill for their copy editing and help compiling permissions. You saved me!

Thank you to TPP Cohorts 4 and 5: Josh, Liza, Mike, Brooke, Mo, Hana, Ty, BethAnn, Jenn, Katey, Naomi, and Natalie. You taught me how to be a teacher again and reminded me that I had lots to give but more to get. I've never had a better job in my whole life. Thank you for standing up for what matters most in schools and classrooms and always practicing. I love you.

A special thanks to Jenny Lyon for loving and caring for my boys while I kept one foot in the doors of schools. Thank you to the Nan-Man, Evan Duggan, for teaching my children "Through the Green Glass Door," how to stay alive in the pool, how to make crystals, and the scientific names for insects while I was writing. They won't want me back next summer!

Thanks to the best tale-spinners I know, the Charms—Colleen, Tommi, Sheila, and RuthAnne—for honing my storytelling craft over the past twenty years. Laughing with you and trying desperately to make you guffaw has been a highlight of my life and is the foundation of the stories in this book.

Thanks to my families, the Lundgrens, the Rachbachs, and the Bennetts for pitching in with Bennett-boy care, showing an interest, and being proud.

Thank you to Jonna Mulqueen, cheerleader extraordinaire and role model for the perfect mother. Thanks for your honesty and dedication to making the world better than you found it. I want to help create schools that deserve Lily, Chloe, and Violet.

Thanks to Augie, Theo, and Charlie for being blindingly beautiful rays of sunshine and good guys who take care each day. To the moon and back, My Loves.

Thanks to Mo for, well, for, ummm, for . . . yeah, you know. Thanks for carefully reading my drafts late at night—telling me what was boring, what was too much, what was kind of funny, and what was just right. Thank you for making time. Thank you for 51 percent. Thank you for making happy children. Thank you for making my belly shake with laughter. Thank you for 33 in 30. Thank you for dancing. Thank you for sushi and movies. Thank you for sharing me. Thank you for hoarding me. Thank you for making me feel lucky every minute of every day. I love you more.

The bummer about the big-wedding process is that inevitably, you forget to invite your mother's second cousin. If I've forgotten to thank you and you have been a really important influence on my life as an educator or writer, please fill your name in here:

Thank you, _____. You are the best.

Thank you, _____. You are so smart.

Thank you, _____. I owe it all to you.

Love,
Sam

CHAPTER ONE

Why Workshop?

What does it look like when students are doing the *work* of thinking? The *work* of learning? The *work* of achieving? The *work* of becoming better human beings? Literally and metaphorically, it looks like a *workshop,* a place where *works*—concrete demonstrations of understanding—are created.

The classroom as workshop has been around for a lucky generation of learners. The classrooms and children that Donald Graves first wrote about in his landmark study *Writing: Teachers and Children at Work* (1983) showed that with thoughtful planning, whole chunks of the school day could be turned over to children to do the work of learning to write by writing. In the preface, Graves writes, "Teaching and writing are highly complex acts. For this reason, the book will not present 1-2-3-4, step-by-step teaching methods. Rather it will introduce *help in the context of everyday teaching* that fosters children's writing fluency" (1983, v, emphasis added).

My, how far we've come. Or have we? What began as stories of classroom practice with student work, talk, and thinking shining brightly lately has devolved into a bureaucratic obsession with superficial practices for easier systemwide implementation. Workshop has been relegated to harsh time constraints, descriptions of activities to do in minilessons, or strict pacing guides that tell teachers how a workshop should unfold over the year. The problem is, with these cursory structures, the focus is *still* on what comes out of the mouths of teachers instead of what comes out of the mouths of students. We have a problem of broad implementation with shallow understanding of the potential of what a classroom as a *literal* workshop means. The superficial orthodoxy around the procedures of workshop has distracted us from the core values of *why* workshop works.

A workshop has it roots in learning from the dawn of human existence. Once one caveman learned to make fire, he *showed* the next caveman *how.* He didn't say, "I have fire. Now go make one." Throughout history, a workshop has been a physical *and* mental space to organize human learning. Think master and apprentice. Think making things.

Think transferring the skills and knowledge from one generation to the next through demonstration and the creation of products that have *use* in the world—products that help further the course of human progress.

The list of musts connected to workshop instruction have become longer than the original stories of *why*. The workshops of Donald Graves, Lucy Calkins, and Nancie Atwell revolved around some key ideas: student choice, student voice and ownership, student responsibility for learning, reading, writing, and thinking for big chunks of time, and building a community of learners. We need to get back to the whys of workshop to help students be the people we desperately want and need in the world—engaged citizens who are readers, writers, talkers, and thinkers. We've just begun to exploit the potential of the classroom as workshop. Let's get back to the whys in this age of standards-based education and high-stakes accountability. We need workshop now more than ever.

Introducing—next generation workshop.

What Happens Inside Workshop?

In their groundbreaking article about assessment *for* learning, "Inside the Black Box," Black and William write,

> *In terms of systems engineering, present policies in the U.S. and in many other countries seem to treat the classroom as a black box. Certain inputs from the outside—pupils, teachers, other resources, management rules and requirements, parental anxieties, standards, tests with high stakes, and so on—are fed into the box. Some outputs are supposed to follow: pupils who are more knowledgeable and competent, better test results, teachers who are reasonably satisfied, and so on. But what is happening inside the box? How can any one be sure that a particular set of new inputs will produce better outputs if we don't at least study what happens inside? (1998, 140, empasis added)*

What happens inside, indeed. What happens *inside* classrooms is the most intriguing, grueling, exhilarating, life-giving, energy-sapping, heart-breaking, joy-filled, complex, and intellectually demanding work in the world. In order to study what happens inside, we need classrooms with wide-open doors where we can gather together and listen closely to the words of students and their teachers. We must study the things that happen *between* the inputs and outputs. We must get back to Graves' context of *everyday teaching*—the daily systems, structures, routines, and rituals that help children become better readers, writers, problem solvers, and thinkers—truly, the better adults we need to engage in and lead our world.

That Workshop Book: New Systems and Structures for Classrooms That Read, Write, and Think presents stories from *inside* classrooms—classrooms with real students in real schools. Classrooms like yours.

These classrooms are places I want to linger all day because students are doing the work of learning. Students are reading, writing, talking, laughing, thinking, pausing, reading, figuring, and writing some more. The classroom walls are filled with their thinking, their drawings, their charts and graphs, their diagrams, their commentary. The working hum of these classrooms is the sound of happily, intensely engaged learners. I feel compelled to pull up a chair next to students in these classrooms and say, "Tell me what you are doing so I can do it too!"

There are many intertwining essentials to next generation workshop (a whole book's worth in fact!), but at the heart of it is one crucial concept: teaching as listening.

Teaching as Listening versus Teaching as Talking

Teaching requires careful listening, that is, paying close attention to those we are trying to teach. The teacher must be able to turn to her students to learn how to reach them. . . . Really good teachers know this. They can hear in a student's voice interest or understanding or fear, can see in a student's writing, drawing, and math notebook pages evidentiary traces of that student's thinking, like rabbit tracks in the snow.
(Fredrick Erickson in Schultz 2003, ix)

This book is filled with concrete examples of teachers listening to teach. Each day in these classrooms, students read, write, and talk about important content in order to learn *how* to read, write, talk, and develop their dispositions as thinkers. Teachers listen all along the way to students' writing, their conversations, their stories, and their questions. Teachers' literacy instruction, content knowledge building, and skill practice is based on what they hear from students. Instead of "What am I going to do tomorrow?" these teachers ask, "How do I know what my students know and are able to do?" and "How will I use what I learned about students today to help them learn more tomorrow?"

The question "How do I know what my students know and are able to do?" has the power not only to change how we spend our time as teachers but also to change the nature of schools. This question makes school about *learning* instead of about teaching. If a teacher is constantly pursuing the answers to "How do I know?" the school day builds around *what comes out of the mouths, pencils, and actions of students* instead of what comes out of the mouths of teachers. If "How do I know?" guides a teacher's daily practice, teachers can no longer say, "I taught it. It isn't my fault if they didn't get it."

The question "How do I know?" is filled with infinite possibility to change both students' and teachers' experiences of school. Teachers hear often that assessment should drive instruction. Unfortunately there aren't enough school leaders who can articulate what it means on a day-to-day, teaching moment–to–teaching moment basis. This is what assessment-driven instruction means to me: teachers and students are the ones who know best what students know and can do. Test scores and other formal assessments do tell us part of the picture, but it is far from a complete picture. We need to *increase our repertoire of ways we know* and begin to shout what we know from the rooftops of every school in this country.

My purpose is to help teachers articulate all the other ways, in addition to standardized test scores, that they know what students know and are able to do, as well as teach students to articulate it themselves. If we don't want to be judged solely by test scores, we had better start sharing, with each other, our students, and the outside world what we *do* know about students from spending our days with them. In 1996 the National Commission on Teaching and America's Future based their entire report on three simple premises. The first was, "What teachers know and can do is the most important influence on what students learn" (1996, 6). We matter most. Let's start proving why.

Teaching as a Persistent Pursuit

> *There's no such thing as the perfect lesson, the perfect day in school, or the perfect teacher. For teachers and students alike, the goal is not perfection but persistence in the pursuit of understanding important things. (Tomlinson and McTighe 2006, 56)*

That Workshop Book is about the constant, daily pursuit of understanding important things. All day long, the teachers featured here have structured classroom time to try to answer "How do I know?" and the other questions that stem from it embedded in the teaching *cycle* of assessment, planning, and instruction (see Figure 1.1).

✳ **Figure 1.1** Teaching as a Cycle

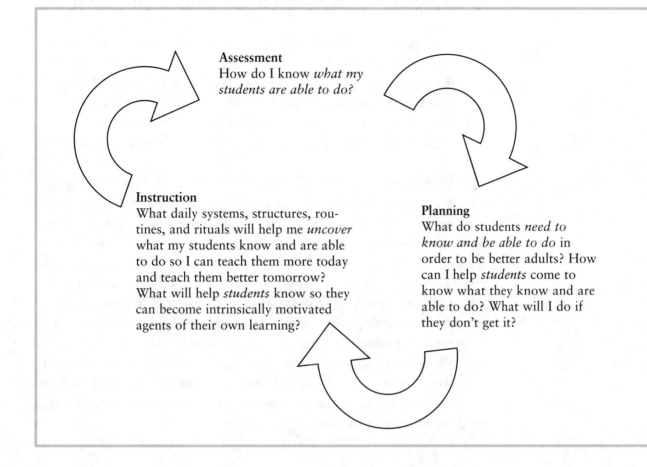

Assessment
How do I know *what my students are able to do?*

Instruction
What daily systems, structures, routines, and rituals will help me *uncover* what my students know and are able to do so I can teach them more today and teach them better tomorrow? What will help *students* know so they can become intrinsically motivated agents of their own learning?

Planning
What do students *need to know and be able to do* in order to be better adults? How can I help *students* come to know what they know and are able to do? What will I do if they don't get it?

Too often, teaching is spoken of only as what happens when teachers are in front of students. Direct instruction is actually a very small part of teaching. Take another look at the questions embedded in the teaching cycle of assessment, planning, and instruction. The answers to these questions are not dependent on a single great lesson. These questions cannot be answered with any single teaching practice. Teaching and learning are so complex that these questions can be answered only by *multiple* daily opportunities for students to read, write, and talk, and for the teachers to listen to individuals, small groups, and the whole class—in small ways and big ways over time. These questions can be answered only if teachers know their students deeply—as people *and* as learners—with layer upon layer of daily interactions combined with careful listening, close study, and heartfelt care.

So, what does listening to teach look like in daily practice? Next generation workshop.

Workshop: The Key to Listening to Teach

> *It is significant to realize that the most creative environments in our society are not the ever-changing ones. The artist's studio, the researcher's laboratory, the scholar's library are each deliberately kept simple so as to support the complexities of the work-in-progress.* They are deliberately kept predictable so the unpredictable can happen. *(Calkins 1983, 32, emphasis added)*

✳ Workshop is a *predictable* structure, routine, ritual, and system that allows the *unpredictable* work of deep reading, brilliant writing, mind-changing conversations, inspirational epiphanies, and connections of new to the known—that is, learning—to happen. Workshop is the key to listening to teach for many reasons, but not for any *one* reason. It is a complex system of intertwining events that lead to students doing the work of learning *and* demonstrating their understanding of essential content and skills.

In a workshop, as students are busy doing the work of learning, it frees teachers to do their work as learners. As students read, write, think, and talk, teachers do the work of learning about their students: what students know, what they can do, and what they need to be successful adults.

Workshop is a *structure*, a *routine*, a *ritual*, and a *system* that helps teachers answer the question "How do I know?"

Workshop as Structure, Routine, Ritual, and System

Too often, workshop is spoken of *only* as a structure for learning. As a structure alone, workshop will never work. Workshop is essential to listening to teach because it is a structure, a routine, a ritual, and a system. Structure. Routine. Ritual. System. Why do these words matter in a learning environment? How are they the same? How are they different? Let's peel back the layers.

Workshop as a Structure

✳ *structure* (n.)—something arranged in a definite pattern of organization (Merriam-Webster's Collegiate Dictionary 2001)

Workshop is a way to *structure* class time that gives students the bulk of time to do the work of learning. As a structure, whether the chunk of time

Figure 1.2 Workshop as a Cyclical Structure

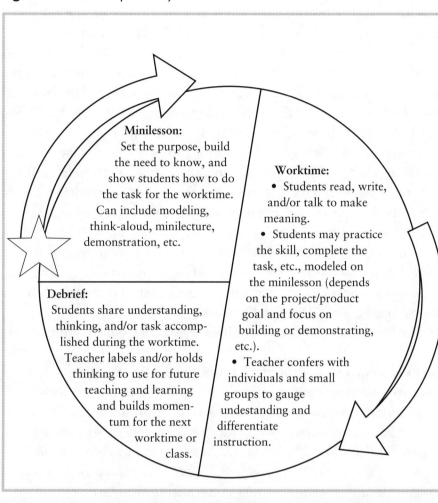

Minilesson:
Set the purpose, build the need to know, and show students how to do the task for the worktime. Can include modeling, think-aloud, minilecture, demonstration, etc.

Worktime:
• Students read, write, and/or talk to make meaning.
• Students may practice the skill, complete the task, etc., modeled on the minilesson (depends on the project/product goal and focus on building or demonstrating, etc.).
• Teacher confers with individuals and small groups to gauge undestanding and differentiate instruction.

Debrief:
Students share understanding, thinking, and/or task accomplished during the worktime. Teacher labels and/or holds thinking to use for future teaching and learning and builds momentum for the next worktime or class.

is 48, 60, 90, or 120 minutes, workshop is composed of three parts: a short minilesson, a student worktime, and a debrief (see Figure 1.2). In the past, workshop has been described as a cycle of a 10- to 15-minute minilesson, a 30- to 60-minute student worktime, and a 10- to 15-minute debrief. Lots of teachers tried it. Some succeeded. A lot more failed and gave it up for really good reasons. Here are a few I've heard:

★ "It's impossible to do all three parts in a forty-two-minute class period!"

★ "Students can't (or won't) work for the full time and my class explodes in chaos!"

★ "How do I say everything I need to say in fifteen minutes?! I have a lot of content to cover!"

All are often-cited reasons to abandon workshop. Still, I believe there are more compelling reasons to take another look.

The reason the workshop structure is presented as a *cycle* is because a teacher may rotate through the cycle several times during one class period. My colleague Peter Thulson calls this the catch-and-release model of workshop (see Figure 1.3).

Picture the rhythm of a fly fisherman. During the minilesson, the teacher (or fisherman) has the students "out of the water." The trick is to throw them back into the river before they stop breathing and die. Clever, huh? That is why the word *mini* before *lesson* is important.

During the worktime, student stamina for work may wane, and it is time for another "catch" from the fisherman. So, we pull students out of the river of learning and give them another round of teacher talk—to show students *how* and remind them *why* the task we are asking them to do is important. But, and this is a big but—ONLY FOR A FEW MIN- UTES! It is crucial to throw them back in to reading, writing, and talking *before they stop breathing*. Students need lots of time to swim in texts and talk in order to learn. If teachers are doing all of the talking, they are the ones swimming—and doing all the work.

In *How People Learn,* the National Research Council writes,

> *In all domains of learning, the development of expertise*
> *occurs only with major investments of time, and the amount*
> *of time it takes to learn material is roughly proportional to*
> *the amount of material being learned. Although many people*
> *believe that "talent" plays a role in who becomes an expert in*
> *a particular area, even seemingly talented individuals require a*
> *great deal of practice in order to develop their expertise.*
> *(2000, 58–60)*

Workshop teachers work toward that clean, golden ratio of 15-45-15 (the fifteen-minute minilesson, the forty-five-minute worktime, and the fifteen-minute debrief—a common structure in my neck of the woods) because it is nice and tidy and helps keep the focus on students. But we all know that learning is anything but tidy. The basic structure of the 15-45-15 workshop is essential *only* as a foundational agreement to structure the bulk of class time around what comes out of students' mouths and pencils instead of what comes out of the mouth of the teacher. David Perkins powerfully states the obvious: "Learning is a consequence of thinking" (1992, 8). Thus, if we expect students to learn, they must have chunks of time dedicated to reading, writing, and talking to think. In order for workshop to work, *a teacher must believe* that what comes out of students' mouths and pencils is more important than anything a teacher could say.

Think of your own classroom for a moment. How many minutes are

Figure 1.3 Workshop as a Cycle of Catch and Release

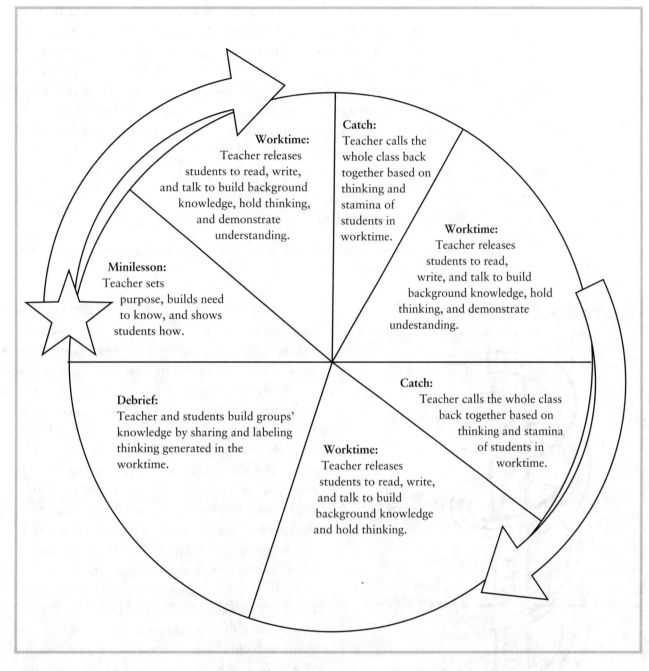

dedicated to students reading, writing, and talking? How many minutes are dedicated to teacher talk? If a teacher truly believes that *student think-ing matters most*, then student voices dominate the bulk of time in any class period.

With a catch-and-release-style workshop, even if the students aren't working for forty-five minutes straight, the majority of classroom time should still be used for students to do the work of reading, writing, and talking, so that the teacher can *listen to students' thinking* in order to know students deeply, teach them more, and teach them better tomorrow.

This basic paradigm shift—flipping the definition of teaching as talking to teaching as listening and allocating classroom time accordingly—sits at the core of the structural shift in the use of time in a workshop. When workshop works, the bulk of the classroom time is dedicated to students reading, writing, and talking, not listening to someone else talk.

The structure of time in a workshop is only the beginning. Why does workshop as a *routine* matter so much?

Workshop as Routine

routine (n.)—a regular course of procedure; habitual performance; ordinary (Merriam-Webster's 2001)

Figure 1.4 Workshop as Routine

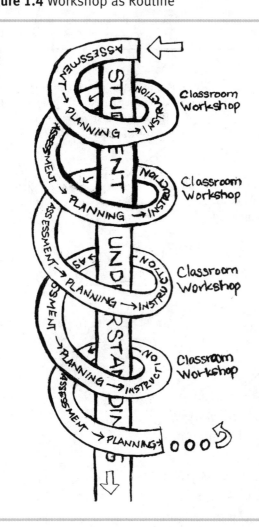

When workshop works, it is a *daily routine* that sits at the core of a teacher's practice (see Figure 1.4). As a *routine*, the workshop is the regular order of events in classrooms where students are doing the work. It is the habitual sequence of events that guides a teacher's planning. It is the ordinary way teachers know that they will *make* time to listen to individual students and small groups to figure out what they know, what they are able to do, and what they might need tomorrow to continue to build their background knowledge and extend their thinking, no matter the subject. Workshop as a routine is essential for both teachers *and* students.

If a teacher knows, on a daily basis, that she has (approximately!) fifteen minutes to demonstrate not only *what* knowledge she wants students to build during the worktime, but *how* she wants them to build it, how does that change her planning? If she knows that each day she has the opportunity to talk to many of her students one-on-one, to read their writing, and to talk to them about how they are making meaning, how does that change her ongoing assessment practices? How does it inform her planning for the next day? If you plan with the routine of workshop in mind, you are consciously and intentionally planning for students to make meaning. You are consciously and intentionally *setting up the predictable on a daily basis* (the workshop structure) *so the unpredictable* (students thinking and making meaning) *can happen.*

The routine of workshop is essential for students because if students know that every day, without fail, they will be expected to read, write, and talk to make meaning of the world around them, they are more likely to take the risk to attend to making meaning.

With workshop as a daily routine, students know their teacher will give them a chunk of information and show them how she makes meaning in reading, in writing, in history, in science, in thinking. Students know they will have time to go deep with a text, talk about it with their classmates, and write to think about it. If students know that each day they will have a debrief and will be expected to share and celebrate the thinking that came out of the worktime, it helps them stay on task.

If students know to expect the routine of a workshop each day, it frees up some brain space used for the anxious questioning, "I wonder what social studies will be like today? I wonder which of the words coming out of the teacher's mouth I am supposed to remember? I wonder if I will be called on and not know the answer?" With this freed-up brain space, students can pay attention to the big ideas and the big work of making meaning by reading, writing, and talking.

OK, so workshop structure is important (check!), and the routine of workshop is important (check!). What about workshop as ritual?

Workshop as Ritual

ritual (n.)—a system of rites; a ceremonial act customarily repeated (Merriam-Webster's 2001)

> *I'd always hated when a teacher forced us to invent something on the spot. Aside from the obvious pressure, it seemed that everyone had his or her own little way of doing things, especially when it came to writing. Maybe someone needed a particular kind of lamp or pen or typewriter. In my experience, it was hard to write without your preferred tools, but impossible to write without a cigarette. I made a note to bring in some ashtrays. (Sedaris 2000, 85)*

Now, for the magic. Think about other rituals in your life, such as holiday celebrations or religious services—*ceremony* sits at the heart of a ritual. Ceremonies are filled with predictable patterns—a "system of rites." As we experience a system of rites over and over, they take on emotional significance.

Minilesson, worktime, debrief. As a *ritual*, a workshop in which students are doing the work has a spirit of sacred celebration to it—a celebration of student thinking. If each day, a teacher focuses on students *making meaning* of important content —meaning that is inspired by the content of the minilesson, listened to during the worktime, and then labeled and celebrated in the debrief—then student thinking sits at the heart of each minute of the school day.

✳   The rituals *within* a workshop emulate the way readers, writers, and thinkers in the world operate. When an author gets ready to write, he gathers his tools, sits in his favorite window, and may put a few inspirational texts beside him. A reader may sit in her favorite chair with a hot cup of tea and then call her best friend to discuss the *Times'* style section every Sunday. Workshop is filled with rituals for the readers, writers, and thinkers that live there each day—a specific time for author's chair, access ✳ to high-quality tools of the trade, time for book talks, a favorite spot, a favorite mentor text for inspiration to write—it's all there. Ritually.

It is a *teacher's conscious sense of the importance of the ritual of workshop* that helps make it work. No other activity takes precedence. You can't fake it—it can't be just something you *have* to do, it has to be something you *want* to do because you believe it is central to learning. You have to believe in it—in the desire and the ability of students to read, write, think, and make meaning of the world around them and the celebration of their thinking at the center—for workshop to work.

Structure. Routine. Ritual. How is workshop a system?

Workshop as a System

✳ *system* (n.)—a regularly interacting interdependent group of items forming a unified whole; serving a common purpose (Merriam-Webster's 2001)

Workshop is a system (see Figure 1.5) because it must be *all three parts*—minilesson, worktime, debrief—orchestrated with purposeful reasons in a purposeful manner in order to "serve a common purpose."

In order for workshop to work, students need the bulk of the time to read, write, and talk, bounded by explicit instruction in the minilesson *before* the worktime and a synthesis of thinking and learning *after* the worktime. Here come the layers of complexity: during each part of the workshop, not only does the minilesson feed the worktime, which feeds the debrief, which feeds the minilesson the next day, but during each part of the workshop, the teaching cycle of assessment, planning, and instruction must also come into play.

Figure 1.5 Workshop as a System

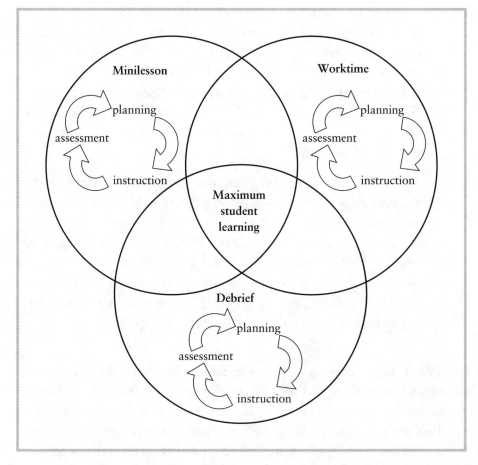

One of the misconceptions of workshop is that teachers have only fifteen minutes in the minilesson to teach. Teachers don't teach just in the minilesson part of a workshop. As teaching consists of assessment, planning, and instruction, teachers teach the whole way through the workshop:

★ During the *minilesson* teaching can look like setting a purpose, demonstrating a skill, doing a think-aloud, showing students how to make meaning from a difficult text, presenting information, modeling the entry points to an assignment, building a context for facts or information, demonstrating a process, listening to student questions to gauge student understanding of a task or process . . . the possibilities are endless if you have a clear purpose.

★ During the *worktime* teaching can look like listening to a student read for fluency and comprehension, listening to a group discuss a text, recommending a text, having a conversation with individuals or small groups, asking, "How's it going?" to gauge student understanding, reading student thinking in response to a text and asking follow-up questions, planning next steps for instruction based on patterns of assessment (what you are figuring out by listening to student talk and student writing), labeling student thinking ("You just did what good readers do! You asked a question when you got stuck!"), helping a student get unstuck by asking a question, giving explicit information, offering expert advice . . . the possibilities are endless as long as listening is at the core.

★ During the *debrief* teaching can look like sharing student thinking and work, synthesizing student thinking, labeling patterns from the worktime, making connections from the minilesson, setting the stage for the next day, holding student thinking on an anchor chart to propel the next day of thinking, summarizing the purpose, asking students to self-assess, sharing student questions raised during the worktime . . . the possibilities are endless if you believe that student thinking matters most.

Workshop works as a system because while teachers listen to students talk about their reading and writing, they are assessing what students are getting and beginning to plan their next minilesson. While teachers label student thinking, they hear patterns that emerge and decide what students need that very minute to move forward on the continuum of understanding and what type of texts or experiences they might need later in the week to deepen their thinking. Teaching happens each minute workshop is in session because teachers show students *how* each step of the way.

Workshop as structure. Workshop as routine. Workshop as ritual. Workshop as system. Overlapping, crisscrossing, intertwining, multilayered, and gloriously complex.

Why Do Routines, Rituals, Structures, and Systems Matter So Much?

Structures, routines, rituals, and systems are at the heart of every learning-filled classroom where students are doing the work. I stress the importance of the workshop being all four because it is so much more than how teachers structure the time for learning in their room. If it were just about the 15-45-15 time structure, everyone would be doing it perfectly without a hitch and we wouldn't be worried about student achievement, love of books, or engagement for learning. In classrooms where workshop works, there is something magical about how it all comes together. These four elements—structure, routine, ritual, and system—are about the little things that happen every day in the classroom that add up to the great big thing: students doing the work of learning.

Learning is not about one great lesson or one great activity teachers design for students to do. It is about the little things teachers ask students to do every day, like read, write, and talk, that add up to the big things like making meaning from text and adding meaning and purpose to life. Workshop as a structure, a routine, a ritual, and a system is the *key* to being able to answer the question "How do I know?"

The Power of a Good Story

> The stories people tell have a way of taking care of them. If stories come to you, care for them. And learn to give them away where they are needed. Sometimes a person needs a story more than food to stay alive. That is why we put these stories in each other's memories. This is how people care for each other. (Lopez 1998, 60)

This book is filled with stories of teachers and students *inside* classrooms that use workshop as a structure, a routine, a ritual, and a system. Each chapter is a new story of one day's workshop in a yearlong sequence of workshops— a profile of a teacher and his or her students tackling an important idea and reading, writing, and talking to make meaning.

My ability to relay these stories from *inside* workshop classrooms grew out of six years of looking closely and listening carefully to teachers and students in dozens of schools in the Denver Metro area, first in my work as a staff developer for the Public Education and Business Coalition (PEBC), and currently as an instructional coach at the Rocky Mountain School of Expeditionary Learning (RMSEL). The stories you'll encounter here sprang from my attempts to name what I saw and heard in these classrooms—things that help students learn better, do better, and *be* better human beings.

As I was collecting stories from *inside*, I studied the stories of other educators—Nancie Atwell, Donald Graves, Harvey Daniels, Steven Zemelman, Arthur Hyde, Ellin Oliver Keene, Stephanie Harvey, Anne Goudvis, Cris Tovani, Debbie Miller, Jean Piaget, Lev Vygotsky, Grant Wiggins, Jay McTighe, Katie Wood Ray, Michael Fullan, David Perkins, Ron Ritchhart, Kurt Hahn, Ron Berger, Sonia Nieto, and Eleanor Duckworth. Their stories are ones I continue to consult on a weekly basis.

I am definitely a person who needs "a story more than food to stay alive," and so I want to share these new stories to help more teachers do this incredibly difficult, lifesaving, world-bettering work on a daily basis.

Stories that affect our lives are complex and multilayered. We can read them again and again and make new meaning each time. Learning that affects our lives is much the same—we can encounter powerful practices again and again and uncover something new each time. The workshops presented here are not patented or flawless. They are not meant to be replicated in their entirety. They are meant to give you a vision of what teaching and learning in these classrooms look like. These stories are packed with countless ideas for you to assimilate into your practice. If you can see it, you can do it.

As I recorded these stories, I imagined you were *inside* the classrooms next to me, noticing what I noticed, hearing what I heard, wondering what I wondered. Classroom systems are complex, so as I wrote, I also realized that you might notice and wonder different things about these stories. That's the goal of this book—to *feed* you with stories of real teachers and real students in real classrooms; there are multiple layers, multiple ideas, and thus, multiple take-aways from each story. How hungry are you?

The Structure of This Book

> *The reader [is] in serious trouble most of the time, floundering in a swamp, and [it is] the duty of anyone attempting to write English to drain this swamp quickly and get the reader up on dry ground, or at least to throw a rope. (E. B. White in Strunk and White 2005, xvii)*

So, here's my attempt to throw a rope. Each chapter is a story of the inside of one classroom over time. Each story includes as much of the thinking, the planning, the instruction, the assessment, the talking, the reading, the writing, the reflection, the messiness, the chaos, and the fun as possible. At the heart of each of these stories is a model of a classroom workshop.

Specifically you'll see

- ★ a classroom observation email from me to the teacher
- ★ a transcript of one day's workshop: minilesson, worktime, and debrief
- ★ teacher thinking and reflection
- ★ student work produced as a result of the workshop we listened in on

★ student work produced as a result of several workshops over time
★ students' reflection on who they are as readers, writers, thinkers, and learners
★ lots of commentary from me

Throughout each story, you'll have a very special tour guide: the Teaching Fairy. She will flutter in anytime the teacher or student work needs some extra careful attention. The Teaching Fairy will help *uncover and label* the work of teaching and learning that resides at the heart of this book. So, when you see the fairy, *stop, look, and listen.* She will help you make meaning, and hopefully make you laugh a little along the way.

Each chapter is a complex story, but not the complete minute-by-minute teaching and learning over an entire unit. Here is where the fun comes in. I've told these stories as narratives on purpose. Each story is loaded with great ideas for you to use in your own planning, assessment, and instruction. But when and most importantly *why* you replicate the practices profiled is the hitch.

More than any single practice, it is the systems, structures, rituals, and routines of each teacher's classroom that cry out for replication. It is the (seemingly) small, ritualized routines and daily practices that matter most to student learning. The littlest things make the biggest difference—think grain of sand and oyster. Crucial systems, structures, routines, and rituals happen *inside* classrooms that think. Each story is packed with examples of these routine practices that you can make your own.

Inside the Classrooms

This book consists of the stories from inside six different classrooms. By looking closely and listening carefully inside these classrooms, I uncovered a distinct rhythm. Regardless of the grade level or content area, listening closely, I heard

Tinkerbell, Schminkerbell! I'm the Teaching Fairy and I'm the real deal. Teaching is the hardest job in the world and we all need an extra hand (or brain) from time to time. Although my kind are usually known for mischief, I'm really just here to help—to ask questions, to guide, to support, and to provide a good-natured laugh at the unending complexities of our daily lives with children.

Education is the key to eradicating poverty, war, racism, disease, and unhappiness. With all that seriousness, if we didn't laugh—loud and often—we'd just lie around and cry all the time.

In our current reality, where teachers feel like they are in a constant state of emergency, we have to focus on things that inspire joy and passion and thinking and collaboration and LEARNING to survive. That's what I'm all about! Labeling the good so we can do it more!

Also, I guess I won't be disappointed if by the end of this book you have a conversation in your classroom or see a piece of student work and ask yourself, "What would my Teaching Fairy think?" That would be OK, I guess. If you must. OK, get back to reading Chapter 1! See you soon!

boom-bapa-boom-bapa-boom-bapa-boom—workshop. Over and over again workshop emerged as the structure, system, routine, and ritual that mattered most to student learning. The workshop was the rhythm that carried every other note of instructional practice and allowed the voices of children to speak loudly, clearly, and convincingly that they were thinking to make meaning. In each chapter we'll listen in together as teachers assess, plan, and instruct with the workshop in mind.

In Chapter 2, you'll meet Peter, a first-grade teacher who is the King of Routine. Peter's belief in the capabilities of six-year-olds to make meaning of the world shines through as he confers with Helena and helps her make sense of difficult text, following her passionate quest to answer "What makes a bird a bird?"

Chapter 3 tells the story of Katie's second and third graders thinking deeply about homelessness and developing understanding through empathy as they read, write, and talk about the guiding question "Why are families homeless?"

Chapter 4 recounts the story of Jen, the Princess and the Pea of Relationships, as she confronts the question "How do I know my fourth- and fifth-grade readers are growing?" with evidence from more than her heart and her gut.

In Chapter 5, we'll spend a few weeks in Ali's fourth- and fifth-grade writers workshop and be inspired by her students' collaboration, careful attention to craft, and perseverance to write inspired essays about the topic "The Best Part of Me."

In Chapter 6, we'll meet Josh and listen to his sixth-through eighth-grade students wrestle with the complex ideas of justice and revenge through a study of the Sand Creek Massacre and a memorial design project.

In Chapter 7, we'll follow Jenn on her journey to help her sixth- through eighth-graders become twenty-first-century citizens. I'm quite sure a student from this class will win the presidential election of 2032 *and* be able to write his or her own inaugural speech.

The closing chapter of the book will help answer the question "Where should I start?" and offer resources for next steps and further study.

Why Do I Get to Tell Teachers What to Do?

When I began writing this book and showed a chapter to a colleague, she said, "I think it's great, but I know you. I think teachers will ask, 'Why do you get to tell teachers what to do?!'" Great question, Katey! Thanks!

In my job as an instructional coach I spend the bulk of my days inside classrooms, looking closely and listening carefully to help teachers help students *think* better, *learn* better, *perform* better, and *be* better human beings. After each observation, I record my noticings and wonderings in an email to the teacher that has multiple purposes:

1. To label what I see and hear so the teacher can repeat practices that help students learn.

2. To push the teacher's thinking about why he did what he did and what he intends to do tomorrow based on what he figured out today.

3. To invite the teacher to reflect a bit in writing. This is based on my belief that writing is thinking, and through writing to me, the teacher will be better for students in the future. It is also a great way for me to document a teacher's growth in thinking over time to gauge my own effectiveness as a coach. Am I helping? How do I know? Their written reflections are one way I know.

Each chapter begins with one of these observation-based coaching emails and will give you a glimpse into my life as an educator and the relationships I've built with teachers. The longer I coach, the more I realize that my job almost exactly parallels the experience that each of the teachers has with his or her students.

I didn't start out wanting to help teachers figure out how to help kids learn. My own experience as a teacher began with middle school students in San Francisco. I started teaching social studies, then morphed into a humanities teacher, and then I began experimenting with the integration of technology and project-based learning. After spending a year as the curriculum-technology integration specialist at my middle school, I began to believe that my middle school students didn't need computer projects to help them demonstrate their understanding as much as they needed to know how to read, which led me to a study group with some colleagues of the landmark book *In the Middle* by Nancie Atwell (1998). As my colleagues and I began to see changes in our students based on our experiments with the workshop model, we were asked to share what we were learning with others and I became a district literacy coach. Then I met

Ellin Keene (cowriter with Susan Zimmermann of *Mosaic of Thought* [1997]) and my life as an educator changed.

Ellin was the keynote speaker at a four-day Thinking Strategies Institute at the Public Education and Business Coalition (PEBC). Well into her talk in front of eighty teachers, a participant raised her hand and asked, "Can you tell us about text-to-text connections?" I sighed and got ready to hear what I had already read in her book, but instead I bolted upright when she responded, "You know, I wish I had never written that! I used to think labeling the connection was important, but now my thinking has changed." A nationally known author saying her thinking had changed?! *What?!*

In my years of teaching, in all the one-shot workshops that were my experience with staff development (even the ones I'd led) I had never, ever, *ever* heard a presenter say, "Yeah, I used to think that, but I don't think that anymore." We're allowed to say that out loud? We don't have to have it all figured out? This learning business is more complex than one, two, three . . . do this on Monday and your students will learn? I was instantly hooked. I needed to know more about this woman and the organization she led.

Soon after, I became a staff developer for the PEBC. At last count, I have had the opportunity to be in more than 150 classrooms, kindergarten through twelfth grade, in all kinds of schools.

Over the past sixteen years I've built a lot of background knowledge about classroom practice and have been surrounded by people who are smart, funny, and passionate about making schools great places for kids and adults. So, back to our question, "Why do I get to tell teachers what to do?" I don't want to tell anyone what to do. What I do want to do is share what I've noticed and wondered about and share my current thinking about how we can help students learn more, do more, be more, and perform better.

This book is a *testament to* and a *chronicle of* the complexity of the daily journey of teachers and students inside real classrooms and real schools. I hope these stories are food for thought that give you ideas and energy to try something new on Monday. And Tuesday. And Wednesday. And Thursday and Friday, too. I hope these stories feed you again and again, anytime you need an extra burst of brain food to keep fighting the good fight. Teaching is about our minds, our hearts, and our guts. I hope this book reaches all three. Please turn the page and join me *inside*.

CHAPTER TWO

Peter's Writer-Readers

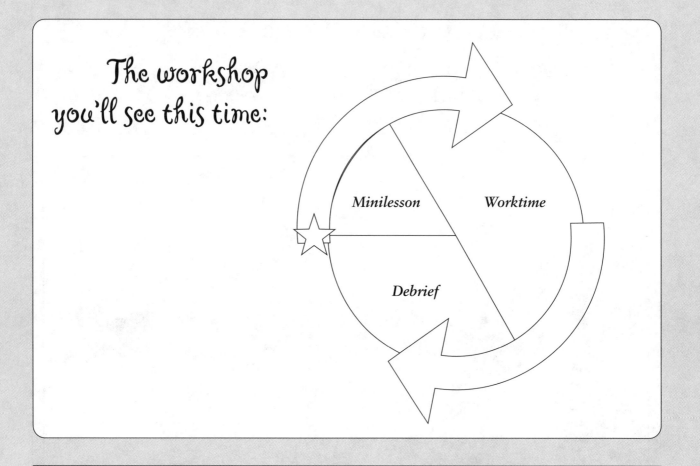

The workshop you'll see this time:

Minilesson

Worktime

Debrief

Workshop duration: 60 minutes

Minilesson (12 minutes):

★ *Teacher sets content purpose:* To recognize letter patterns in words—*he* to *she* to they.

★ *Teacher sets process purpose:* To model sentence structure and determining importance.

Worktime (30 minutes):

★ Students are reading choice books and finding an interesting sentence to share in the debrief.

★ Teacher is conferring.

Debrief (18 minutes):

★ Students share sentences from their reading time.

★ Teacher listens and capitalizes on teachable moments by labeling thinking, making connections, and listening for patterns of understanding to determine what students get and what they need.

Hi Peter,

Thanks for having me in your classroom today. What I noticed today are things you intentionally design on a daily basis: the systems, structures, rituals, and routines that make your classroom incredible soil to learn and grow. Your conversation with Helena brought to mind the learning-to-read versus reading-to-learn conversations that are such a debate in early literacy these days. It seemed such a seamless process for you and for Helena today. I wanted to have a video camera to capture the power and joy and learning all rolled up into one five-minute conversation.

Here is an excerpt from the script of your conference with Helena during worktime:

> **Helena:** I found the barred owl in this book!
> **Peter:** Did you learn anything new about the barred owl? I see the word *song* here in bold. What did those words tell you about the song of the barred owl?
> **Helena:** It says: " Call is d-d-drawn- out . . ."
> **Peter:** Do you know what that means? That is interesting . . . eight or more syllables. Let's count them together on your fingers. "Who-cooks-for-you?-Who cooks-for-you-all?" I count nine.
> **Helena:** What is this word? "De . . . scen . . . ding."
> **Peter:** Descending . . . descending means going down . . . How can the sound go down?
> **Helena:** Dowwwnnnnnnnnn [her voice trails down . . .]
> **Peter:** So, with the song of the barred owl it might sound like "Who cooks for you allllllllllll" [voice going down]. You can share that with the other kids in the circle in a few minutes.

And during the workshop debrief with the group:

> **Peter:** Empty your hands and look at Helena. Helena, what did you discover about the barred owl's song during reading workshop today?

Helena: The first part of its song stays up and the end goes down. It says here in this book "Usually eight or more drawn-out notes [adds in bird song] 'Who cooks for you? Who cooks for you all?' Call is drawn-out, descending."

Peter: Wow, Helena. Thank you. OK, first graders, let's all be barred owls.

Whole Class [in unison]: Who cooks for you? Who cooks for you all?

Theo [first grader]: But Peter, who does cook for you?

End of script.

A few questions for you, Peter:

- What did you *notice* today about Helena as a reader? As a writer? As a learner? As an ornithologist?

- What do you *wonder* about her as a reader, writer, learner, and ornithologist?

- What systems, structures, rituals, and routines best help you know what students know and how they have grown in their learning and skills?

I know your life is really full right now, but please take a few minutes to respond via email. Just write for ten minutes and push Send. Holding your thinking today will help give me a window into your brain about what matters most to you as a teacher and a learner and will give us a great start on our debrief conversation tomorrow.

Thanks for having me in today. It is going to be a fun coaching cycle this spring.

Talk soon,
Sam

The Morning Routine

Between 8:00 and 8:30 A.M. every day, Peter's first-grade classroom is buzzing with activity. Students bound into the room and immediately stop at the job board to see what their morning responsibilities entail. Today the Black Eagle Launchers team is responsible for the calendar, so Charlie gets right to work writing the number nineteen on a card to post the date. The Magic Cake team is responsible for the turtles, so Addie adds some pellets to the turtle tank, then consults Emery about the blooming algae problem. They decide that the turtles need some fresh water, so they grab a bucket and begin to siphon the brackish sludge. The Stingray team is to straighten the classroom library, and as Bryce gets to work organizing the alphabet books, he pulls one out, and starts to quietly sing the alphabet song and sound out the *f* words he knows. Julia plops down next to him and together they start to brainstorm some more *f* words, beginning with the *ffff*ish tank that Joshua has decided needs some maintenance.

Where is the teacher? Ahh . . . if you look closely, you'll see a slightly larger head among a group huddling around a book on a table. Max has brought a book about Yellowstone National Park to share with his classmates, and a group is intently studying a photograph of a bald eagle in flight. Max explains that the wingspan of the eagle is seven feet, which, he says, "is longer than Peter!" The whole group, Peter included, exclaims, "Whoa!" in unison.

A first-time visitor to this classroom may be startled by the industriousness of these six-year-olds. But, since the first week of school, each morning has looked the same. Although there are a dozen activities going on, there is a predictable rhythm to the start of the day in this classroom. Everyone has a role, everyone has a responsibility, and the room feels full of possibility.

It may look informal, but Peter has some very formal reasons for beginning the day in this very student-centered, student-directed way. Peter shares,

Choice time in the morning is essential to my classroom. A good way for children to get good at making choices is for them to practice making them on a daily basis. It is my job to make sure that there are rich things for them to do. They need to be surrounded by rich distractions—on the walls, on the bookshelves, on the side tables—to help them make interesting choices. As they choose each morning, it is a great time for me to connect with individuals and check their gauges—I want to help each child radiate at his own particular frequency.

Promptly at 8:30, the musical notes of a recorder fill the air, and like the children following the pied piper, students quickly finish what they are doing and scurry over to the chalk circle on the rug in the front of the classroom.

The Minilesson

Peter began, "Good morning, first graders. I wonder if someone would like to read the words for us on the whiteboard with a loud, loud voice."

> **Grace:** [in a loud, loud voice] "Every day he got better and better." Hey, *every* sounds like *Emery*.
>
> **Peter:** Yes, Grace, you are right. Emery, will you write your name on the board so we can see what is the same and what is different? Let's take a look at that.
>
> [Emery jumps up and writes her name above *every*.]
>
> **Peter:** Wow. Every. Emery. Look at that. Wow. Thanks, Emery. Thanks, Grace. So, "Every day he got better and better." Does anyone recognize where those words come from?
>
> **Charlie:** From read-aloud! From *The Trumpet of the Swan*! He's talking about Louie!
>
> **Peter:** Yeah, that's right. Louie, practicing on his trumpet and each day he got better and better. I'm noticing in here, each day you are getting better and better. Does anyone else notice that?
>
> **Nicholas:** Yeah, at writing!
>
> **Peter:** Great example! Each day, Nicholas got better and better. What if I add an *s* in front of *he*. Now what does this say?
>
> **Astoria:** Each day *she* got better and better.
>
> **Peter:** That's right. Each day *she* [pointing to Astoria] got better and better—at the monkey bars on the playground . . . at writing letters. What if I erase the *s* and add a *t* in front and a *y* in back of *he*?
>
> **Garret:** They! Every day *they* got better and better.
>
> **Peter:** That's right. Every day *they* [pointing around the circle] got better and better. Thanks, Garret.

PETER'S MINILESSON

Structure and Content

Instruction:

★ 12 minutes long

★ Teacher sets content and process purposes:
   • To use a familiar text, the class read-aloud, to practice looking at patterns in words with similar letters and sounds—*he* to *she* to *they*. *Every* to *Emery* was a great bonus!
   • To demonstrate choosing a sentence out of a text to share that has significance for the reader.
   • To prompt students to think strategically about their book choice for reading time.

Teaching Cycle Implications

Assessment and Planning:

★ Peter will confer during the reading time to see individual growth in knowledge and skills.

★ Peter will use the knowledge he gains about students during conferring time, and look for patterns, to plan a minilesson the next day.

Today, during reading workshop, I want you to get better and better at reading. I'd like you to read for half an hour today and I'm going to give you a job. After reading time, when we come back to the share circle today, I want everyone to be ready to share a sentence they think is interesting from their book. I chose that sentence from *The Trumpet of the Swan* because it made me think of you.

You have lots of new books to choose from today. There are some new books about birds on the bird shelf, and I've also restocked the song books, so you might find a new favorite in that bin today. Who has thought about what book they want to read today?

And as the children shared their choices—Dr. Seuss, Cynthia Rylant, Miss Mary Mack (to name a few favorites)—they scurried to the shelves, retrieved their books, and got to work—reading. Over half of the class headed to the shelf nicknamed the bird tower, filled with picture books, field guides, poetry books, and nonfiction stories, all about birds. The class was immersed in a yearlong study of birds, trying to answer the guiding questions "What makes a bird a bird?" "How can birds fly?" and "How do birds' bodies affect how they live?" Let's listen in on the worktime of this readers workshop.

Figure 2.1 The Owl's Visit and Helena's Response

"I saw Toni. The girl showed her owl. She let us get really close."

The Worktime

As students began reading their books, Peter circulated around the room and conferred one-on-one with students to see how they were decoding (learning to read) and making meaning (learning to read and reading to learn), building his own background knowledge about them as readers and thinkers and meeting their individual needs along the way.

Helena, still excited by a class visit from a barred owl the previous week (see Figure 2.1) and by a story she had written from the perspective

Hi again! During the conference with Helena, Peter helped her navigate the conventions of nonfiction text. He helped her notice words in bold print and see how the book was organized in categories of birds and then in specific categories of information about each bird. He helped her decode text by connecting the subheadings in the text—"Song," "Behavior," "Breeding," and "Nesting," all in capitals and bold—to her prior knowledge about what birds do. Not bad for a five-minute conference!

of a barred owl during writing workshop the day before (see Figure 2.3), chose to read the Smithsonian handbook *Birds of North America*, by Fred J. Alsop III (2001, 366) (see Figure 2.2).

Peter approached Helena and she shared, "Peter! I found the barred owl in this book!"

Peter: Did you learn anything new about the barred owl? I see the word *song* here in bold. What did those words tell you about the song of the barred owl?

Helena: It says: "Call is d-d-drawn- out . . ."

Peter: Do you know what that means? That is interesting . . . eight or more syllables. Let's count them together on your fingers. "Who-cooks-for-you?-Who-cooks-for-you-all?" I count nine.

Helena: What is this word? "De . . . scen . . . ding."

Peter: Descending . . . descending means going down . . . How can the sound go down?

Helena: Dowwwnnnnnnnnn. [Her voice trails down.]

Peter: So, with the song of the barred owl it might sound like, "Who cooks for you all-llllllllll" [voice going down]. Great! You've found your sentence! You can share that with the other kids in the circle in a few minutes.

Reflecting on this conference, Peter shared,

I was thrilled that the visit from the barred owl [See Figure 2.1] gave Helena both the inclination and the stamina to make her way through the difficult text and gain some new knowledge. Her new knowledge about the song of the barred owl not only helped her understand the ways birds are different from other animals, but also how birds differ from one another, and led her to develop understanding about the guiding question "What makes a bird a bird?" Her interest in the topic fueled her effort and helped her grow as a reader and an ornithologist.

Peter continued to meet with other students during the half-hour worktime. He talked to ten different students, asking some to read aloud and asking others to read their favorite sentence that they might want to share in the circle time debrief. Peter shared his thinking about the goal for this worktime:

My goal with having the students pick out a sentence to share was multifold. Looking for a sentence helps them understand what a sentence is. I want them to get accustomed to seeing and hearing a complete thought and look for the patterns of a capital letter to start and a period to end. This feeds their writing time as well. This minilesson is paired with the minilesson for writing time.

Before the debrief, I am circulating, helping them prepare. When I come upon a conference like Helena's, I am thrilled! It was a great teachable moment for her and turned into a great one to share with the whole class in the debrief.

Let's listen in. . . .

The Debrief

During the debrief, Helena came back to the circle with her learning about the song of the barred owl. Peter had written the song of the barred owl on the board with a drawing of the corresponding notes going downnnnnnnnnn.

Peter: Empty your hands and look at Helena. Helena, what did you discover about the barred owl's song during reading workshop today?

Helena: The first part of its song stays up and the end goes down. It says here in this book, "Usually eight or more drawn-out notes [adds in bird song] 'Who cooks for you? Who cooks for you all?' Call is drawn-out, descending."

Figure 2.2 Helena's Reading Choice

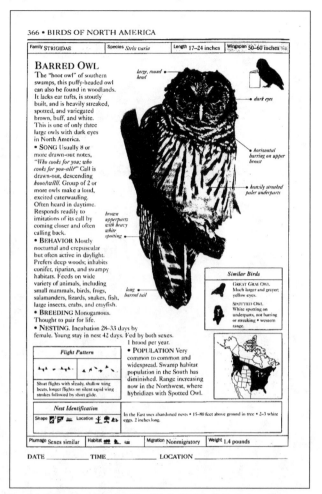

Peter: [pointing out the words and graphic on the board] Wow, Helena. Thank you. OK, first graders, let's all be barred owls.

Whole class [in unison]: Who cooks for you? Who cooks for you all?

Peter: Who else has a sentence they would like to share?

As other students shared sentences from their reading, Helena continued to study the page about the barred owl with a look of deep concentration. It was hard for her to break the spell when Peter's voice ended the workshop with "OK, first graders, thank you for sharing those interesting sentences. I'm excited to see if you use any of the language you liked today during your writing time after recess. Please line up."

The Pulse of Workshop Emery Every Day

*Knowing what to expect is an important step towards
students taking charge. (Peter Thulson)*

If you walk into Peter's classroom *any* day, you will see a workshop as structure, as system, as routine, and as ritual. As a basic *structure,* you will see minilesson, worktime, debrief. Every day. Actually, this pattern is repeated multiple times every day. For reading. For writing. For science and social studies. For math. Minilesson, worktime, debrief. At least three times a day, for every subject. As *routine* and as *ritual,* it is a way of being for students and for their teacher. This is a classroom of, for, and by learners. Students and teacher alike. It is a magical place of the working hum.

As a *system,* workshop teaching for Peter doesn't happen just in the minilesson. If you shadow Peter during the worktime, you will hear rich conversations with his first graders about how they are making meaning from text, how they are matching sounds to print, and what they are learning about birds or the story they have chosen to read that day. Peter listens carefully to *assess* what his students are getting as well as what they need. It is the *just-in-time instruction* during these conversations that matters most to helping each student move forward on the continuum of understanding. He then *plans* to highlight and share the ahas of individuals that will help the whole group learn and grow during the debrief. Assess, instaplan, just-in-time instruct, assess, instaplan for the debrief—the teaching cycle in the worktime.

Peter shares this thinking,

*In my workshop I try to have a thread that I pull all the way
through. The workshop creates the conditions for wonderful
things to happen, and over time, I've learned that it improves*

*the conditions for wonderful ideas if my students and I have
that central thread at the forefront of our minds. Yet, I have
to tug gently all the way through to the share session. As the
teacher, I have to exploit the opportunities that come up to
support the work of the readers and writers, even if they
aren't holding onto my particular thread. I have to be sure to
honor whatever learning comes up during a workshop session
and be ready to jump on it and use it as an opportunity to
drive the next steps for each learner.*

During the debrief, Peter asks students to share their discoveries and
the important thinking they had during the worktime so that the whole
class can benefit and grow their thinking and understanding. As students
share, he continues to assess what they got and plan for the instruction in
the minilesson the next day. Assess, plan, instruct—the teaching cycle in
the debrief.

Peter describes the pulse of his workshop like the beat of a heart. He
starts the beat in his minilesson. With this explicit instruction, he builds
students' capacity to do work without him during the worktime, and the
beat continues away from his central artery. When students flood back to
the circle to share what they did, he can label things, point out connections, and celebrate their hard work. It is this back-and-forth pulse of the
workshop that is the rhythmic heartbeat of Peter's classroom of, for, and
by learners.

What Did Peter Learn About Helena?

*We make inferences about what students know, understand
and can do based on information obtained through assessment. Although educators sometimes loosely refer to an
assessment as being valid and reliable, in fact a more precise
conception has to do with the extent to which the results of
an assessment permit valid and reliable inferences. Because all
forms of assessment have inherent measurement error, our
inferences are more dependable when we consider more than
one measure. In other words, reliable assessment demands ✂
multiple sources of evidence. (Tomlinson and McTighe 2006,
60, emphasis added)*

What did Peter learn about Helena today as a reader? As a writer?
As a learner? What will he do with this information? How will it inform
what he will do tomorrow? How did he structure this unit and this lesson

to enable Helena to read a text above her "normal" reading level? What other ways throughout the day does Peter know what Helena knows and is able to do? How will he share what he learned with Helena and her parents? How does *Helena* know what she knows and is able to do? What difference will that make to Helena's learning—to her success as an adult?

I've shared with you that Peter has not only *one* workshop a day but several. That adds up to a lot of listening to teach. During writers workshop the previous day, Helena had written a story from the perspective of a barred owl (see Figure 2.3).

So, let's listen closely to Helena by looking carefully at three pieces of evidence: her caption on the picture of her with the barred owl (Figure 2.1), her story about the barred owl (Figure 2.3), and her conversation with Peter about the song of the barred owl (the script that opens the chapter). First the *what*: What can we infer about her as a reader? As a writer? As a thinker? As a learner? And then the *so what*: How can our inference help us teach her better tomorrow? What does she need most to help her grow in her knowledge and skills?

Helena as a Writer

Helena's owl story leaves us more tracks in the snow to learn about her as a writer and a learner. In her story (Figure 2.3) she is integrating perspective taking, "I was the owl / I saw a spider / It looked tasty," and the facts she knows about owls—that they have special feathers and quiet feathers—and putting it in context of the owl surprising the spider.

Peter said, "I felt that told me that she didn't just have declarative knowledge that an owl has special wings and quiet feathers, but she had an understanding that it meant that the owl could catch the spider without being heard. She is using the scientific content to construct a narrative."

Reading and Writing Grade by Grade states, "[In first grade] writers begin to show an intention to really connect with a reader by, for example producing text that strives to be interesting or surprising" (*New Standards®* 2004, 112). Helena's story certainly is evidence of meeting this standard of writing purposes and resulting genres. Peter was delighted with the final page. He shared,

> *I'm really intrigued by her use of literary language. She says, "It moved a muscle" and then skips to "It was yummy." She allows the reader to make an inference there. It may not have been deliberate, but I imagine a smile on her face as she wrote that. Especially as she ends with "I felt happy." It seems like*

Figure 2.3 Helena's Story

I was the owl. I saw a spider. It looked tasty.

I tried to get the spider. I was so quiet that I got the spider.

There are lots of important things to notice about Helena's work and the classroom systems, structures, routines, and rituals that support her as a writer and reader. These systems and structures also support Peter—his ability to know her and, thus, to know what she needs to grow as a writer and a reader.

Next to her name is a date stamp. Each day Peter date stamps student work and collects it in "Works in Progress" folders at each table. Each week, Peter culls through the working folders and takes out any work that is not part of a student's current narrative to put in the student's master file. Peter feels that it is essential for students to have a "manageable" narrative in their writing folder so that students are more likely to be able to know where to go next with their stories. This ties back to that sense of agency that he strives to cultivate in the learners in his classroom.

This system is also tied to his instruction. Before he releases students to write, he suggests that they go back and reread their stories so it will help launch them into their writing. If they can figure out where to go next, they don't need him by their side to get started. Peter explicitly asks them to replicate the habits of writers in the real world—read what you wrote yesterday, and figure out where to go next.

Students get to choose the paper they write on. Space for a picture is crucial for these young writers because it is another scaffold for them to write independently. The picture can become the inspiration for the text, and after the text is written, the illustration can be a powerful trigger to remind the student what the text says, just like in a picture book. The pictures are also a great place for Peter to start with when he is conferring with his writers. When students first begin to write, it is Peter's job to help them elaborate and use their oral skills to improve their narrative. Peter begins many of his writing conferences with "Who is this? Tell me what is happening here."

Helena's language use and conventions in this story also give us clues to what she knows and is able to do. She is using mostly capital letters but some are lowercase. She is fluent with her phonetic spelling. She wrote forty or fifty words in a single session (thirty to forty minutes) and shows a fair amount of fluency. The first five words are all conventionally spelled. She spells it and to get and was conventionally every time.

She is using spaces between words. She is discriminating among vowels—with an i and an a in quiet. She is using y as a consonant and the second time she has put a y in kwiyat.

New Standards states that by the end of first grade students should "produce writing that contains a large proportion of correctly spelled, high-frequency words and write text that usually can be read by the child and others—regardless of the scarcity of correctly spelled words—because most of the perceived sounds in unfamiliar words are phonetically represented" (1999, 137). Helena is doing this and more! Bravo, Helena! Bravo, Peter!

Figure 2.3 Helena's Story (continued)

And I am scary. I have special wings and quiet feathers.

It moved a muscle. It was yummy. I felt happy.

an understanding that the element successfully reaches its goal in the narrative and shows success of the story.

Peter's delight with his students is evident throughout each day. He is filled with delight because he expects that his students will surprise him each day. He sees his job as setting up the conditions—the systems, structures, routines, and rituals—to be delighted, and he is rarely let down by the learners in his classroom.

What Can We Infer About Helena as a Reader?

When students understand that, together, the sounds of language and the sense of stories can help them become word problem-solvers, the puzzle of reading and writing begins to come together. (New Standards 2004, 92)

Paying careful attention to Helena's reading, writing, and talk allows Peter to make inferences about what Helena knows and is able to do and what she *needs* from him to help her know more and do more tomorrow.

During the conference, Peter learned a few new things about Helena and confirmed other things he already knew about her as a reader, writer, and learner. When he first approached her and saw that she had the field guide open to the page of the barred owl, he realized that she had made a connection from the barred owl's visit earlier in the week and had identified it in the guide. He knew the text would be too difficult for her, so he helped her navigate the nonfiction text by drawing her attention to the ways in which the text was organized. He pointed the topic heading in boldface—"Song"—a word she would know, to encourage her to make some meaning within that chunk of text. Peter explained some specifics from the script of the conference with Helena:

Her cue with the book was the image of the barred owl after seeing the barred owl in the classroom. She was using a book with text well beyond her skills, and even more than that, it was intimidating for her. She tends to be a cautious reader. She was excited about seeing the barred owl but she needed me to see it and verify for her what she was seeing. Knowing that it was a difficult text, I wanted to affirm her success and start with the assumption that she had gotten something out of it, so I used her excitement to get her to attend to the words next to the picture. She knew "Who cooks for you" from the owl's visit, so she could really see it once I called her

> Peter has set up a simple portfolio system to help students (and their parents) know what they know, what they are able to do, and how they have grown throughout the year. Student-led conferences twice a year provide the purpose and audience for these portfolios.
>
> Each portfolio opens with a letter from the student about himself and his accomplishments. There are sections for reading, writing, math, art, and this year "All About Birds." Each is filled with important evidence that shows both growth and mastery. The whole portfolio is filled with photographs of the learners at work—many with student-written captions and commentary— a great scaffold for the student-led conversation at conference time.

attention to the word *song.* Recognizing it in print made the whole sentence readable to her.

That was fluent reading that she wouldn't have done without me there prompting her and expecting it of her. There was an awful lot unfamiliar to her that I needed to scaffold for her by providing the synthesis and vocabulary. It was a very scaffolded session. I helped her make meaning with incomprehensible text, but her role was decoding and using prior knowledge. I supplied synthesis, vocabulary, and determining importance for her, but the meaning she made was all hers, and she was able to share with confidence in the debrief.

In the book *Reading and Writing Grade by Grade*, the authors posit that first graders should "listen to and discuss every day at least one book or chapter that is longer and more difficult than what they can read independently" (New Standards 2004, 106). Helena's discussion with Peter helped her gain confidence in herself as a reader and also helped her build new vocabulary, which will help her be a risk-taking reader in the future. She will return to the field guide again, and while we want her to also read books at her independent reading level, the fact that she doesn't fear picking up a big, thick, heavy nonfiction text and try to make meaning from it bodes well for her future as an insatiable reader of a wide variety of genres.

With large chunks of time to read, write, and talk with her peers and with Peter, Helena is well on her way to meeting and exceeding expectations in January of first grade. How do we know? We follow the tracks she leaves in the snow and pay very careful attention to everything we see and hear.

How Helena Knows

Peter has multiple systems, structures, routines, and rituals in place for students to be metacognitive and reflect on their own progress as learners. On a daily basis, Peter asks students to reflect on their learning in the debrief of workshop. Also each day, students save their work in folders, which they later comb through to select pieces for portfolios for use in student-led conferences (twice a year) and in a final portfolio presentation to their second-grade teacher. During these more formal reflections—at goal-setting conferences in September, at student-led conferences in December and March, and at their final portfolio presentations in June—students write about themselves as learners. In March, after choosing work to include in her portfolio to show to her parents at the conference, Helena wrote a letter to them about her progress. She wrote:

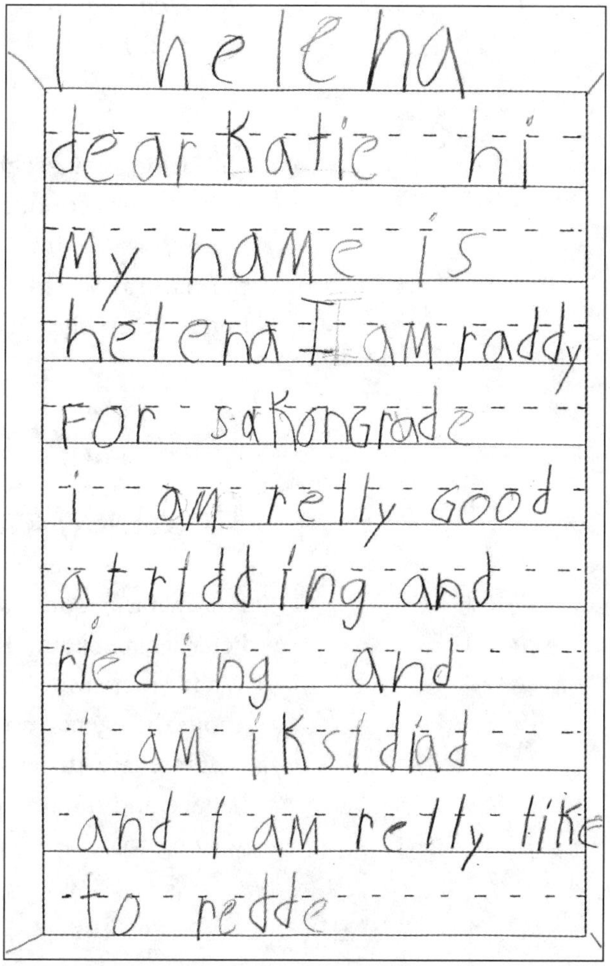
I helena
dear Katie hi
My name is
helena I am raddy
for sakongrade
i am relly Good
at ridding and
rleding and
i am iksidad
and i am relly like
to redde

Figure 2.4 Helena's Portfolio Introduction Letter

Dear Mom and Dad,

I've been reading good. And writing good too. And I went to Castlewood Canyon. We went all the way to the top of the canyon. I was not tired. I saw a red tailed hawk. It was cool. I saw a crow it was cool. I used to not know about birds. Now I know a lot about birds. I used to not go on the monkey bars. Now I can do the monkey bars now. Last year I didn't see birds. Now I see birds.

And in June, in a letter (see Figure 2.4) to her new second-grade teacher, she wrote,

Dear Katie,

Hi my name is Helena I am ready for second grade I am really good at writing and reading and I am excited and I really like to read.

Her letter continued,

And I am good at math and I like doing math too and I like doing reading and writing it is cool being a second grader and

I like it really much. I like studying birds. It is really fun studying birds. You study birds' feathers and beaks. It is really fun. I hope we do more fun things in second grade.

So, by the end of first grade Helena has learned a lot about herself and a lot about school. She can read, she can write, she's a mathematician, she has confidence in herself as a learner and monkey bar navigator. She knows it is important to look at feathers and beaks closely, she thinks the natural world is cool, and she is excited about school because she knows learning is fun. Now she sees birds. Wow. Now she sees birds.

Peter's Systems, Structures, Routines, and Rituals

Following is some scaffolding for the story of teaching and learning in Peter's classroom. Remember, whole-scale replication is not the point. What practices were intriguing to you? What practices match your beliefs about the agency and capacity of children to think and learn? The beauty is, there are dozens of entry points. Pick one that matches what you believe and the rest will come. Do you want to start with date stamping? Writing folders? Here are a few other ideas for places to start:

Systems, Structures, Routines, and Rituals Highlighted in Chapter 2	Narrative description found on page	Ideas to help you get started	For r chec resources
Building classroom community • morning circle • closing circle • classroom jobs	27	Think about how you want your days with children to begin and end. What matters most? Be intentional with your community-building time. What is the first thing you want students to experience in your room each day? What is the last thing you want them to experience and carry home with them? What little things over time will add up and make a big difference? Learning to care for animals and plants makes children better adults. Take the time to teach children how to communicate in circle time. Observe colleagues that are known for a positive classroom climate. Reorganize the physical space and materials in your classroom so students can have access to materials, work in pairs and small groups, and curl up and read a good book. Read, read, read. Ask the students how they would like to start each day. What routines can you hand over to children in your classroom? Harness the power of twenty-four to thirty of them and one of you! Take time to build community—it will help students read, write, and think better.	*Journey Towards the Caring Classroom* (Frank 2004) *Being Good* (Wolk 2002) *Reading with Meaning* (Miller 2002) *About the Authors* (Ray and Cleaveland 2004)
Writing folders and writing files	35	Writing folders should be accessible to students. Peter keeps the students' folders in the center of their work tables next to a bucket of sharp pencils. Writing files are for the teacher to use to track growth over time (biweekly or at progress report time) and/or to pull back out when it is time to choose work to go into the portfolio.	*About the Authors* (Ray and Cleaveland 2004) *In the Middle* (Atwell 1998)

(handwritten notes in left margin:)

Morning:

Table Group Jobs — sort, straighten

* Library — return, repair

* Calendar / # Day — date, straws - notation, coins - $ notation

* Mail / Papers / Homework — pass out papers, write homework - ✓ everyone's

collect homework

*Lunch — cross off, read to anyone, tally each area, ~~collect homework~~ (✝) L Leader / Caboose

Systems, Structures, Routines, and Rituals Highlighted in Chapter 2	Narrative description found on page	Ideas to help you get started	For more information check out these resources
Portfolio assessment	35, 38, 39	Start small. Collect work in a central space—don't send it all home. Plan time for students to look back at work and talk and write about what they notice about themselves as readers and writers. Invite students to participate in or lead their parent conferences. Base the conference on the student work.	*Best Practice* (Zemelman, Daniels, and Hyde 1998)
Conferring	30, 36, 37	Start small. Start simple. Release students to read and write for seven minutes. Get eye-to-eye with students and show an interest in what they are doing. Listen.	*How's It Going?* (Anderson 2000) *About the Authors* (Ray and Cleaveland 2004) *In the Middle* (Atwell 1998)

CHAPTER THREE

Katie's Humanitarians

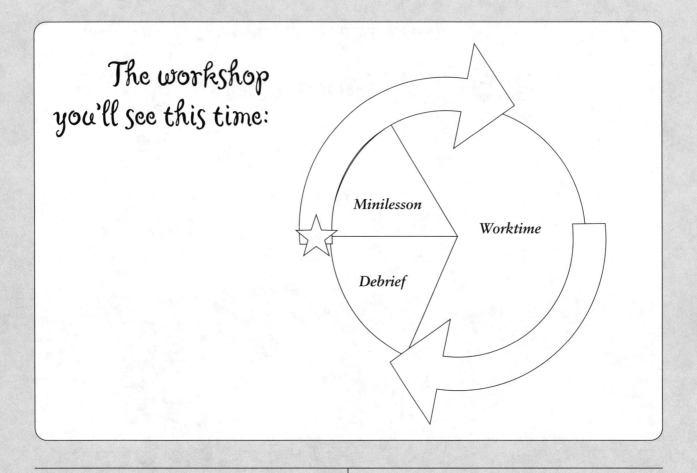

The workshop you'll see this time:

Minilesson

Worktime

Debrief

Workshop duration: 75 minutes

Minilesson (20 minutes):

★ *Teacher sets content purpose:* To build student background knowledge through listening to a short text and recording student thinking in an anchor chart (group construction of knowledge) and in their reading journals (individual construction of knowledge) around the three guiding questions of the unit: (1) Why are families homeless? (2) What support do they need? and (3) How can I show empathy?

★ *Teacher sets process purpose:* To keep a conversation going in book groups in order to make more meaning and help each other get smarter.

★ *Teacher models use of graphic organizer to hold thinking.*

Worktime (40 minutes):

★ Students meet in book groups to discuss and record their thinking in a graphic organizer about a text they read the day before.

★ Teacher circulates and confers with small groups.

Debrief (15 minutes):

★ Teacher asks students to respond to the guiding questions based on the text they discussed in their book groups.

★ Teacher asks students to record any new thinking in a different-colored pencil.

★ Teacher labels thinking and makes connections to the big ideas of the unit.

★ Teacher asks students to synthesize and reflect on the process purpose of making meaning in a small group.

Dear Katie,

Thank you so much for having me in your classroom today. It was incredible to hear the depth of the second and third graders' conversations about homelessness.

A few things I noticed:

- Your guiding questions posted prominently (and beautifully, as always!) on your wall: Why are families homeless? What support do they need? How can I show empathy? ✳
- You asked students to hold their thinking from each story they read with a graphic organizer that is linked directly to the guiding questions. I saw students excited to hold their thinking—they were writing with a purpose and checking back in their journals, comparing their reflections from other texts.
- I heard students specifically refer to each other's thinking—showing they were listening to each other's ideas.
- I heard students asking a lot of each other and of the book. I heard students ask, "Do you think homeless people get worried?" "How do they pay for gas?" "Where did the car come from?" "Do you think she got that job because of luck or support?" and "Don't they need an advocate?"

What I wonder:

- How are you tracking shifts in student thinking over time?
- What does empathy look like to you?

I'm excited to talk to you about this tomorrow and interested to see how the character-based vignettes turn out.

Talk soon,
Sam

Better Classrooms and Gardens

When you enter Katie's classroom, you may be confused and think you have entered a photo shoot for the cover of *Better Classrooms and Gardens* (her classroom is, in fact, the model for the cover of this book)! A tree stands in the center of the room, beautiful leaf-shaped words hanging from every branch. Beneath the tree is a papasan chair, the perfect size for the two second graders currently cozied up with a book from the extensive classroom library. Painted along the top of the classroom is the class mantra, which you can hear if you enter the classroom around 8:05 A.M. Katie begins, "If you are a dreamer. . . ." and immediately twenty-four seven- and eight-year-old voices join in with a poem inspired by Shel Silverstein:

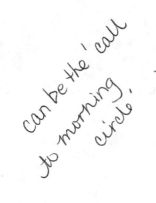

> . . . *join in,*
> *If you are a dreamer, a reader, a writer,*
> *A thinker, a wisher, an all-the-time talker,*
> *If you're a good listener, come sit in my circle,*
> *For we have some stories to share and to spin.*
> *Join in!*
> *Join in!*

And by the final, rousing "Join in!" the students are seated in a circle, ready to begin their day of learning together.

Surrounded by poetry, photographs of themselves reading, writing, and exploring, and evidence of their thinking on anchor charts lining each wall, the children begin the ritual of greeting each other, reading the schedule, and sharing a hope for the day.

This year the class is engaged in a yearlong study of shelter. In the fall, students learned the art and science of building: physics, geometry, electricity, energy flow, architectural plans, perspective, spatial relationships, materials, and roles in the building industry. This spring, they will think about shelter from a humanities perspective and tackle the issue of homelessness.

Million Dollar Murray

"Homelessness with second and third graders?!" you exclaim. Well, yes. And here's why. It's all because of Murray.

Malcolm Gladwell's article in *The New Yorker* titled "Million Dollar Murray" begins like this:

[handwritten note in left margin: can be the 'call to morning circle.']

Murray Barr was a bear of a man, an ex-marine, six feet tall and heavyset, and when he fell down—which he did nearly every day—it could take two or three grown men to pick him up. He had straight black hair and olive skin. On the street, they called him Smokey. He was missing most of his teeth. He had a wonderful smile. People loved Murray.

His chosen drink was vodka . . . On the streets of downtown Reno, where he lived, he could buy a two-hundred-and-fifty-milliliter bottle of cheap vodka for a dollar-fifty . . . if he was broke he could always do what many of the other homeless people of Reno did, which is to walk through the casinos and finish off the half-empty glasses of liquor left at the gaming tables. (2006, 96)

By most accounts, Murray fits the standard profile of whom people think about when they think of the homeless.

Maybe it is just me, but alcoholics on the street do not seem like an ideal topic for eight-year-olds to study. OK, it's not just me. One parent shared with Katie before the unit started, "I'm not sure I want my child exposed to the harshness of the world like this just yet. Why do you have to study homelessness? How is this an appropriate topic for second and third graders?" Good question.

Gladwell's article helped Katie answer it. Powerfully. As the article illustrates, Murrays are a very small percentage of the homeless population in this country. The largest number of homeless are those who are homeless for a very short time. In fact, a researcher in Philadelphia found that 80 percent of the homeless are in and out of the shelter system very quickly. He explained, "In Philadelphia, the most common length of time that someone is homeless is one day. And the second most common length is two days. *And they never come back.* Anyone who ever has had to stay in a shelter involuntarily knows that all you think about is how to make sure you never come back" (Gladwell 2006, 98, emphasis added).

EIGHTY PERCENT. Never come back. Who are *these* people? How did they end up at a shelter? It was this statistic that could help battle stereotypes and misconceptions with children and adults and provide the basis of the study of homelessness with second and third graders. Katie had the inspiration and support she needed to dive into the topic with her students. She developed three guiding questions to focus her study and help students understand this complex topic:

★ Why are families homeless?

★ What support do they need?

★ How can I help?

✳ Planning with the End in Mind

> *A student who really understands can explain, can interpret, can apply, sees in perspective, demonstrates empathy, and reveals self-knowledge. (Wiggins and McTighe 2005, 84, emphasis added)*

Katie's next step was to figure out concrete ways her students could demonstrate knowledge and understanding of the guiding questions while building reasoning and writing skills. A main Colorado state literacy standard states, "Students will recognize the power of language and use that power ethically and creatively." What product or performance would ask students to use the power of language ethically with the knowledge and skills they would gain over time during this study of civic responsibility?

As she brainstormed ideas, Katie thought it was important not to simply ask the students to raise money for a shelter or donate items as a way to show that they understood the problem. While those actions would constitute a great service-learning project, those actions alone wouldn't demonstrate students' complex understanding of the topic, nor allow students to demonstrate their "ethical and creative" use of language.

Katie turned to a resource she often uses in this stage of planning, the Rubric for the Six Facets of Understanding, by Wiggins and McTighe (2005). This rubric outlines six concrete aspects of what understanding looks like: explanation, interpretation, application, perspective, empathy, and self-knowledge. In their rubric, Wiggins and McTighe describe the development of empathy from egocentric to mature (178):

EMPATHY				
Egocentric	**Decentering**	**Aware**	**Sensitive**	**Mature**
Has little or no empathy, beyond intellectual awareness of others; sees things through own ideas and feelings; ignores or is threatened or puzzled by different feelings, attitudes, views	Has some capacity or self-discipline to walk in others' shoes, but is still primarily limited to own reactions and attitudes, puzzled or put off by different feelings or attitudes	Knows and feels that others see and feel differently and is somewhat able to empathize with others	Disposed to see and feel what others see and feel; open to the unfamiliar or different; able to see the value and work that others do not see	Disciplined; disposed and able to see and feel what others see and feel; unusually open to and willing to seek out the odd, alien, or different; able to make sense of texts, experiences, events that seem weird to others

Katie's eyes were immediately drawn to the word *empathy*. Wiggins and McTighe define a mature sense of empathy as "Disciplined; disposed and able to see and feel what others see and feel; unusually open to and willing to seek out the odd, alien, or different; able to make sense of texts, experiences, events that seem weird to others" (178). That seemed to raise the stakes a bit as far as students being able to demonstrate their understanding. Thus, Katie decided to change the third guiding question from "How can I help?" to "How can I show empathy?"

Doing Her Own Assignment

Katie's first idea was to have students write letters to children who were homeless; students could send these "little notes of hope" to a shelter to distribute—a real-world audience (check!) and a real-world purpose (check!). The letters could serve a few purposes—they could explain that there were many people in Denver that were working every day to help them, they could let the readers know that there were other kids who understood their problems and were thinking of them, and writing the letters could be concrete proof of a small kindness making a big difference.

It sounded great, for content (knowledge of reasons families are homeless), skill (practice in letter writing as a text type), and understanding (emotional support that children who are homeless need). But Katie wanted to try to write a letter herself *first* to see if this was the product that would allow students to fully demonstrate their understanding.

So, during a planning period while the students were at morning recess, she sat down and began to write. Katie tried to put herself in the shoes of an eight-year-old writing to another eight-year-old. After about fifteen minutes, she had tears in her eyes (an appropriate response when you are demonstrating empathy!), but something didn't feel right.

Katie reflected, "The letter format wasn't allowing me to get to the heart of what I know about homelessness. There are so many different reasons families' webs of support break. This letter was supposed to be a way for my students to demonstrate their understanding, but by trying to show my content knowledge in the letter, I was ignoring the person I was writing to."

Instead of content, her letter was filled with questions. She didn't want to offend the recipient by pretending that she knew just how it felt to be homeless. And the format, while personal, still allowed Katie to remove herself and set herself apart from the child who was homeless—not an empathetic response at all.

The letter format was *too* personal, and without knowing the story

Project Design Alert!
Taking the time to do your own assign-
ments is an essential component in the
teaching cycle. It is the quickest and easiest
way to test yourself on what matters most:

- *Does this project (essay, letter, pamphlet,*
  lab report, etc.) exist in the real world?
- *Is it something that a person in this pro-*
  fession (citizen, social worker, scientist,
  historian, mathematician, etc.) would do
  to communicate?
- *Does it help students demonstrate knowl-*
  edge, skills, and understanding?

Doing your own assignments is also
essential to the planning process because as
you complete the project yourself, you keep
track of the thinking and process steps you
go through to create it, and you have your
minilessons authentically scaffolded . . .
bang, boom, wow! Show them how!

of each recipient, without having a relationship with each child, Katie couldn't imagine asking her students to assume they knew what the homeless children were thinking or feeling.

The original purpose of the letter was not to make students feel bad or guilty. But because a letter can be a very personal form of communication, and the students wouldn't be able to know the recipients of their letters, it made the whole idea fake. Katie knows the power and influence of a real purpose and a real audience on students' motivation, engagement, and ability to demonstrate skills, and the letter was *not* going to work. For all of these interconnected reasons, the letter was the wrong project.

The thinking generated by trying to do her own assignment prompted Katie to think differently about a final product that could represent *more than* students' standing outside the problem and looking in. Developing a final product that would demonstrate understanding *and* serve a real-world purpose in this instance was going to take some careful consideration.

Planning to Build Students' Background Knowledge: Collecting Resources

In the meantime, Katie began scouring websites, bookstores, and libraries for a variety of texts about homelessness she could use with her second and third graders. Katie decided to use a book club structure to help students build their background knowledge around the three guiding questions, "Why are families homeless?" "What support do they need?" and "How can I show empathy?"

Within a few days, she had compiled a variety of texts at all different reading levels. Her resources included picture books, novels, poetry, nonfiction texts, literature from local shelters, and Denver's Road Home Plan for ending homelessness in Denver.

Katie also found three expert contacts: Tom from the St. Francis Shelter, Leon from the Gathering Place Day Shelter, and Jamie from the Denver mayor's office, all of whom agreed to come speak to the students about homelessness in Denver. These experts became key to building students' understanding of homelessness as well as an excellent real-world audience for students to demonstrate their growing empathy.

Katie's search for resources also led her to a great idea for students' final products! Listed on a website of resources on homelessness for kids, she found *Changing Places: A Kid's View of Shelter Living* written by three caseworkers from Virginia. The caseworkers wrote from the perspectives of children they knew that had passed through the Virginia shelter system. The book begins:

> *Dear Readers,*
>
> *The three authors of* Changing Places *met while working together at a family shelter in Virginia. We watched and were involved with children as they came in, as they claimed their new roles within the shelter and as they moved on. Often the comings and goings were marked by insecurity and fear, sadness and confusion. We were touched by the depth of feelings exhibited in behavior, though only occasionally expressed in words.*
>
> *The friends in this book put words to some of those feelings. They were created to speak directly to the children we were meeting . . . We attempted to validate the wide range of emotions they might be feeling, so as not to define what they should be feeling . . . Children in the middle of family crisis often see themselves as essentially different from other children. They feel that they alone have been chosen for these burdens and that there must be something wrong with them. They may also feel responsible. We hoped this book would be one step toward breaking that isolation. (Chalofsky, Finland, and Wallace 1992, 6, emphasis added)*

The book is creatively structured to parallel the stages that children who become homeless go through in their shelter experience, told in their voices. There are three main sections, "Arriving," "Staying," and "Leaving," each with a series of vignettes of children's individual stories. Katie shared her thinking behind using the book to scaffold student learning:

I was initially thrown for a loop when I realized my students wouldn't be able to interview children or families who were homeless because of privacy issues. This book contained the personal stories I was looking for. They were true, powerful stories of kids—authentic pieces of information about children going through the experience of being without a home. In order to meet the goal of students developing empathy, it was so important to me that they saw homelessness through the eyes of a child, not an adult. I am so thankful to the authors of that book. I don't think the students would have learned as much without that text as a resource.

The text became a resource for more than the content of the unit. It also became the mentor text for the final product, the way students would demonstrate their understanding of homelessness. The structure, a three-part narrative—arriving, staying, and leaving—was a great format to help students organize their thoughts and demonstrate their content knowledge of how families become homeless and the support they need to get back on their feet and eventually into their own homes. It would meet the goal of students using their powers of literacy "ethically and creatively" (from the Colorado state standards) and would be a way for them to demonstrate being able to "see and feel what others see and feel": the definition of empathy.

This text was an important piece of the puzzle that helped Katie design the final product students would write to demonstrate their understanding. Let's listen in and see how Katie built students' background knowledge to take on this important project. . . .

★ The Minilesson

Katie's students are sitting in a mush around her, reading journals in hand. Next to her is an anchor chart (see Figure 3.1).

Katie begins,

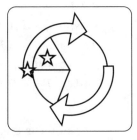

Today we are going to begin to build our background knowledge about homelessness. I'm going to read a story called Someplace to Go, *by Maria Teste and Karen Ritz [1996]. As I read, I'd like you to think about the questions that are written up here on our anchor chart and on the chart in your reading journals. "Why*

is this family homeless?" "What support do they have?" "What support do they need?" and "How would you feel if you were a part of this family?" If, while I'm reading, you have some thinking to share about any of these questions, write them on the chart in your journal and we'll share out at the end of the story.

As Katie reads the story, about a mother and son who are homeless, students listen intently, many beginning to record their thinking in their reading journals. There are intermittent "Ohs!" as students make meaning and find answers to the guiding questions based on the story of Davey and his Mom. When Katie finishes reading, she gives students a few minutes to record their individual thinking in their reading journals. Then she begins to discuss the text with the whole class and capture the children's thinking on the anchor chart up front.

She begins, "OK, who has some thinking to share?" and the students clamor to help her fill in the anchor chart and share their interpretations of the text. Figure 3.1 shows the chart Katie and the class created together.

KATIE'S MINILESSON

Structure and Content

Instruction:

★ 30 minutes long
★ Teacher sets content purpose: To build student background knowledge through listening to a short text and recording student thinking in an anchor chart (group construction of knowledge) and in their reading journals (individual construction of knowledge) around the three guiding questions of the unit: (1) Why are families homeless? (2) What support do they need? (3) How can I show empathy?
★ Teacher sets process purpose: To keep a conversation going in book groups in order to make more meaning and help each other get smarter.
★ Teacher models use of graphic organizer to hold thinking (see Figure 3.1).

Teaching Cycle Implications

Assessment:

★ Use of anchor chart will help guide instruction day to day and be a visual representation of growing knowledge about the guiding questions.
★ Individual charts in journals will help when Katie confers with individuals about their understanding and will help her know how each student's thinking is growing over time.

Planning:

★ Katie knows that for this "building background knowledge" stage of her unit, her minilessons will include sharing a new text about homelessness and recording student thinking around the same guiding questions.
★ As students' understanding of the complexity of homelessness grows, so will the sophistication of the conversations the whole group and the small groups have about the texts, and she will have to consider adapting the text level and content to students' growing understanding.

Figure 3.1 Class-Constructed Anchor Chart

Date: _____

Our thinking about . . .
Someplace to Go, by Maira Teste
and Karen Ritz

We think this family is homeless because . . .
Davey's mom lost her job at the paper mill.
The paper mill closed.

Support they have
- Shelter/clothing
- Brother, Mom, Davey have each other
- Zack
- Soup kitchen
- Friends (Josh)
- School
- Jobs (little money)
- Hope

Support they need
- A dad could help them
- Someone else to keep them company
- More money (better job for mom)
- Fun things to do
- More clothes
- More family (?)
- A home of their own

How we would feel:
Horrible and scared to be alone; sad and angry to not have a home or a dad, thankful for family, nervous, lonely, excited for my brother, confused, happy that I had food and friends, and family, happy that I have somewhere to go.

> *Each student had an exact replica of this anchor chart stapled into his homeless study journal.*
>
> *A space for the date is very important so Katie and her students can track the growth of their knowledge and thinking over time. By the end of the building background knowledge phase, Katie and her class had constructed multiple charts that showed the growth and complexity of their thinking around the guiding questions.*

> *The "How we would feel" section at the bottom helped students put themselves in the character's shoes as they read each story and acted as a scaffold for discussions of empathy.*

This anchor chart hangs on the wall as a concrete representation of the class' thinking on one day. As the class reads multiple stories, and charts their thinking for each, the quantity and variety of responses will grow—responses that they will need to refer back to later they when they craft their own profiles of homeless children as a demonstration of their understanding, the culminating product of this unit.

The Worktime ✳

After listening to her students' responses, Katie sends them into worktime with the following challenge:

> **Katie:** Today, in your book groups, I would like you to continue the discussions you began yesterday on the book *A Shelter in Our Car* by Monica Gunning and Elaine Pedlar. You may fill out your charts together. Figure out how you can support one another to get your job done.
>
> I'd like you to try to keep the conversation going for twelve minutes today. What are some things that can help you keep the conversation going, Enzo?
>
> **Enzo:** We can ask a question.
>
> **Katie:** Good. Anyone else?
>
> **David:** We can share a quote that we liked.
>
> **Elise:** We can make a connection to what someone else said.
>
> **Katie:** Great. OK, choose your text, find a spot in the room that is comfortable for your group, and get started.

Katie releases the students into their book groups. As each group reads and talks about the text over the next few days, Katie will circulate and join in the conversations to push their thinking when needed. Her main role during the worktime is *teacher as listener*—figuring out how each group, and each student, is making meaning and coming to understand the guiding questions more deeply. She uses what she hears to help guide her planning for the minilesson the next day, to recommend different texts to different students or groups, or to figure out where misconceptions lie and do some relevant just-in-time instruction. Let's listen in on one of the groups discussing the book *A Shelter in Our Car*, by Monica Gunning and Elaine Pedlar (2004):

An important teachable moment! Not everything a person reads is going to be interesting. Is the text too hard for Harris, or is he bored by the conversation surrounding the book? As a reader, how do you decide whether to stick with a text because it is important to make meaning or give up? Katie has some thinking to do about Harris. . . .

Ah! Katie is on it! And Harris confirms her suspicions with his response—he is confused. So, what are the implications for instruction? For now, Katie decides to ask Harris to do some thinking and writing about it in his journal. She has faith in Harris and in the groups' abilities to help Harris with his big questions. By not answering Harris directly, she is asking him to do the hard work of thinking and giving responsibility to the group to make meaning together—with support, of course. She assures Harris, "I can help you . . . but I want you to do a little thinking [by writing] about it first." Katie also wants the group to take some responsibility to help Harris make meaning. Students have to need each other to make meaning for book groups to work. She also knows that if this group has this many lingering questions, the rest of the groups probably do, too, and they can talk about it as a big group during the debrief.

Angie: How did the dad die?

Zoe: The book never tells us. I'm thinking that he died in Jamaica, and then the mom came to America to get a better job.

Harris: So, they had money to come over here, but now they have a car and no money for gas? I don't get it. This is boring.

Katie: [interjecting] It is OK to be confused or to wonder or to think it is a boring story.

Harris: It isn't really interesting . . . it should go a few pages more so we could see more of the story.

Angie: I like it better when they don't add all the details because then you need a prediction and you can make up your own ending.

Katie: So, Harris, are you left with too many lingering questions? Is that what is frustrating you right now? What is the big question that is driving you crazy right now?

Harris: I don't get it! The dad died—how? Why are they in America from Jamaica? What happened in Jamaica? What happened here? Why can't they live half here and half there if they miss it so much?

Katie: Wow. Your group is doing some amazing thinking and you have some really big, important questions that I think you can figure out together. Harris, my challenge for you is to write a little bit about why you think this book feels so frustrating to you. Please write for a little bit and you and I can have a conversation about it in a few minutes. I can help you figure some things out, but I want you to do a little thinking about it first.

I'm going to confer with another group, but start holding your thinking in your journals so you can share it in the debrief.

The Debrief

Katie calls the class back to the circle and asks students to have their reading journals open to their graphic organizers. She begins, "Make sure you have a colored pencil to add new thinking to your sheet. I'm wondering why you think this family is homeless? What does the text tell us?"

Elise: It could be that the dad made all the money. We know that the dad died.

Enzo: I think the dad died and the mom couldn't afford the rent.

Augie: She regained it though.

Katie: Yeah, Augie, she gets that job and she goes to college, so she isn't only trying to work and make money but she is also trying to learn. Josh, what are you thinking?

Josh: Maybe the dad was the greatest support with money and they don't have enough now.

Enzo: I think Jamaica was their greatest support.

Katie: Wow, Enzo. Interesting thought. So from the text, we know the dad died and we know that the mom is going to college too. I challenged some groups to think about their own support webs and make some inferences.

If you have been a listener, I want you to be a speaker now.

Brodie: They have shelter in their car and at the end they have a hotel.

Katie: Do you think this family can be happy in the U.S. or do they have to go back to Jamaica? That might be a lingering question for us. Let's put ourselves in their shoes for a second. How would we feel? If you share a feeling or emotion, back it up. I want to hear from Harris or Niijama. Put yourself in Zettie's shoes. What is it going to feel like?

For Successful Book Groups

Before diving directly into building background knowledge on homelessness, Katie spent time sharing the content-based purpose of book group conversations: to learn more by talking and listening to one another. We are smarter together.

Thus, in order to get smarter together by talking, their daily process purpose when meeting in book groups was "How can we keep the conversation going?"

The students brainstormed ways to keep the conversations going and modeled how to have a good conversation with a small group in a fishbowl format (a small group on the inside modeling the process, and a group on the outside recording what they noticed and what they wondered about the process).

They began the first day with a familiar text and five ideas for how the keep the conversations going.

Each group puts their "Book Club Reminders" in the middle of their discussion circle each time they meet:

- *Sit eye-to-eye and knee-to-knee.*
- *Ask questions.*
- *Tell stories and make connections.*
- *Share our feelings.*
- *Share mental images.*

Empathy alert! Going for the big idea, building their understanding, and asking them to back it up with evidence like real social scientists do!

Lorenzo's comment is evidence of students listening to each other and learning from each other—one of the little things that makes a big difference over time. Through modeling careful listening, Katie has built a culture of listening with her students.

A new idea emerges from Elise! New thinking is being generated through discussion. And Katie makes sure to label it and hold it in the anchor chart to come back to later.

Harris: Sad because she doesn't have a home.

Elise: I wouldn't feel sad. I would feel proud that I am part of that family and proud that I survived.

Katie: Wow, this hasn't come up yet. Yeah, of all of these sad and bad things that happened, you survived.

Josh: I feel like I'd be jealous because when I would see people with a whole family, I'd think, "What makes them so special; why do they have a whole family and I don't?"

Lorenzo: I'm kind of disagreeing and piggybacking. I'd be thankful for the mom but still jealous of people that had a dad.

Katie: Yeah, it is possible to feel both at the same time. So, we will read another story tomorrow, but while they are fresh in your head, I would like for you to jot down your lingering questions and fill out your group reflection on "How was your conversation today?"

✳ And with those words—an invitation to students to write their thinking in their journals "while it is fresh in [their] heads" so the thinking can be recorded in order to propel them into learning the next day, Katie's workshop comes to an end.

Who is doing the work in this classroom? Who is doing the reading? Who is doing the writing? Who is doing the talking? Who is doing the learning?

Let's follow other tracks in the snow to learn more.

How Katie's Students Know

When pupils acquire an overview of [a clear picture of the targets their learning is meant to attain] they become more com-

mitted and more effective as learners . . . [T]heir own assessments become an object of discussion with their teachers and with one another, and this discussion further promotes the reflection on one's own thinking that is essential to good learning. (Black and William 1998, 143)

Even the last few minutes of Katie's workshop are filled with purposeful learning. In the last three minutes, students write to hold their lingering questions from their group discussion as well as reflect on the quality of that discussion. In Katie's class-closing statement, she asks students to fill out a group reflection on the quality of their conversation today (see Figure 3.2). This is more of a checklist (as opposed to a complete rubric) than a lengthy reflection, but it helps remind students of the purpose for the book groups. It is also a great reflective tool for them to think about the bigger questions "Did I do the very best I could do today?" "Did I make meaning for myself?" and "Did I help others make meaning today?"

Imagine if adults took a few minutes every day to answer these questions. What would our world look like? I know it is a small step, but I believe that it is a small step that makes a big difference over time. Again, with both *process* and *product*, Katie is helping students become better human beings.

When students understand and *value* the purpose behind the things we ask them to do, they don't balk. Talking with classmates, hearing their thinking, asking questions, challenging assumptions, and asking for clarification makes us all smarter. How was our conversation today? How did we do? What will we try to do better next time? We need each other to be smarter, so we'd better try to have a better conversation next time. Next time. Ritual and routine. System and structure. Back to our original questions: How do we know what our students know and are able to do? How do they know what they know and are able to do? Let's keep listening to find out. . . .

Figure 3.2 Group Reflection Checklist

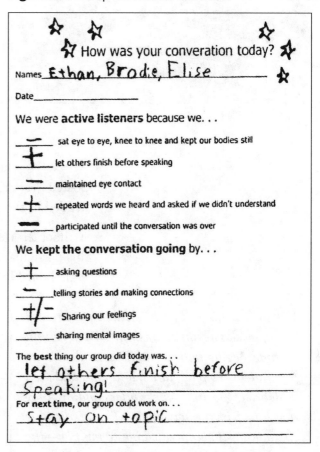

The Walls Are Alive with the Evidence of Learning

Figure 3.3 Posted Guiding Questions

The walls in Katie's classroom speak loudly. I can walk into her room any day and based on the whiteboard and walls, within a few minutes, I can infer what learning her class did yesterday, what they worked on today, and where they are going tomorrow. Katie is *that deliberate* with her instruction, assessment, and planning. There are a variety of artifacts for me to consult to make my inferences:

★ Artifact 1: The guiding questions are prominently and beautifully posted (see Figure 3.3). This tells me where the students are headed in the long term.

★ Artifact 2: The whiteboard greeting and schedule tell me where this particular day fits in the big picture. Figure 3.4 shows how the whiteboard looked on the day we listened in on the book groups.

Katie's teaching day is structured around multiple classroom workshops. Each chunk of time begins with a minilesson, then time for students to read, write, and talk, and then a debrief to share the understanding they developed in the worktime. The predictable that allows the unpredictable to happen—the magic of students coming to know.

Figure 3.4 Katie's Morning Whiteboard

Dear Amazing Crew,
I heard you had a great day on Friday. I can't wait to hear about it. Today we will begin science inquiry. Do you know what inquiry is?
Love, Katie

Daily Schedule
8:15   meeting
8:30   homeless workshop
10:00   snack/recess
10:30   readers workshop
11:15   math workshop
12:15   lunch/recess
1:00   *Gregor the Overlander*
1:30   science inquiry workshop
2:45   clean up/closing circle/song
3:00   home/aftercare

★ Artifact 3: The walls are *filled* with anchor charts (as modeled in the classroom vignette) created during different minilessons, from *all subject areas, clearly labeled* with titles and dates and filled with student thinking.

★ Artifact 4: High-quality student work blankets the walls (Figure 3.5).

★ Artifact 5: The chalkboard tray is lined with texts about homelessness, as is the display bookshelf that borders the circle area. This display gives me a clue about the variety of texts students are reading to build their background knowledge.

★ Artifact 6: Next to the bookshelf is the treasure chest of all treasure chests—students' homeless study journals, filled with their day-by-day developing knowledge, skill, and understanding.

I can pick up any journal and see the sequence of learning day to day and week to week. I can see the titles of texts that spurred bursts of students' thinking. I can infer the ideas that came out of group conversations and whole-class debriefs. I can read questions a student wanted to ask the guest speaker from the St. Francis Shelter and also what the student thought was important about what the guest expert shared. I can see what students think about how their group conversations are going from the filled-out checklists stapled onto a page (see Figure 3.2). I can read questions and feedback Katie has for individuals based on their writing. . . . and on and on and on. My learning about a student from the journal I have in my hands is limited only by the richness of what Katie asks the kids to read, write, and think about. Rich inputs, scaffolded well, lead to rich outputs. What goes on inside the black box of students' brains shouldn't be a mystery if we show them how to make meaning by reading, writing, and talking to think.

Figure 3.5 Student Work on Katie's Wall

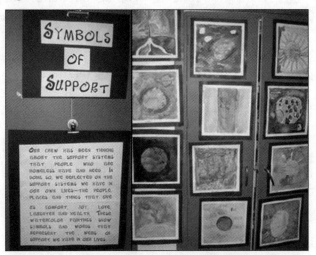

Our crew has been thinking about the support systems that people who are homeless have and need. In doing so, we reflected on the support systems we have in our own lives—the people and places and things that give us comfort, joy, love, laughter, and health. These watercolor paintings show symbols and words that represent the webs of support we have in our lives.

One Place for Everything: Enzo's Journey of Understanding

It is fascinating to follow Enzo's tracks in the snow—the journey of his understanding about homelessness through his homeless study journal. One of his first entries is his initial thinking about the guiding question "Why are families homeless?"

His first quick-write to the guiding question shows an interesting mix of thinking about the links to resources ("People lose their jobs. . . . They couldn't pay for their mortgage . . . They get really sick.") along with stereotypes ("People drink too much. . . . Homeless people sleep in garbage cans") (see Figure 3.6).

Over the next few weeks, Enzo reads, writes, and talks about homelessness with his classmates, and through his writing we can track developing subtleties in his thinking. In the script of the book group conversation, Enzo was the one to say, "I think Jamaica was their greatest support," when the class was discussing the needs of the homeless family from the book *A Shelter in Our Car*. In his journal that day he wrote: "If I were a member of this family I would feel scared because the people at school were mean to me and I would feel bad because my dad was dead and feel grateful for still having a mom." This is evidence of his meaning making from listening to the text as well as to his classmates' comments during the group discussion. Through the structure of the homeless study journal as a place to hold student thinking, Katie is able to track the connections Enzo is forming as he builds his background knowledge and his brain works as fertile soil for the seeds of empathy to take root and sprout.

More importantly, *Enzo* can read back through and use his *own knowledge and thinking* as he prepares to take on the persona of a child who has lost his home and write a personal narrative, the final culminating project Katie has designed for students to demonstrate their understanding.

Figure 3.6 Enzo's Essential Thinking on the Guiding Question

> Why are families homeless? to
> People lose their jobs and
> become homeless.
> They coudnt pay for their
> morgej.
> They get ralley sick.
> People drick to much.
> homeless People sleep in the
> garbeg cans.

Use of a Mentor Text as a Model and Scaffold for the Final Project

Katie's first goal was to get students "into" the lives of the children profiled in the book *Changing Places* to begin to develop their capacity to show empathy. Just like with the book clubs, she organized reading-discussion groups around different children profiled in the book. Each day the conversations centered on the main content questions "How did this family become homeless?" and "What support do they need?" After spending a few days discussing the life of an individual child, Katie asked students to expand on one of the vignettes. Enzo's addition to the arrival story of Lamont is shown in Figure 3.7. Enzo, in both content and tone, jumped right into the flow of the narrative from

Enzo clearly sees Lamont's dependence on his mom in the strange shelter environment. He is also able to develop a sensory image (strange snoring) based on the room full of beds Lamont describes in the original text. Enzo is making meaning from text and able to apply that meaning to continue the narrative flow with strong voice.

Figure 3.7 Enzo Steps into Lamont's Shoes

LAMONT Age 6

"I'm Lamont. Mom and I came to this shelter late last night. I didn't know the lady asleep in the bed next to me, but Mom said I didn't need to be afraid. She said we were finally in a safe place."

I couldn't sleep last night. there were to many people snorring. In the morning me and mom had brekfest I didnt like it much mom said

I should be greatful of what I have I am, but they could at least have pizza on Friday. The beds were lumpy this night and there were people snorring again but I got to sleep.

The "Lamont" text came directly from the book Changing Places: A Kid's View of Shelter Living *(Chalofsky, Finland, and Wallace 1992).*

Starting with Lamont's story and attempting to add to it was important scaffolding for Enzo before he attempted to write a completely new story about a child who goes to live in a shelter.

Students learn to write by studying the craft and process of other writers. The use of a mentor text as a model for students of writing craft, process, and genre is a great way to scaffold student writing.

By carefully studying the craft of writing—the use of language, the patterns of text, the flow of narrative, and so on—students have a variety of entry points for their own writing that honors the difficulty and complexity of the writing process.

Lamont's point of view. Like Enzo's plea for "pizza on Friday," many of the students' stories focused on the unappetizing food at the shelter—a perfect entry point of empathy for them.

Bringing the World to the Class and the Class to the World

> *Students . . . learn from fieldwork, experts, and service in addition to learning from text. They use the natural and social environments of their communities as sites for purposeful fieldwork and service connected to academic work. Students working in the field are active investigators using the research tools, techniques of inquiry, and standards of presentation used by professionals in the field. . . . In addition to having students conduct research outside the school, teachers bring experts from the community into the classroom. . . . These experiences maximize students' motivation to learn. (Expeditionary Learning, Core Practice Benchmarks 2003, 14)*

Along with the texts they were reading, Katie knew the students would need some real-world experience to make their personal narratives come to life. Katie scheduled two experts, employees from local shelters, to speak to the students and answer questions, as well as a trip to the St. Francis Center for students to see firsthand what a shelter looks like, sounds like, and in some cases (as Enzo noted in his journal) smells like (see Figure 3.8). "Write what you know" is the mantra of every author, and students needed to see a shelter with their own eyes in order to write powerfully about the experience from the perspective of a child who had lost his home.

Figure 3.8 Notes from Enzo's Visit to St. Francis Center Shelter

I notice:	I wonder:
• It is big • There are a lot of people • Most of the people have shoes • Some people are missing teeth • There were lots of supplies like toothpaste stacked up and other toiletries • It smelled harsh	• Why didn't we see the beds? • Why were there more men than women? • Is there a lockout time? • How many people are here? • Do you help them get jobs? • Do the kids go to school? • Can all people come?

During each expert's visit, the guiding questions helped students ask questions that would build their understanding and develop a sense of empathy for homeless children and their families. Toward the end of May, Katie was able to get a representative from the Denver mayor's office to speak to the students about Denver's Road Home Plan—an ambitious plan to end homelessness in Denver in ten years, which was profiled in Malcolm Gladwell's *New Yorker* article (2006). Katie shared,

> *My students were amazing when Jamie, a representative from Mayor Hickenlooper's office, came to speak to them about Denver's Road Home Plan. During the question-and-answer part of his talk, the students spoke with such eloquence and passion, sharing statistics they had learned and giving him examples of what homelessness feels like from a kid's point of view. He couldn't believe it. He said, "I rarely meet adults with such a deep understanding of homelessness, and I've never met more socially conscious children." I know it is an informal assessment of their understanding, but believe me, they get it!*

Although the guest experts' visits were not set up intentionally for the purpose of assessment, Katie's intentional *planning* for student access to experts throughout their study turned out to be an excellent way to both excite *and* demonstrate student thinking, perspective taking, and empathy.

Let's listen carefully to Enzo's attempt to demonstrate his understanding through writing a story from the perspective of a child who has lost his home. . . .

Enzo's Story: "Friends in a Shelter"

What counts as literacy? How can we learn about, appreciate, and make use of the narrative affiliations of potentially alienated boys? How can we tap the interests that exist on the other side of the partition? I am convinced that these boys can be reached if we are willing to interrogate our own values and open ourselves to a more comprehensive view of narrative choice. (Newkirk 2002, xxi)

In Enzo's progress report from the fall, Katie wrote, "Enzo enjoys writers workshop and takes initiative. However, when given a choice, he rarely deviates from his battle-based comic creations. I support Enzo's comic writing, but in order to build his writing fluency, I will continue to encourage him to share his thinking and ideas using more words and fewer pictures." Flipping through eight pages of the rough draft of Enzo's "Friends in a Shelter" from his homeless study journal, I would not recognize the writer Katie described in the fall.

Before Enzo began writing, he used a web to brainstorm the main character, Joe, for his homelessness story (see Figure 3.9).

After students brainstormed the skeleton of their character's story, they met with a partner to talk it through and get the creative writing juices flowing. Katie described Enzo's process:

Enzo went through an amazing transformation this spring with his writing. He and Augie [another third grader] latched on to the idea that if they were homeless, the greatest support they would need would be a friend in the shelter. That idea was a

> *Once again, Katie scaffolded the prompts to match the guiding questions. Purpose. Focus. Purpose. Focus. When you know where you are going (as a teacher and as a student), it is easier to get there!*

Figure 3.9 Enzo's Character Brainstorm

Your name Enzo

My character's name   Joe

My character's age   13

My character is homeless because . . .
Support my character has and needs . . .
If I were this child I would feel . . .

*spark that fueled their writing for weeks! Each day during
writers workshop, they would lie next to each other in the
corner and talk and write and talk some more. Then they'd
rush over to me, thrust their journals at me, and say, "Read
this. Is it funny? We want it to be funny, but not too funny.
We know it is a serious story, but if we were in the shelter
together, we would make it fun."*

*In the fall, during writing conferences with Enzo, I would
have to literally drag words out of him. I would say over and
over, "Tell me more about that," and he would write one
extra word. This spring, the collaboration with Augie and his
insistence on telling Joe's story realistically was so important
to him. The ownership and pride he took in this story was
incredible. There was so much feeling in his writing, unlike
anything else he wrote with me in two years. The writing
habits and stamina he developed during this process are going
to fuel his writing life for a long time.*

We'll take a closer look at Enzo's story, but first, I think it is important to talk a bit about boys and literacy. As the mother of three boys, I find it a particularly interesting topic. My eldest son's first literary masterpiece, written on his first day of kindergarten, was titled "Poop!" which also happened to be the only word written on each of twelve pages of the book besides "And he. . . ." It was also beautifully illustrated in full color.

Why does this matter? It matters because as teachers, we have to maintain a delicate balance of high energy, positive intent, and chaos in the service of momentum. One of my favorite books on the topic of boys and literacy is *Misreading Masculinity: Boys, Literacy, and Popular Culture*, by Thomas Newkirk. In the chapter titled "Making Way for Captain Underpants," Newkirk writes,

*Humor is an illusive topic. Explain it too much and you kill
it. The humor of kids in school is primarily oral and
physical. . . . It is primarily subversive, mocking adult author-
ity. . . . And male humor in particular deals with the body in
ways that are designed to make adults uncomfortable—that's
part of the point. It flaunts the code of embarrassment or
shame; it directly attacks the social conventions that says
which body parts must be covered, which bodily acts must be
hidden from public view, and which bodily noises must be
silenced. This humor is a field of energy that surrounds what
we do in classrooms; it fits into the cracks and open moments
in the hallway, before official work begins. . . . It is the*

adhesive that connects a generation, more powerful and appealing—more ancient and enduring—than most of the official learning in schools. (2002, 145)

This matters because I believe that what worked for Enzo as a writer had as much to do with the flow of Katie's writing workshop as it did with the importance and relevance of the topic. The collaboration with his best buddy, lying on their stomachs in the corner, debating scenarios of misbehavior and mischief at the shelter, helped Enzo incorporate a sense of normalcy into his story. The physical and emotional space Katie allows in her classroom—the overwhelmingly positive, humor-filled energy of seven- and eight-year-olds that she allows to fill every pocket of air—is as big a part of the success of her writers workshop as the important topic she asked the students to read about, think about, talk about, and ultimately write about.

A Note About Writing Assessment: Assess What You Teach

If you're ever bored at a faculty party and want to stir the pot a bit, bring up the subject of assessing writing. Although I agree that there are some basic standards for comprehensible written communication and ways of writing that are more powerful than others, I am a huge egalitarian when it comes to the written word. Take this passage, for example:

> *I may say that only three times in my life have I met a genius and each time a bell within me rang and I was not mistaken, and I may say in each case it was before there was any general recognition of the quality of genius in them. I have met many important people, I have met several great people but I have only known three first class geniuses and in each case on sight within me something rang. In no one of the three cases have I been mistaken. In this way my new full life began. (1993, 6)*

Are you holding yourself back from marking it up with your red pen? This passage is by Gertrude Stein, from *The Autobiography of Alice B. Toklas*, one of my favorite books of all time. Stein said she tried to separate language from its direct representation of objects in the same way that abstract painters tried to separate painting from mere representation. Once you get into the flow of her language, you can't put the book down. When it was first published it became an immediate best-seller and launched Stein into a realm previously held only by gangsters, baseball players, and movie stars.

Why does this matter? This matters because young Gertrude's English teachers complained of her wayward syntax and made her write papers over and over and over. This matters because if not for Gertrude's resilience, we might not have her books today. The point is, writing is tricky and assessing writing is trickier. As educator and author Vicki Spandel writes, "So much of assessment is about identifying problems. But courage is what writers need most" (2006, 16). Rejoice to that!

Katie explicitly used a mentor text that was full of voice, had a purposeful organizational structure, and was written in the first-person narrative. So, along with the Colorado state standard of "using the power of language ethically and creatively," Katie should assess around voice, organization, and the characteristics of first-person narrative. My point? ASSESS WHAT YOU TEACH.

The "6 + 1 Trait of Writing" rubric is one that is used nationwide, so for the fans of 6 + 1 Traits, I have added some labeling of Enzo's work using language from this common assessment tool. But, be cautioned: there are many ways to identify good writing. What matters most is a teacher's use of *real models of writing* to help students learn the craft of writing. Look at a piece of great writing with your students and try to label *why* it is great. Ask your students to emulate the craft that made the model piece of writing so clear and powerful. Once again: TRUST YOURSELF, trust your students. Make sure students know the goals of communication their writing is supposed to meet (real model, real purpose, real audience), and then explicitly teach what you want to assess.

How Do We Know What Enzo Knows and Is Able to Do?

So, what did Enzo write? How did he demonstrate his understanding of why families are homeless, the support they need, and how he can show empathy? Enzo's story begins: "Hi I'm Joe and I'm 13 years old. Right now, I live at the St. Francis Center with my dad. We are homeless right now because my Mom got sick and me and Dad used all our money for medical bills." He goes on to relate how he met Bob (aka Augie) and his dad at the St. Francis Center. As in the mentor text, Part 2 is titled "Staying," and Part 3 is "Moving to a Different Place." Let's take a look (see Figure 3.10).

This story is *one* way Katie knows what Enzo knows and is able to do. Here is a list of the other evidence of thinking and understanding she has asked him to create along the way:

★ watercolor of "My Web of Support" (see Figure 3.5)

*Skill development alert! Seamless incorpora-
tion of dialogue to illuminate a narrative and
propel the plot. Strong sense of voice.*

*Katie was excited to see the inklings of
emotion in Enzo's narrative: "me and Bob
were a little sad," and "I felt safer . . ."
something new for Enzo in his development
as a writer.*

*A mature sense of empathy is described as
"able to make sense of . . . experiences,
events that seem weird to others." Enzo
meets the standard here by showing the
resiliency of Bob and Joe taking a difficult
situation in stride. He makes the reader
believe that this is how he and Augie would
handle this situation—make the best of it, be
themselves, and help each other feel safe.*

Figure 3.10 Enzo's Final Product

Staying

The next day I showed Bob
and his dad around. While
me and Bob were walking
we made a deal "hey Bob, if
me and my dad get a home
you and your dad can come
live with us" I said "and if
we get a home you guys can come
live with us" Said Bob we Shook
on it. Later that day me and
Bob were alittle Sad
So we went into the
Shower room and knocked on
a window we heard a voice
Saying "Cut it out you darn
kids" We ran away giggling.
At breakfast Bob said a
funny joke, Unluckily I had
a big drink of milk and
Spat it all out laughing.
After breakfast we Sat by the
entrance seeing People walk by. I've
felt Safer since I moved
into the Shelter.

From 6 + 1 Trait rubric: "Sentence Fluency—Sentences vary
in length as as well as structure. Fragments, if used, add
style. Dialogue, if present, sounds natural."

From 6 + 1 Trait rubric: "Voice—The writer speaks directly
to the reader in a way that is individual, compelling, and
engaging. The writer crafts the writing with an awareness
and respect for the audience and the purpose for writing."

Figure 3.10 Enzo's Final Product (cont.)

Moving to a different Place

It's been one month since Bob and his dad moved in. MY dad has some money but its not enough for a home. I told him about me and Bobs deal. The next day me and Bob met up. I said my dad has a little money, he said his dad had some money so we could get an apartment to live in. So we went and told our dads my dad said its fine so me and Bob met up again. Bob said its fine with them. I said it was fine with us. The next morning our dads had a talk. They finally told us to get our coats. Bob got his bike I got my scooter. we were moving to find a home. we saw a place for rent. We went to the owner and asked how much the rent was. He said "300 bucks" we had enough, So we bought it we rushed to the shelter, we got all our stuff and rode back to our new home.

From 6 + 1 Trait rubric: "Ideas and Content—Insight—an understanding of life and a knack for picking out what is significant—is an indicator of high-level performance."

From 6 + 1 Trait rubric: "Ideas and Content—The writer seems to be writing from knowledge or experience; the ideas are fresh and original."

Enzo allows the dads to have a say in the matter . . . but the idea to live together and pool resources was all his and Bob's—the power of collaboration! Enzo's narrative is a testament to the power of a child's voice, especially in a situation where adults and children usually feel powerless.

Enzo's narrative demonstrates some understanding of the amount of monetary resources needed to get a home and logical problem solving of combining resources with another family to make a home possible.

"Bob got his bike. I got my scooter." Again, some typical eight-year-old boy behavior in a situation that is anything but typical in Enzo's personal experience.

★ in his homelessness study journal:
- initial reflections on the guiding questions (see Figure 3.6)
- anchor charts created for each text the class read and talked about (see Figure 3.1)
- letter to a child from the mentor text
- story based on a child from the mentor text (see Figure 3.7)
- brainstormed questions for the guest experts; notes from those visits
- "What I Notice/What I Wonder" chart from shelter visit (see Figure 3.8)
- planning web for homelessness story (see Figure 3.9)
- rough draft for homelessness story

Katie has multiple ways to know what Enzo knows and is able to do. These artifacts help Katie reconstruct the story of Enzo as a learner—both *what* and *how* he came to know. His final product is a delight, but not surprising because Katie's assessment, planning, and instruction unfolded in a way that helped Enzo connect new information to known information and showed him how to both grow and demonstrate his thinking and understanding each step of the way. Based on conversations, prewriting, access to rich texts, collaboration, and long chunks of time for writing, Katie knew Enzo would create something wonderful and amazing. But still, her predictable systems and structures allowed the unpredictable to happen. Katie said,

> *This project game me ahas on many different levels. On a personal level, I was very concerned about the topic. I wanted it to be real, but not scary. The thing that I learned through this project, the thing that surprised me most, was that you can have amazing real-world conversations with young kids that are honest and open and age appropriate about a very serious adult topic. There is a need to protect the students, but to make them aware of what is happening in the world and to get rid of stereotypes—that will have an impact on them for a long time. I watched stereotypes melt away with this project. Seven- and eight-year-olds can develop a deep understanding of who the homeless are and what they need. I of course wonder what impact this will have on them in the future, but I know their thinking has affected me profoundly.*

On Denver's "Road Home" website (*www.denversroadhome.org*), there is a page for frequently asked questions. One reads,

Q: As an honest, hard-working, tax-paying citizen of Denver, what does this plan ask and expect of me?

A: Get Involved. *Call 2-1-1 and become a volunteer or give to help end homelessness. Please do NOT give to panhandlers and advise your friends against giving. Give instead to solutions that will have a lasting impact on the lives of homeless people. Encourage groups and organizations where you are a member to get involved in mentoring a family that is homeless. Consider helping a person permanently exit the streets by offering a job for a person who is working to get off the streets. Give to solutions to homelessness through the Community Appeal managed by Mile High United Way. Donate today to programs that will have a lasting impact on the lives of panhandlers and the homeless.*

I believe that the students in Katie's classroom will be the citizens that answer this call and have a lasting impact on those in need.

Katie's Systems, Structures, Routines, and Rituals

Following is a scaffold for the story of teaching and learning in Katie's classroom. Remember, whole-scale replication is not the point. What practices were intriguing to you? Which practices match your beliefs about the agency and capacity of children to think and learn? The beauty is, there are dozens of entry points. Pick one that matches what you believe and the rest will come. Do you want to start with a compelling guiding question? Doing your own assignment? Student book groups? Here are a few ideas for places to start:

Systems, Structures, Routines, and Rituals Highlighted in Chapter 3	Narrative description found on page	Ideas to help you get started	For more information check out these resources
Doing your own assignments	49, 50	• Try it. Write down the steps you had to go through to complete the assignment. Use your steps as the minilessons for a few days to show students possible entry points to the assignment. • Use your work as a model to give students a vision for a high-quality final product.	*Culture of Quality* (Berger 1996) *Understanding by Design* (Wiggins and McTighe 2005) *How People Learn* (National Research Council 2000)
Academic journals—one place for everything	53, 56–59, 61–66, 72	• Buy/add to your student supply list a composition notebook. Have students put all notes, worksheets, graphic organizers, reflections, entrance and exit tickets, and so on inside (glue, tape, staple—whatever strikes your fancy). • Every few weeks, give students time to read through their journals to see how their knowledge and skills have grown over time. • Have students use notes, thinking in graphic organizers, and so on to sythesize their thinking in final products/projects.	*Best Practice* (Ch. 8) (Zemelman, Daniels, and Hyde 1998) *Integrating Differentiated Instruction and Understanding by Design* (Tomlinson and McTighe 2006)
Anchor charts	52, 53, 54–55, 61	• Buy a giant sticky note pad. • Each day/week, think about the key idea/skill you want students to take away—it usually is a good topic for an anchor chart. • Think about topics/ideas you want students to have access to throughout a study unit that they can come back to again and again. • Think about how the walls of your classroom can speak volumes about what happens inside—what matters most? When you figure that out, ask students about it and hold their thinking on an anchor chart!	*Strategies that Work* (Harvey and Goudvis 2000) *Reading with Meaning* (Miller 2002)

Systems, Structures, Routines, and Rituals Highlighted in Chapter 3	Narrative description found on page	Ideas to help you get started	For more information check out these resources
Using a mentor text for writer's craft and product design	49, 50–52, 63, 69	• Ask yourself, "How does a [insert real-world job title here] demonstrate his understanding of a topic?" Find that demonstration of understanding at a library, online, or from a colleague's bookshelf. Or, write one yourself.	*Understanding by Design* (Wiggins and McTighe 2005) *About the Authors* (Ray and Cleaveland 2004) *Study Driven* (Ray 2006)
Book groups	55–59	• Prepare students to talk about text by sharing with them *why and how* talking about books with others helps them make meaning. • Explicitly label what a good conversation looks like and sounds like. • Try a fishbowl conversation with a few students to show the class what it looks like.	*Reading with Meaning* (Miller 2002) *Mini-Lessons for Literature Circles* (Daniels and Steineke 2004) *Strategies that Work* (Harvey and Goudvis 2000)

CHAPTER FOUR

Jen's Readers

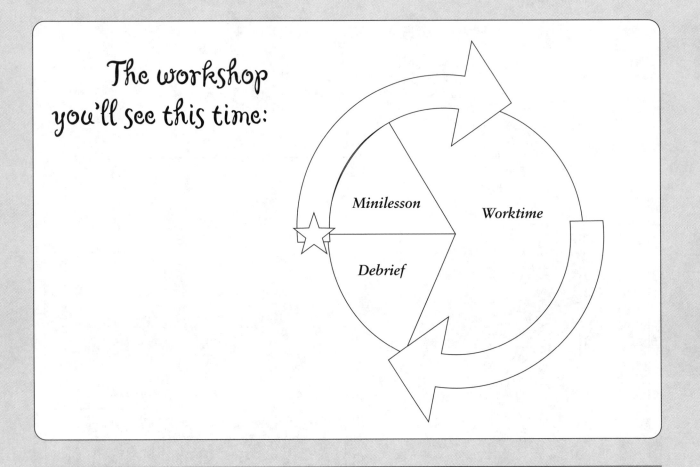

The workshop you'll see this time:

Minilesson

Worktime

Debrief

Workshop duration: 75 minutes

Minilesson (13 minutes):

★ Teacher reviews the purpose of keeping a reader's notebook throughout the year.

★ Teacher models the type of thinking she is hoping to see in students' reader's notebooks by highlighting the thinking of one student in the class.

Worktime (45 minutes):

★ Students read choice books and record their thinking on sticky notes next to the text that spurred the thought.

★ Teacher confers.

Debrief (17 minutes):

★ One student shares how she recorded her thinking during the worktime.

★ One student shares his synthesis of the series books he is reading.

★ Teacher labels the student thinking she hears and thanks students for being her teachers every day.

Hi Jen,

Thanks for inviting me into your classroom a for read-aloud of *Gregor and the Curse of the Warmbloods* today. The energy around a good story in your classroom is palpable. It is a great time of day for all.

What struck me most was the conversational tone, pace, and flow of your read-aloud and the natural pauses to discuss parts with your fourth- and fifth-grade students. I don't think this can be underestimated. It is both fun and interesting for students to talk about books with you.

I see many incredible long-term effects from your daily read-aloud time. You are re-creating the emotional and intellectual pleasure of "lap time" reading as well as bringing your students into the grown-up world of sitting around the dinner table for hours having fascinating conversations—another life-enhancing habit to cultivate!

Over and over again I'm convinced that it is less about what a person knows and more about how a person comes to know it that makes a better adult. Read-aloud time in your classroom is helping students come to know in so many gentle yet targeted ways day after day after day—it's kind of like water falling into a crack in a rock and drip . . . drip . . . drip . . . creating a canyon!

Here is an excerpt of the script from your opening conversation today:

> **Jen:** How is read-aloud time working for all of you? I've been thinking a lot about it lately and I need to hear your thinking about it to get smarter.
> **Zoë:** It is more fun to read with a big group. You get to hear what everybody else thinks and it helps you make connections.
> **Brian:** Jen, when *you* read, it helps me sort the different voices in my head. It helps me when I read by myself because I can hear you in my head sometimes.
> **Jen:** Wow, Brian, I'm wondering . . . if you are losing interest in a book, would that work? What if you made different voices talk in your head? What if you added more animation in that voice in your head when you read?

Eliza: I kind of do voices. I try out different accents when I get lost and it makes me laugh and I keep going.

Brian: I do that with my kindergarten reading buddy.

Jen: So do you agree with what Zoë was saying—that this book wouldn't be as good if you were reading it by yourself?

J.J.: I do like to read by myself, too, but Jen, you have a really good Boots voice [character in the book]. That is why we don't like when substitutes are here!

Jen: Thanks, J. J. Let's dive back into the book. From that part we read yesterday *I'm* thinking that the author has missed the mark with Frill . . . what is the point of that character? I'm thinking, "Why did the author waste her time describing him if he doesn't have anything to do with the story?"

Victoria: I think Frill is going to become a hero in the end.

Jen: So you think the author is setting Frill up here? Ohhh. In the last book we read, remember it was the tiny details that made a big difference . . . let's add that prediction to our anchor chart. [Jen writes on the anchor chart behind her: "Frill—a small character that will make a big difference? Why does the author spend so much time describing her?"]

Tyler: I think that Frill is going to do a lot of stuff and then she is going to die.

Jen: Thanks for your prediction, Tyler. Let's keep reading and find out! Here we go. . . .

End of script.

So, Jen, this conversation left me wondering:

- How do you hope this explicit labeling from the *Gregor* story will play out in students' own reading?
- How might it concretely show up later? What will it look like in their reader's notebooks, their conversations in book groups, or in their writing?

I'm thinking, if you know what you are looking for, it is easier to find it . . . of course a good rule for shopping, too. ☺

Please write to me a little bit tonight if you get a chance. I love to capture your thinking over time and then show you later how brilliant you are. Let's touch base tomorrow in person. Let me know what time is good for you.

Talk soon,
Sam

Jen Is Crying

As if an ear-splitting siren has gone off, the news travels throughout the halls of school: everyone's favorite teacher and colleague, Jen, is crying. School is not in session today. It is September and it is goal-setting conference time, the first of three student-led conferences held each year.

The fact that Jen is crying is not a shock, because she cries at the drop of a hat. What is shocking is the reason. She's crying because she just had a tough run-in with a parent who wanted to know how Jen would challenge his daughter academically this year. We are all in shock. A parent not falling down and weeping at Jen's feet, thanking her for inspiring his child to be a lifelong reader and thinker? What's going on?

Jen is an institution at her school. She is the hub of communication and the walking embodiment of teacher as learner, voracious reader, and inspiring writer. If anyone of any age in her K–12 school (adults included) needs a book to read, she is sent to Jen for a recommendation. She has won Teacher of the Year for Denver Public Schools, she is National Board Certified, and she was nominated for Disney's Teacher of the Year (for which she gained the nickname Mickey for several months while the decision was pending).

Not only is she the font of all knowledge about matching people to books, but I also like to describe her as the Princess and the Pea of Relationships. If there are any "peas" of discontent between colleagues at the school, she feels it to her core (I'm sure she even develops bruises). She is kind of a voodoo doll for *un*collegiality.

As we hope with all teachers, her behavior in the world of adults is mirrored in her life as a teacher. The teaching belief that guides each minute of her day is "I must know my students deeply to teach them well." For Jen, the cycle of assessment, planning, and instruction is intricately tied to knowing her kids, and if a teaching practice won't help her know them better, forget it!

So, this is why the parent's questions sting *deeply*. At the core of his questions sits, "How well do you know my daughter AS A LEARNER?" On the spur of the moment, Jen couldn't answer, and thus, she can't stop crying.

Luckily, Jen, as the center of the school's relationship universe, doesn't have to figure it out alone. *All* of her colleagues want to help her stop crying.

What's All the Fuss About?

Over the next few days, the story got passed around and discussed at length. The questions the parent was asking were not just for Jen; he had thrown down the gauntlet for all of the teachers. The questions were some of the same ones that sit at the core of this book:

★ How does Jen know his daughter is growing as a reader?
★ What specific skills does his daughter need to improve in order to grow as a reader? How will Jen explicitly help his daughter learn those skills?
★ How does his daughter know she is growing as a reader?
★ How does her parent know?

Assessment as Magic: Knowing Students Deeply

Oscar Wilde wrote in a time when grown men wrote very seriously for young readers. For instance, Hawthorne and Longfellow in America, and in England Lewis Carroll, Robert Louis Stevenson, and Rudyard Kipling all wrote stories and poems for children to read.

They did not do it offhand, or with a sly smile, but in earnest, with all the skill and wisdom they had, as if their lives depended upon it, which in a way they did. For if men do not keep on speaking terms with children, they cease to be men, and become merely machines for eating and for earning money. (Updike 1955, 235)

Jen is *on speaking terms with children.* All of her teaching practices stem from the belief that she must know her students deeply to teach them well—to put books in their hands, to know when to push them and when to pull them, to know just what they need at the perfect teachable moment. If you ask her what reluctant readers need most, she will say, "Relationship is everything—oh yeah, and they need good books."

Throughout the years, as countless children and their parents will tell you, she's inspired students to become lifelong readers. In each case, she was the spark that set the passion for reading ablaze in students' hearts. A very telling piece of student writing comes from a reader's notebook in Jen's class. After filling three pages with detailed descriptions of the "coolest" part of the book he was reading, a fourth grader wrote, "P.S. Jen, you win. I am kind of enjoying reading. So you win. This time."

In a reflection for National Board Certification, Jen wrote,

> The ultimate priority for me is to know my students deeply. This is the most basic foundation to my teaching and the foundation behind my uniqueness as a teacher. . . . Every day, without fail in my classroom, we begin our day in a circle. The circle itself is important because the circle is a symbol of collaboration and of equality. We start as a community. In this circle, we take the time to share news and check in with each other. This is one of the most important ways that I begin to know my students deeply. I know their lives outside of school. I know what is important to them and I know what they care about. I can look in my students' faces and hear from them how they are coming to school that day. This helps me know who may need some extra attention.

So, it was this thoughtful, dedicated, inspiring teacher who was being challenged on her assessment practices. It wasn't that she couldn't answer the parent's questions. She *could* answer them from her gut and her heart. The problem was, she didn't have any concrete evidence to *show* the parent what she knew to be true about his child in her head. Good teachers just know, right? Isn't that part of the art of teaching? Well, yes, and no. Mostly no. It isn't enough.

Assessment by Heart and Gut

I recently read Philip Pullman's *The Golden Compass* (1995). The book is named for an instrument central to the story, an alethiometer—a sort of compass that reveals the truth when you ask a question, but only a few people on earth can read it and usually only after years and years of study with a book of symbols. Lyra, the eleven-year-old protagonist, is suddenly in possession of this instrument and begins to read it quite easily. Pullman writes,

> He handed the instrument back to Lyra, and added:
>
> "May I ask a question? Without the books of symbols, how do you read it?"
>
> "I just make my mind go clear and then it's sort of like looking down into water. You got to let your eyes find the

right level, because that's the only one that's in focus.
Something like that," she said.
     "I wonder if I might see you do it?" he said.
     . . . She sat still, letting her mind hold the three levels of
meaning in focus, and relaxed for the answer, which came
almost at once . . . When [the instrument] had completed the
movements several times, Lyra looked up. She blinked once or
twice as if she were coming out of a trance.
     . . . "Would you tell me how you read that?"
     . . . "I just see it all like that, you see," she said. (1995,
153)

Many brilliant, amazing teachers, when you ask them how they
know what their students know and are able to do, would answer the
same way as Lyra. They know their students deeply and can tell you stories about them, their lives, their habits as students, their likes and dis-
likes, but when you ask them, "*How* do you know?" they answer, "I just
see it all like that, you see." It is a tremendous start, but in this age of
accountability, when we need literate, thinking world citizens more than
ever, we need to know more in order to help *students* know more, do
more, be more, and perform better.

Relaying the story of the parent conference, Jen shared, "I was stuck.
I didn't know what to say to the parent. I go so much by my gut and my
instinct when it comes to what students need. It is good when my gut is
good but it doesn't help me all of the time. I really want to figure this
out."

So, she decided to spend some time thinking about these questions:
"How do I know *all* of my students are growing in their skills and understanding of reading?" "How do I help students make the 'invisible' skills
of reading comprehension 'visible'?" "What can I do to help students read
better?" Finding answers to these became Jen's quest for the year.

The Quest Begins

Jen began by brainstorming a list of how she knows her readers are growing over time. She wrote:

★ They choose to read more sophisticated books over time.

★ They have rich conversations about books.

★ Their reading stamina increases over time.

★ They know what to do to make meaning when they get stuck.

★ They make inferences about writer's craft.

★ They are able to articulate how reading makes their life better.

★ They always have a book, or multiple books, going.

★ They can identify landmark books—books that affected them intellectually and emotionally and know why and how.

★ They understand the rhythm of a book. They are able to stick with a book and wait out the tough parts because they know the routines of the author or genre.

★ They understand the "diet of a reader." They know the pay-off of an instant gratification book vs. a difficult book, or a candy book vs. a main course book. What sticks with you over time?

★ They hold thinking in their head from reading to reading.

As Jen looked back over the list, she realized, "Wow!" Not only are there many concrete, *visible* ways for her to know, but there are multiple ways for her to track, both quantitatively and qualitatively, what these reading habits look like over time.

Jen *did* have it all in her head, but when the parent pressed her in the conference, she couldn't articulate it on the spot and hadn't collected concrete evidence to support what she knew about his daughter. So, now what?

Working with a few of her colleagues, Jen decided to brainstorm different ways to collect evidence for each habit as well as the implications for planning, instruction, and assessment. (See table pages 86–87)

Over and over again, reader's notebooks were the structure that emerged as a way to explicitly track student thinking over time. This was a structure that Jen had used before in her classroom, but she had never intentionally organized them explicitly to track the specific ways to know. So Jen decided to start with a *revamping* of her reader's notebooks.

The Reading Notebook Revamp

Jen reflected about the reorganization of the reader's notebook structure in an email:

> *My reader's notebooks were something I loved and held dear to my heart. I looked forward to reading them, and once I*

Documentation of Conversation About Making the Invisible Visible

How Readers Grow	Evidence *Might* Look Like?	Implications for Planning, Instruction, and/or Assessment?
Choose to read more sophisticated books over time	A reader's bibliography that students keep throughout the year with date, title, author, genre, number of pages, and a brief reflection on "What I learned from this book . . ." or "What this book made me think about . . ."	• Add structure to reader's notebook (first five pages?) • Create a board for students to recommend books to each other • Goal-setting implications? • Individual conferring conversations based on book choice • Minilessons about book choice
Have rich conversations about books	• Scripts of student conversations when they are in book clubs • Scripts of student-teacher discussion during read-aloud time • Creating a dialogue from teacher to student and student to student in the reader's notebook	• Minilessons on how to have a good conversation • Model of an adult book club? Fishbowl of teachers talking about books? Middle schoolers? • Add dialogue structure to reader's notebook
Reading stamina increases over time	• Ask students to keep track of their uninterrupted reading time during readers workshop and maybe even at home? • Do all students need to track this?	• Add structure to reader's notebook? • Parent involvement? How to not make it punitive? Write explanatory letter to parents.
Know what to do to make meaning when they get stuck	• Sticky note evidence of getting stuck/getting unstuck (asking questions, making connections, etc.) in their reader's notebook • Ask students to reflect on this question over and over	• Model in multiple minilessons (spiral throughout the year) • Keep an anchor chart of student-generated responses to "What do I do when I get stuck?" • Make this a recurring question for reflection in the reader's notebook
Make inferences about writer's craft	• Script discussions from read-aloud time • Script discussions from book groups • Explicitly ask students to reflect on this question in their reader's notebooks	• Point out writer's craft over and over during read-aloud time; ask students to remark on it when they hear it • Model writer's craft in multiple minilessons over time • Careful scripting/documentation during worktime (What system/structure will work for me? How will I keep this consistent? How will I track individual students?) • Make this a recurring question for reflection in the reader's notebook
Are able to articulate how reading makes their life better	• Ask students to explicitly reflect on this question in their reader's notebooks	• Model and share stories (written and oral) from my own reading on a regular basis • Make this a recurring question for reflection in the Reader's Notebook • Think about including this question in portfolio reflection and passage presentations
Always have a book, or multiple books, going	• Reader's bibliography	• Add structure to reader's notebook (first five pages?)

Documentation of Conversation About Making the Invisible Visible (continued)

How Readers Grow	Evidence *Might* Look Like?	Implications for Planning, Instruction, and/or Assessment?
Can identify landmark books—books that affected them intellectually and emotionally and know why and how	• Reader's bibliography (add books from past?) • In reader's notebook? • Presentations?	• Structure for reader's notebook? • What might this look like for students presenting over time? A structure to add to morning meeting once a week?
Understand the rhythm of a book. Are able to stick with a book, wait out the tough parts, because they know the routines of the author or genre	• Reflect on this explicitly in reader's notebook? Multiple times throughout the year?	• Model in minilessons, think-alouds, share stories from my own reading • Develop a menu of questions students can reflect about in their reader's notebooks • Individual reading conferences
Understand the "diet of a reader." Know the pay-off of a hard book vs. an instant gratification book . . . a candy book vs. a main course book. What will stick with you over time?	• Reader's bibliography • Explicit reflection question in reader's notebook	• Add structure to reader's notebook (first five pages?) • Develop a "menu" of questions students can reflect about in their reader's notebooks? • Individual reading conferences
Hold thinking in their head from reading to reading	• Explicit question to ask/talk about during individual conferences during reader's workshop	• Model in minilessons/think-alouds how I do this when I read • Develop a menu of questions students can reflect about in their reader's notebooks • Individual reading conferences

found the time to write to kids, I found it a great way to connect to each kid—or at least for me to feel connected. It was like writing a secret note. But while I was still holding onto a somewhat fantastical notion of how great they were, if I looked at the kinds of things I was learning about kids as readers, the structure was falling flat. Kids were mostly writing me the same kinds of things—summaries of the book and maybe a wonder or two. It was methodical in many ways but I couldn't let go of it because I wanted a way to connect with what my kids were reading.

Based on my list of "How Readers Grow" I decided to change a few important things about the way I did reader's notebooks. For one, their letters to me about their reading are no longer homework. They happen in the classroom during a readers workshop. In the classroom, I want them to slow down their reading a bit and focus on how they are making meaning so they can talk to me about it when I confer with them. At home, I want them to read for fluency and pure pleasure.

A second change is that I ask kids to use sticky notes each time they read their choice books during workshop. I ask kids to keep track of their thinking on stickies and place them next to the text that spurred the thought. Then, at the end of the week, they can transfer these sticky notes to their reader's notebooks to use as a basis for their synthesis letter to me about how they are making meaning while they read and reflect on how they are growing as a reader.

Aha! We see Jen's beliefs driving her practice here—relationship, relationship, relationship. The reader's notebooks were a great way to get to know her students deeply as people and a great way to build relationships with them—the bond of a "secret note." The problem was, the journals weren't telling her much about her students as readers other than if they could retell the plot. . . . It was not enough, and so she restructured the general format to meet her goal of tracking students' growth as readers over time.

Instead of just letters back and forth, the notebooks would now include:

- *the explicit purpose of the reader's notebook in student-friendly language (see Figure 4.1)*
- *a checklist for what it means to choose a just-right book (Research says that in order for students to become independent, proficient readers, they should be spending the majority of their time reading books that they can read with a high level of reading accuracy, fluency, and comprehension [Allington 2001, 47].)*
- *A chart to record their "personal landmark books":*

Book	When I Read It

- *a reading log:*

Title/Author	Date Started/Completed

- *Sticky note thinking, recorded directly next to the text that spurred the thinking in the book throughout the week, and then moved to the reader's notebook once a week when the student used the sticky note thinking to compose a synthesis letter to Jen about his thinking that week—based on the list of purposes and Jen's list of how readers grow.*

Let's take a look at Jen's restructured reader's notebooks and follow her journey of coming to know her students deeply as people *and* as readers.

The Assessment Tool Drives Instruction

So Jen refocused her reader's notebooks so she could use them not only to know students as people but as a way to know concretely how her students were *growing* as readers. *The restructuring of the reader's notebook as her main assessment tool became the driving force behind the instruction in her daily readers workshop.* As she wrote in her reflection, the first big change was that the students wrote their reflections in the worktime of a readers workshop, instead of writing their reflections after their nightly reading at home. This allowed Jen to use the minilesson to model the type of reflection she was looking for before she released students to read, to confer with them during the worktime about the depth of their reflection as they read, and to share student thinking about their reading as a model for others during the debrief of the reader's workshop.

This chapter opened with the story of an invested parent asking Jen some really important questions about his daughter's learning. Jen responded with an intentional restructure of her reader's notebook so she would have concrete evidence to *know* and to *show* his daughter's (and all of her fourth and fifth graders') growth over time.

With a combination of heart, gut, head, and now "differently intentional" structure, Jen began her quest to know *more* about what her readers knew and were able to do. Let's look carefully and listen closely to the journey of Jen and a few of her students.

We'll begin with Jen and fifth grader Eliza. We'll listen in on two simultaneous dialogues, the first between Eliza and a book, and the second between Eliza and Jen. Let's listen and learn. . . .

Figure 4.1 Inside Cover of the Reader's Notebook

> **READER'S NOTEBOOK**
>
> *Purposes*
>
> ★ To have a record of what I have read over the year
> ★ To keep track of my reading stamina
> ★ To keep track of my thinking about a book so that I remember it well
> ★ To keep track of what kind of thinking strategies I use when I read so I can improve my reading
> ★ To keep track of the kinds of books that challenge me
> ★ To keep track of my thinking so I can use it for future writing—either stories from a book I love or writing about a book I love

Jen's Red Thread: An Extended Relationship

The red thread is used in a variety of cultures as a metaphor for connecting, binding, and uniting. . . . The red thread [for

*teachers] is a metaphor for the central goals and guiding pur-
poses that connect, bind, and unite our practice, giving it its
cohesiveness. These most deeply held instructional values and
goals take precedence over other agendas and exert a great
deal of influence on our teaching. . . . Knowledge of our red
thread gives us power to shape it in the direction we want it
to go. (Ritchhart 2002, 207)*

*Knowing my students as readers is about an extended rela-
tionship. I want a relationship with them about who they are
as people and as part of that I want a relationship with who
they are as readers and what they care about. I want that so I
can build their appetite for books and present them with a
broader menu of things to read and to care about. (Jen
Wood)*

Eliza's first reflective entry looks much like Jen's old structure for
having students write about their reading—basically, retelling what has
happened and asking a question. Eliza writes,

Inkheart by Cornelia Funke

8/30   9 pages

Dear Jen,

*What's happening now is Mo and Meggie got to Meggie's
Aunt Elinor's house. Before they left Meggie saw her dad with
a book wrapped in brown paper. I wonder what that has to
do with the story? I can't wait to read more.*

—Eliza

When Jen introduced the new reader's notebook structure, she
explained to students that she wanted their sticky notes and reflective synthesis letters to let her inside their heads to see *how* they were thinking
when they were reading. The next page in Eliza's reader's notebook has
four sticky notes that read:

★ Learn along with Meggie
★ Writer is mysterious
★ Meggie wants to find things out
★ Mo is hiding a book from Meggie

Jen listens to Eliza's thinking on the sticky notes and decides Eliza
needs a model for the kind of questions and connections she is looking for.

Jen writes:

> *Dear Eliza,*
>
> *I imagine you are finding out about the book now. That is part of what Mo doesn't want her to find. I see that* Inkheart, *like* Gregor the Overlander, *is mysterious and you find things out along with the character. What other books have you read where that is the case? Is that always true of a book? Can you think of a book where that doesn't happen?*
>
> *Do you have specific reading goals this year about reading a certain number or genre of books? What do you think will challenge you as a reader this year?*
>
> *Love, Jen*

The dialogue continues when Eliza writes back:

> *Dear Jen,*
>
> *Most of the books I've read have been kind of mysterious, but not all of them have been like* Inkheart. Inkheart *is really mysterious, kind of scary, and the author doesn't give you hints. You learn along with Meggie. A book that's not like that is* Beyond the Western Sea *because it is a different genre so it's not as mysterious. The author also kind of gives you hints and you're not always with the main character, but I still like it a lot.*
>
> *My reading goal is to read five more books by the end of the year and finish* Inkheart *by October break. Those are the answers to your questions.*
>
> *—Eliza*

Jen is trying to make meaning from Eliza's brief thinking held on the sticky notes to model how connections help a reader make meaning. Jen uses Gregor the Overlander, *the book the class is reading during read-aloud time, to model the use of a connection as another way for Eliza to share her thinking.*

Jen models both the tone and format of a letter filled with questions to elicit some reflection from Eliza. Her questions specifically point to concrete ways Eliza can extend her thinking about Inkheart *and about herself as a reader.*

So, no new information about Eliza, until bingo! A new book title and a new genre! And yahoo—a goal, set by Eliza herself. Eliza is trying really hard to meet Jen's expectations. This letter isn't the deepest of reflections, but it is a start. It will be interesting to see what Jen has to say.

The next few pages of Eliza's notebook hold six sticky notes with the following thinking:

★ Q: Is Dustfinger bad? A: No. Mo read Dustfinger out of Inkheart.
★ Q: Why is Inkheart so important? A: Because Capricorn wants to make sure he doesn't go back in it.
★ Dustfinger works for Capricorn!
★ Q: Does Mo know Dustfinger works for Capricorn? A: Yes
★ Q: Is Dustfinger really gonna show them where Mo is? A: ?
★ Q: Does Dustfinger like working for Capricorn? A: No! He hates him.
★ How is Capricorn bad?

What do *you* notice about Eliza as a reader from the thinking she wrote on these sticky notes? What do you wonder? Where would you go next with her? Do you see any opportunities for teachable moments here?

Jen does. Based on the previous synthesis letter and these sticky notes, she responds to Eliza with a letter that is *seven pages long*.

Who Is Doing the Work?

OK, it is time to pause for a systems and structures review. Jen has twenty-four fourth and fifth graders in her classroom. She has made it a priority to keep up a dialogue with students in their reading notebooks on a weekly basis, so she makes time to look at five journals a night. Even at that, the seven-page letter to Eliza had to take at least thirty minutes. Sustainable? No way! Did it help Eliza grow as a reader? Hmmmm. . . . let's listen in to Jen's letter and Eliza's response (see Figures 4.2 and 4.3).

Student Resistance as a Flashing Yellow Light

Despite Jen's enormous efforts, Eliza isn't digging in the way Jen wants her to and *needs* her to in order to grow. The tracks Eliza is leaving in the snow for Jen are not enough for Jen to come to know how Eliza is making meaning below a surface-level understanding of the plot. Jen intuitively knows that Eliza is making more meaning, but Eliza isn't making that deeper level of understanding visible for her.

Figure 4.2 1 of Jen's Seven-Page Response to Eliza

> Eliza,
> I agree that Beyond The Western Sea is different, but I also see your connection that some parts are mysterious or suspenseful. That's what just keeps you reading in any book.
> 5 books is a fine goal for you by January. I also want you to think about yourself as a reader and how you improve as a reader.
> When you are a beginning reader, you take big and obvious jumps in your reading ability — like this!
>
> Read simple books alone
> Read Predictable books by ...
> Read pict ... with books ...
> Read J...

Figure 4.3 Eliza's Response to Jen's Seven-Pager

> Dear Jen,
> I don't really understand what you said in your letter, but I caught some parts of it.
> I didn't mean read 5 books by January, (I don't think I can do that) I meant by the end of the year.
> I can try writing a book review on beyond the western sea and sending it to Stone Soup.
> I think we should actually talk, not just write letters back and forth.
>
> Eliza

This letter may not sound full of a certain tone to you, but if you know Jen, this is about as toney as she gets. The underline of January *in particular makes me giggle a bit. Eliza's goal of reading five books by the end of the year is not going to fly.*

I think one reason this response is seven pages long is that Jen is attempting to model the depth of thinking she is looking for from Eliza. The seven pages are full of juicy quotes, diagrams, and great advice.

But what matters most? What comes out of Eliza's pencil, of course. Will all this great modeling and a precious thirty minutes of Jen's time help Eliza go deeper? Stay tuned. . . .

OK, I know I shouldn't be laughing as I read this—Eliza is being very *sincere in her response—but wow . . . talk about who is doing the work here? Seven pages for this? If you read the last line, you'll see that Eliza also picked up on Jen's tone and isn't happy about it. What happened to her really nice, "I'd go to the ends of the earth for you" teacher? What is up with seven pages of demands?*

The letter hasn't gotten the response Jen was looking for. What's next? It is time for Jen to listen to Eliza.

Eliza knows just what she needs—to talk to her teacher about her reading. It is time for Jen to confer with Eliza so they can get on the same page about specific strategies Jen wants Eliza to try in order to grow in her skills and comprehension as a reader.

Figure 4.4

WHAT GOOD READERS DO
(Adapted from Pearson et. al. 1992)

Research *(and many teachers who explicitly teach these strategies to children and notice amazing leaps in their comprehension)* says good readers use the following strategies to make meaning from text:

1. Ask questions and talk back to the text
2. Use sensory images to "get the movie camera going" inside their heads
3. Infer based on the text and their background knowledge
4. Use their background knowledge to make connections to new information
5. Determine importance
6. Synthesize their thinking in order to answer "So what?" about the text
7. Use a fix-up strategy when they stop making meaning (like rereading with an explicit purpose, asking a question, making a connection, or trying to visualize!)

When students resist our best efforts to teach them, we need to take their resistance to heart. We need to avoid blaming them and take a look in the mirror. Is the dilemma one of *won't* or one of *don't know how*? Eliza's responses tell me that she doesn't understand the type of thinking Jen is looking for. I'm wondering if Eliza gets *why* Jen wants to see what is going on in her head when she reads. Does Eliza know *why* her metacognition matters?

Those of us who learned to read before the 1990s didn't have the benefit of the "knowing what good readers do" research (see Figure 4.4), and some of us became lifelong readers anyway. Why does metacognition matter? Well, it matters a lot, and here's why: metacognition is the key to becoming a *better* reader than you are today, no matter where you start.

One of the misconceptions of reading (and of school) is that there are those who are good at it and those who are not. Many struggling readers wait passively for meaning to arrive, and when it doesn't, they give up. They stop practicing and they never get better. Their mind wanders from the text and they let it keep wandering. Adolescent reading guru Cris Tovani explains this to kids in the most magical way. She says,

> *Does your mind ever wander when you read? Do you ever start thinking about the weekend or what you'll watch on television tonight? You do? Oh, that means you are really smart! You see, your brain hates to be bored, so if the words on the page aren't making any sense to you, your really smart brain starts thinking about other things. The secret that good readers know, that I want you to know, too, is that there are ways to get your brain focused back on the words on the page. There are ways to help your brain stay busy with the text in front of you so you can make your smart brain even smarter. Here's what I do when I'm reading something that I don't get. . . . (classroom observation, 2006)*

Then she puts a difficult text on the overhead and models questioning, or visualizing, or making connections, or some other strategy, depending on her purpose. Explicitly teaching readers how to re-engage with text when the movie camera in their head has turned off or has never switched on in the first place is crucial to helping them make meaning. So often when you ask students what they should do when they get lost in a text, they say, "Reread." Well, if you reread the same way you read the first time, it won't help you make meaning any more than the first read did.

An explicit focus on metacognition—teaching students *how to make meaning* when meaning breaks down—is like a special invitation to the party of lifelong literacy. Metacognition is so important for the students that have been relegated to the pile of "don't get its" and "not good at schools" for way too long, but also essential for students like Eliza who are great readers but *can* and *should* get better. Students say, "Oh, there are things I can do when I don't get it? Show me how!" If they knew better, they'd do better.

There is text that is too hard for all of us, no matter what kind of readers we are. Jen is demanding that Eliza attend to her metacognition because she believes it is key to Eliza being able to read more sophisticated text and make more meaning from the texts she is reading now. Reread Jen's list of how readers grow. One of her ways is "Able to articulate how reading makes their life better." Meaning drives engagement and, oh yeah, making meaning is what life is all about. Jen wants Eliza to not only make the leap but *know* she is making the leap.

Jen reflected on why she was pushing Eliza so hard,

> *I think naming the things a reader does to connect deeply with a book is important so they can do it again and again. I thought about how I needed to push Eliza into thinking about her own growth as a reader beyond just-right books, because for her there are tons of just-right books, but there is so much more she can do with a just-right kind of book.*
>
> *For Eliza it's pushing on genres and thinking about how deeply she is going into a book. I want to see that she is understanding the plot, but I also want her to chew apart how the writer got there. She needs to dig deeper and analyze ideas in order to become a better reader with more sophisticated texts. I want her to personalize the messages from the books in a way that she is then able to expand into a larger menu of books and writers. So, for example, I would love Eliza to be able to say, "I know in this book the thing I loved the most was the writer making you hold more than one story together and telling it from two character points of view. So now I know that in addition to historical fiction genre I am going to look for multiple narratives." Something like that.*

Yeah, *something* like that. I wish my teachers knew my reading tastes that deeply and had put that much thought into the next book I should read! Jen knows her readers so thoroughly because she listens to teach. So, as she listens to Eliza, she realizes that Eliza isn't understanding what she is asking her to do. Also, Eliza isn't the only one not getting it in her class of twenty-four. Remember, there is usually a reason for student resistance. If you believe they would if they could, when they can't or won't, it is time to show them how.

By listening to their sticky notes and letters, Jen hears her students loud and clear. She decides to capitalize on this teachable moment and *show them how*. Jen decides to use a few days of minilessons to kick off students' reading time in workshop by modeling the type of response that shows her what is happening inside their brains while they read. Let's listen in. . . .

The Minilesson

With the kids in a mush around her, Jen puts a transparency of a page from fifth grader Victoria's reader's notebook on the overhead.

Jen: You know that through our back-and-forth letters about your reading and our conversations in reading conferences, we have been talking a lot about how you can let me into your brain to see how you are making meaning when you read. Open the front of your reader's notebook to the list of purposes. Let's review them:

> The purposes of our readers' notebooks are
> - to have a record of what I have read over the year
> - to keep track of my reading stamina
> - to keep track of my thinking about a book so that I remember it well
> - to keep track of what kind of thinking strategies I use when I read so I can improve my reading
> - to keep track of the kinds of books that challenge me
> - to keep track of my thinking so I can use it for future writing—either stories from a book I love or writing about a book I love

> I'm wondering a lot right now about how you can *help me know you better* as readers and how you can *come to know yourselves better* as readers. The best way for you to come to know

yourselves as readers is to think about your thinking in a just-right book.

For me a just-right book is more than words on a page, it is a book that tugs on your heart and makes sparks in your mind. Victoria showed me some tugs and sparks this week and I wanted to show you what she wrote. Here is some of Victoria's thinking while reading *Matilda*, by Roald Dahl, this week [see Figure 4.5].

Let's look at the first sticky note. Victoria writes, "The dad's a lot nicer to the son than to Matilda. Surprised!" Victoria shows me a spark here and I want to know more about that. Why is that surprising to her? Victoria, why was that surprising to you?

Victoria: That was surprising to me because dads aren't supposed to show favorites! And it makes me wonder why he doesn't like Matilda as much. Then I keep reading and see that Matilda is playing all kinds of tricks on her dad and I'm wondering if that is why he isn't very nice.

Jen: Great, Victoria! I need you to write that next time! If you can write that, it shows me that you are making meaning from the book and doing more than just reading words on a page. It is also evidence for you to help you understand how you make meaning, so when you are reading and it just sounds like "blah, blah, blah," you can make a connection or ask a question just like you did with *Matilda*!

So, what are you thinking now? Does the dad have a right to like her brother better? What does that make you think about the world? You are using connections and questions to get you deeper into the story, which helps you make meaning of both the story and the world.

Victoria: Yeah, I wasn't thinking about my life when I was reading it, but I guess it does make sense that her dad is sick of her playing jokes on him.

Jen: Great, Victoria! You just did what good readers do! You made an inference based on what you know about the world—your background knowledge and what you read in the novel.

OK, readers, today during reading time, I want you to practice doing what we watched Victoria do today. Tell me about the

Figure 4.5 A Page from Victoria's Reader's Notebook, Used as a Model for the Minilesson

Matilda

page I started on 52   page I ended on 5?

the dads alot nicer to the son then to matilda.

suprized!

For a little whyle the dad was Being nice But now he lost his temper.

I think matilda is going to play another trick on her pap.

funny!

I think matilda is going to play a trick on her Dad.

funny!

An explicit link to one of Jen's red threads here! She believes that reading makes life better, and she wants to explicitly show students how!

tugs and sparks that happen for you while you read and see if you can tell me how the 'tugs and sparks' help you make more meaning from the book. I'll be coming around to confer with you and we can talk about this more. Get to work!

JEN'S MINILESSON

Structure and Content

Instruction: 13 minutes long
Teacher sets content purpose:
- ★ Teacher refers students back to the purpose of readers' notebooks and stresses the importance of leaving evidence of thinking on the sticky notes in the journal.
- ★ Demonstrates (using student work) how to document thinking more thoroughly while reading.
- ★ Teacher models with a student journal entry the documentation of thinking to give a clearer picture of what is happening in students' brains when they read and make meaning—to help the teacher help them more, and so the student can be aware of when meaning is being made and more fully comprehend the nuances of the text and its application to life. This minilesson clearly connects to Jen's belief that reading is fundamentally about connecting to another world—understanding it better and understanding ourselves better. We teach who we are! It's unavoidable! The red thread is strong!

Teaching Cycle Implications

Assessment:
Students pay careful attention to their thinking process and document it as they read so Jen will know them better and have richer reading conferences with them, as well as be able to prioritize her strategy instruction/minilessons for the whole group and small groups.

Planning:
Students' thinking will help her be strategic in her planning of modeling/minilessons so they unfold for the maximum benefit of a greater number of students—true differentiation and just-in-time instruction.

With those instructions, Jen's readers gather their choice books and their sticky notes and find a comfortable spot in the room to dive into making meaning from text in order to learn more about the world.

The Worktime

During the worktime, Jen confers with individuals about their reading, specifically referring to the points she stressed in the minilesson. In short, targeted three-minute conversations, she asks student after student, "Where are the 'tugs at your heart' with you for this book? What sparks in your mind is the story making? Tell me more." As she goes around she asks a few students to re-copy their sticky note thinking onto a transparency, so they can share it with the rest of the class during the debrief.

After a few conferences, it is Eliza's turn.

Jen responds to Eliza's request to talk, but as she talks, she also *writes*. Jen records the conversation in a chart in Eliza's reader's notebook (see Figure 4.6). Can you infer how the conversation went?

Jen reflected on the cyclical relationship of her conferences and the reader's notebook,

These reading conferences are now working in tandem with the reader's notebooks—each one feeds the other for me and helps drive what I want to do for each child's reading. I am asking better questions in conferences based on what I see in

Figure 4.6 Documentation of Jen and Eliza's Reading Conference

WHAT	(Draft)	• HOW DO I KNOW
Read A Lot	Keep Track w/ a reading log	4 By January
Think Deeply about BOOK	Shallow - details info about plot / Deep - character analysis - thinking about writing	Pay attention Keep track of Stickies
Use characters to think about myself	Am I connecting to a character? HOW ⇒	Reflections
Modeling Writing	Use one trait in my own writing ⇒	Name where you did it
Write about a book	Did you write a book review?	

This one-page chart ends up being a terrific synthesis of the seven-page letter Jen wrote to Eliza. This conversation occurred during the worktime of readers workshop, while other students were busy reading and recording their thinking and reflections in their own reader's notebooks.

This conversation lasted about ten minutes—long for a classroom conference but one-third of the time Jen spent writing Eliza the letter. And from the looks of this chart, the conversation was much more fruitful!

Building relationship through talk is a hallmark of workshop teaching. Jen's letter came from the same place in her heart, but the eye-to-eye, knee-to-knee conversation made a bigger difference to Eliza.

the reader's notebooks and the reading conferences are helping me push kids to share their thinking more deeply in the notebooks. The notes I take during these conferences are powerful because it is what I give back to students to further their learning—it is not what the notes do for me but what they do for them. The notes are a way for me to be sure to listen carefully to what kids are telling me. So instead of thinking about them as assessment for me, I think of the notes as labels for them about the behaviors of good readers— what they are already doing and how they can get better. During each conference, I think, "How do I know what kids know?" Then, I listen and think, "What do I do about it?" Then, I listen some more and ask them questions and learn from what they say.

The Debrief

In the debrief, Jen shares parts of a couple of conversations she had during the worktime:

Figure 4.7 Victoria's Thinking from the Worktime in Her Reader's Notebook

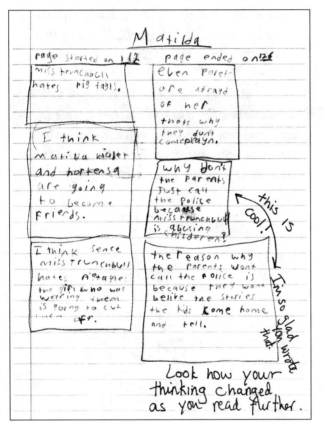

Jen: We started our workshop today by looking at Victoria's thinking—and she was able to record some more of her thinking while she was reading today. Let's take a look at how she did it. Look at this: she is doing what good readers do here—her thinking changes as she gets further into the book. Here Victoria writes, "Even parents are afraid of her that's why they don't complain." I see Victoria making an inference about why the parents aren't calling the police on Miss Trunchbull. That is what good readers do! Then on the next sticky, she asks a question, "Why don't the parents just call the police . . . ?" and then answers it below. Victoria's thinking changed as she got more information. Great job showing your thinking, Victoria! Thank you for allowing me to share that with the class. [See Figure 4.7.]

After sharing Victoria's thinking, Jen wants to share another huge "aha" she had during Nicholas' conference.

Jen: Nicholas, let's share your thinking and our conversation about *The Penultimate Peril,* by Lemony Snicket. I learned something new today, and I want to see if other kids know what you know about the books.

Nicholas: I wrote here on my sticky that Klaus has just run into Charles in the hotel, and I think he is the same guy from *The Miserable Mill,* another Lemony Snicket book, so he should totally recognize him.

Jen: Oh, so you are making connections between the books. I thought they were all the same basic plot. I stopped reading at

Book Six because I was getting a little bored.

Nicholas: [more than a little indignant] Book One through Book Six are the books that introduce all the characters and let you know who is going to be in the story. Those just give you a feel for it. Seven through Twelve are the turning point in the books where it becomes more of an adventure story and not a story about the orphans versus Count Olaf. It is more than that. You should have just kept reading!

Jen: Wow! It sounds like these individual books are really just like one big book?

Nicholas: [with his best "Duh!" look] Yes. That's why I like reading them because it's like one story and you really have to pay attention to each one so you can connect to the next one!

Jen: Thank you, Nicholas. Did you guys know that? [Students answer with a chorus of *yeses* and a few *nos*.] See, Nicholas, some kids didn't know that and I certainly didn't. Thank you so much for sharing your expertise on the Lemony Snicket books. Wow! I learned a lot today about you guys as readers and thinkers. Thank you for being my teachers today. OK, put your books away and get ready for lunch.

Jen shared her thinking in an email that night. She wrote,

> *Nicholas' thinking during debrief today told me that I should not assume anything and listen more! The way he is reading these Lemony Snicket books is much more sophisticated than I ever imagined. This definitely shows a change from his reading last year where he just ate the stories up. Somehow, reading all of the series has helped him prepare himself for reading in a more sophisticated way. I've been encouraging him to choose different texts, but instead he is bringing deeper meaning to the texts he is already passionate about reading.*
>
> *I found it so interesting because as a reader, I view those Lemony Snicket books one way, but he clearly sees them differently. Nicholas has made me think today about what "sophisticated text" means and also what it means to improve as a reader. What a day!*

What a day. For Victoria, for Eliza, for Nicholas, for the rest of their classmates, and for Jen.

The Read-Aloud as Structure, Routine, Ritual, and System

This chapter began with an observation email of Jen's read-aloud time. I would be remiss in discussing Jen's classroom practice without mentioning the centrality of daily read-aloud and its influence on the learning in her classroom each day—a thread through all different subject areas. After observing read-aloud time, I asked Jen:

★ How do you hope this explicit labeling from the Gregor story will play out in students' own reading?

★ How might it concretely show up later? What will it look like in their reader's notebooks, their conversations in book groups, or in their writing?

She responded:

I love read-aloud time. It is a precious time with my crew. They have a fit if we don't have it. On the surface for them and in general appearance, it seems like it is one big relaxation period. But the books we read aloud have always been foundations for many conversations. I think read-aloud is the main thing that fosters reading in my crew. I see evidence of read-aloud affecting their writing all the time. They use language from the book, or a similar character sometimes. It also influences our whole-class conversations—many conversations we have about our group dynamics start with "like in ___ book." I've always loosely used that time as a way to talk about reading comprehension strategies, but this year I have been even more purposeful. Our read-aloud book becomes the anchor text for our readers workshop minilessons. We can all see how the reading strategies unfold and it is a great way for us to analyze together about what makes a really great story. It builds a common understanding for us to have conversations throughout the day, no matter what we are studying.

Jen has read-aloud each day for thirty minutes after lunch recess. As I noticed in my observation, it is a great time of day for all—a culture builder that says loudly, "Books and reading are an important part of *every* day." Like workshop, read-aloud is another nonnegotiable every day. It is a great example of one of the small things Jen makes time for every day that makes a big difference in her students' learning and love of books.

What's Up with Eliza?

Jen continued her reader's notebook structure all year long, and while Eliza showed *glimmers* of deeper thinking and metacognition on her sticky notes, the structure never really clicked with her. She and Jen continued to write back and forth, and continued to confer during readers workshops, and over time, Jen noticed that Eliza was reading a lot more, but the sticky notes were never great evidence of Eliza making deeper meaning.

Let's go back to Jen's red threads—Jen takes the long view and she believed in her heart that if she dug in week after week and continued the dialogue, Eliza would grow. Jen shared, "I think my students know that I am never going to give up on them. Deep down inside, they know that more than anything else."

So, although Eliza never went much deeper on her sticky notes, she did make amazing progress as a reader in her fifth-grade year. How do we know? Let's listen to Eliza's other work.

How Does Eliza Know?

As a fifth grader, Eliza gets to participate in the ritual of Passages to prove to an outside audience that she is ready to pass into middle school. A Passage Panel, comprising of three adults—a teacher, a parent, and a community member—will dedicate two days of their time to be an authentic audience for her. To prepare, Eliza compiles a portfolio with carefully selected pieces of evidence of her mastery of fifth-grade work and also of her growth over time. After Eliza gathers her work, she writes a series of reflections on herself as a reader, writer, mathematician, and scientist. Eliza reveals her learning about herself as a reader in her personal statement:

> In reading, I challenge myself by setting goals and, when I reach them, setting higher goals. Little goals have led up to my big goal of reading twelve books by the end of the year. It's like in a movie we watched called Touching the Void where someone keeps making little goals until he reaches his big goal. I'm also challenging myself by reading harder books. I have read two adult fiction books, and I loved them. I read Flowers for Algernon and The Secret Life of Bees. The

Remember one of Jen's original goals for the growth of readers—"Understand the rhythm of a book. Are able to stick with a book—and wait out the tough parts because they know the routines of the author or genre." Eliza's got it!

Eliza's explicit labeling of the genres she read this year helps her learn about herself as a reader and how she challenged herself to stretch out of her comfort zone. Who wouldn't be proud of this list? What would your list look like from the last six months?

challenging thing about reading adult books is something exciting isn't happening at every second, and the parts where nothing exciting is happening are kind of boring. I challenge myself when I read the boring parts because usually I don't understand them until the end when all the clues come together.

Remember Jen's genre-expansion goal for Eliza? Figure 4.8 shows a record of the genres Eliza read throughout the year.

And that five-book goal? Take a look at her final reading log, in Figure 4.9.

Figure 4.8 Eliza's Genre Chart

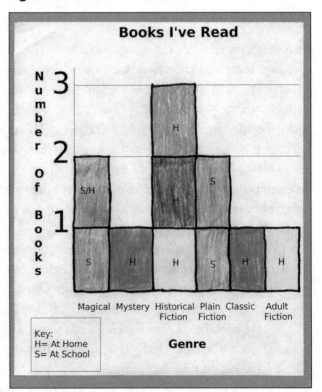

Figure 4.9 Eliza's Final Reading Log

Title	Author	Date	Home	School
Inkheart	Cornelia Funke	8/24/05–11/23/05		✔
A Series of Unfortunate Events book 12	Lemony Snicket	October	✔	
Beyond the Western Sea 2	Avi	August–November	✔	
Charlie Bone and the Castle of Mirrors	Jenny Nimmo	11/26/05–11/28/05	✔	
The Wanderer	Sharon Creech	December–January		✔
My Brother Sam Is Dead	James Lincoln Collier and Christopher Collier	December–January	✔	
Flowers for Algernon	Daniel Keys	Janury–February	✔	
The Devil's Arithmetic	Jane Yolen	January	✔	
The Secret Life of Bees		Unknown	✔	
Montmorency	Elinor Updale	Unknown		✔
Montmorency 2	Elinor Updale	Abandon		✔
The Subtle Knife	Phillip Pullman	April–May		✔
A Corner of the Universe	Ann Martin	May		✔

I think the home-school balance of books is important to note. One feeds the other. Jen's intentional practice to have students read and record their thinking in class, where she can read the thinking they hold on the sticky notes and talk to them about it, seemed to give Eliza confidence to tackle other books at home.

By explicitly naming how readers grow, Jen was able to help students set concrete goals to get better. Another effect of Jen's explicit labeling of how she knew was her intentional practice—in minilessons, in reading conferences, and in debriefs—of showing students how to read better. Although Eliza was a great reader already, it wasn't just up to her to get better on her own so Jen could attend to the struggling readers. Eliza had a partner. She had a guide. She had a teacher, who knew her deeply, as a person *and* as a reader—and Eliza got better!

Red Threads in a Tapestry of Learning

We can learn what's good and what's bad, what's generous and unselfish, what's cruel and mean, from fiction. . . . "Thou shalt not" might reach the head, but it takes "Once upon a time" to reach the heart. . . . I think we should read books, and tell children stories, and take them to the theatre, and learn poems, and play music, as if it would make a difference. . . . We should act as if life were going to win.
(Pullman, in Miller 2006, 54)

Through observing the daily systems, structures, routines, and rituals in Jen's classroom, it is pretty easy to figure out what she cares most about. Her relationships with students drive every move she makes. A second red thread woven into the tapestry of her classroom is that reading makes your life better. Students leave Jen's classroom each June with that belief firmly engrained in their guts, hearts, and heads. But don't just take it from me. Let's listen to one of Jen's former students, who wrote in Jen's recommendation for Denver Teacher of the Year,

To Whom It May Concern,

In my fourth and fifth grade years Jen was my teacher. She was the best teacher I have ever had and I've had a lot of good teachers. No one that I knew of disliked her in my class or in any other. She teaches, but she does it in a fun way. She gets to know her students and bonds with them, not just like, "Hi Jen," but to the point where they would trust her with one of their darkest secrets.

Before I went into her class I wasn't a bad student, I just wasn't good at reading and writing, and she didn't just teach me how to do these things. She taught me how to love them. In third grade I couldn't stand writing and I wasn't a big fan of reading either. Now I read at least thirty minutes every night. Not because it's homework, no, no. It's because I love to. Same with writing. I used to stay away from it as much as possible. Now? Writing and reading are what I do when I'm bored.

Sincerely,
Walker

Thanks, Walker, for the reminder of what matters most. And thanks, Jen, for putting it into practice every day.

Jen's Systems, Structures, Routines, and Rituals

Following is a scaffold for the story of teaching and learning in Jen's classroom. Remember, whole-scale replication is not the point. What practices were intriguing to you? Which practices match your beliefs about the agency and capacity of children to think and learn? The beauty is, there are dozens of entry points. Pick one that matches what you believe and the rest will come. Do you want to start with planning to know what your readers know and are able to do? A reader's notebook structure? Developing a classroom library? Modeling how you make meaning when you read? A compelling read-aloud? Here are a few ideas for places to start:

Systems, Structures, Routines, and Rituals Highlighted in Chapter 4	Narrative description found on page	Ideas to help you get started	For more information check out these resources
Reader's notebooks	85–93, 96–97	Start like Jen did. Make a list of the ways you know your readers are growing and build explicit ways to track those things into student reading journals. Start simple. Track a few things over time and see if it helps you know your students better as people and as readers.	*Writing About Reading* (Angelillo 2003) *Best Practice* (Chapters 2 and 8) (Zemelman, Daniels, and Hyde 1998)
Portfolio assessment	103	Start with folders to collect student work over time. Build in days each quarter for students to look at their work from earlier in the year and reflect on their growth. Use portfolios as the basis for student-led conferences so there is an authentic audience for their work and reflection.	*Best Practice* (Zemelman, Daniels, and Hyde 1998) www.elschools.org
Conferring	98–99, 100–101	Get eye-to-eye with students and start with "How's your reading going?"	*How's It Going?* (Anderson 2000)
Red-aloud time	102	Make 20–30 minutes in your schedule *at least* once a week, if not each day. Start with one of your favorites. (Get multiple copies because many students will pick one up during and after the read-aloud.) Practice your best character voices. Let your students curl up in a circle around you. Re-create childhood lap time reading.	

CHAPTER FIVE

Ali's Writers

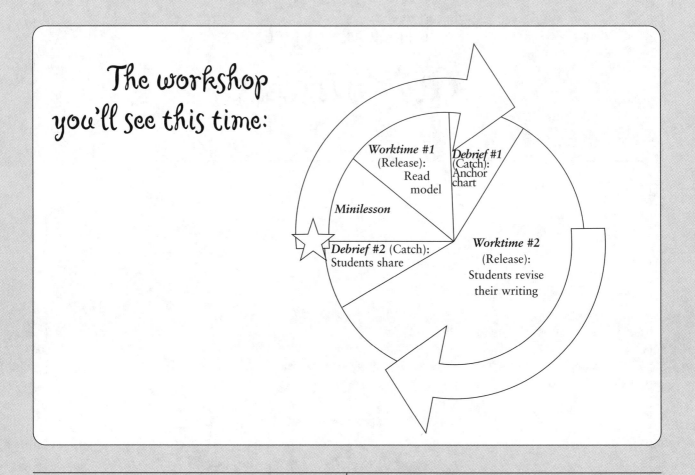

The workshop you'll see this time:

Worktime #1
(Release):
Read
model

Debrief #1
(Catch):
Anchor
chart

Minilesson

Debrief #2 (Catch):
Students share

Worktime #2
(Release):
Students revise
their writing

Workshop duration: 75 minutes

Minilesson (Catch) (10 minutes):

★ *Teacher sets content purpose:* To define sentence fluency by looking at models and labeling where it is used to enhance the quality of a piece of writing.

★ *Teacher sets process purpose:* To use what we figured out about sentence fluency to improve our own writing.

Worktime #1 (Release) (10 minutes):

★ Students read models from other *Best Part of Me* essays.

★ Teacher listens and labels student thinking she hears.

Debrief #1 (Catch) (10 minutes):

★ Students share what they figured out about fluent sentences from reading the models.

★ Teacher creates an anchor chart based on their thinking.

Worktime #2 (Release) (40 minutes):

★ Students write or revise their writing with the goal of fluent writing.

★ Teacher confers.

Debrief #2 (Catch) (5 minutes):

★ Students share their fluent sentences.

Hi Ali,

Thanks for inviting me into your writers workshop this week. I have been inspired to think hard and dig deep to get to the root of your burning questions (and mine too!) about writing. I am so excited to follow this project over the next three weeks.

I'm going to tether my noticings and wonderings to your big question "How do we help our writers write (pick an adjective) powerfully, movingly, descriptively, surprisingly, prolifically, fluently, thoughtfully, feelingly, change-their-life-ingly?" Feel free to add some more adjectives if I missed any that are important to you.

Here we go . . .

Lesson: *Best Part of Me* brainstorm/rough drafts

What I noticed:

- An anchor chart on the wall that outlined "Why do a project like *The Best Part of Me*?"
  - Kids can be authors.
  - To read something new and learn something new about the author.
  - To express feelings.
  - To share interests and opinions.
  - So people will listen to your thoughts.
  - To share your thinking with an audience.
- All students had a model from the book out on their desks while they were writing.

Here are the scripts from two writing conferences:

Conferring with Molly:

> **Ali:** So, Molly, yesterday you were thinking that your hair was the best part of you, but then you decided that gymnastics was such a big part of your life that you wanted to focus on your hands. When you think about your hands, what words come into your head? Read what you have so far.

Molly: [reads from her draft] "My hands help me grab the bars in gym. They hold the pencil when I write. They work together as a team."

Ali: Wow. The line "they work together as a team" is a really strong line. It surprised me because I usually think of people working in a team, not hands. Tell me more about that. I'll come back in a few minutes and see if you can blow that one up in more detail. In about five minutes, I'll be back to hear some more.

Conferring with Christina:

Ali: Christina, tell me about your piece.

Christina: I chose my hands because they help me grab what I want. I wrote, "They help me eat. I would go hungry without them."

Ali: That line tells me what your hands help you *do*. Can you add some details that tell me what is *important* to you? This could be a place where you get descriptive and tell me what really matters to you. What are you telling me is important here? This line tells me food matters most to you. Is that right?

Christina: Yeah. Without food I would die.

Ali: You're right. I'm wondering what else your hands help you do that can tell me more about you? Everybody needs food to survive, but how about a detail that would tell me, "This is Christina, for sure!" See if you can tell me something about yourself that would be unique to *you*. I'll be back in a few minutes to see what you came up with. Great start, Christina.

End of script.

What I wonder:

- Can you write to me a little bit about your philosophy/thinking about conferring? How do you know if a writing conference has been successful?
- So far this year, what have you noticed about the writers in your class? What do you wonder about them? What do you think they need most?

Now, it's your turn . . . just write for ten minutes and push Send. Any glimpse into your brain helps me help you.

I can't wait to hear your thinking.

See you soon,
Sam

The Use of a Mentor Text as Inspiration for Craft and Product

He moons about in the garden, and I have seen him standing doing nothing before a flower for ten minutes at a time. If he only had something to do, I really believe he would be better. (Darwin's gardener commenting on his employer, in Peter Sis', Tree of Life *[2003])*

Inspiration takes many forms. Darwin had his garden. Picasso had his lovers. Maira Kalman has her dog, Max. David Sedaris has Paris. Ali Morgan has the fourth- and fifth-grade authors in her classroom and dozens of shelves overflowing with beautifully illustrated, beautifully crafted, and beautifully written books.

Each day, Ali helps students find their inner Darwin, Picasso, Kalman, and Sedaris by carefully studying the work of real scientists, artists, and authors in the world. Fittingly, Ali spends a great deal of time looking for beautiful and beautifully written books to inspire the authors in her classroom.

The Best Part of Me: Children Talk About Their Bodies in Pictures and Words, by Wendy Ewald (2002), was just the inspiration Ali needed for a beginning-of-the-year project to get to know her students deeply as people and as writers.

The idea was simple and brilliant: students would photograph and write about the best part of them—a powerful, concrete project to get writing flowing from her students. She decided the best way to model fluid, fluent writing would be to write a "Best Part of Me" piece herself. She was excited to dig in *with* her student writers.

Building a Culture of Quality: What Does Good Writing Sound Like?

The most important assessment done in schools is done by students, not teachers. . . . Every student [should] carry around with him or her a picture of acceptable standards, a notion of what his or her work should look like before it is handed in or before it is a finished piece. The picture is a vision of how accurate, neat, thorough, thoughtful, original, and elegant a piece of work should be.

This should be a vital concern of every school: What is the picture of quality in the heads of students? Not our "gifted" students or our "motivated" students, but what is it in all our students? What is it in a student chosen at random in the hallway? And, most important, how can we get into the heads of our students and sharpen that picture as needed? (Berger 1996, 28–29, emphasis added)

At Ali's school, there are five other teachers in addition to her that make up the Lower School Team. They meet once a week to check in, share student and teacher work, and get smarter together. For the first semester, they set a goal of building and refining their common language and common practice around writing instruction. To begin to build a common vision of quality, they decided to share a piece of their favorite writing at their next meeting.

One teacher brought a piece from *The House on Mango Street,* by Sandra Cisneros. One brought a poem by Cynthia Rylant from the book *Something Permanent.* One teacher brought a passage from a novel, *The Icarus Girl,* by Helen Oyeyemi, and another brought a passage from *The Pilgrim at Tinker Creek,* by Annie Dillard. Ali chose a piece from the read-aloud she was doing with her class, *The Islander,* also by Cynthia Rylant. Each teacher took turns reading his or her choice aloud and then brainstormed a list of qualities that the pieces shared:

Writing We Admire

Things we notice:
★ Effective use of repetition (for a specific reason)
★ Efficiency—the writers don't waste words
★ The writers focus closely on moments (explode the moment)—this helps us to feel the emotions of the characters
★ The writers have self-awareness/insight—seeing through what the character is thinking
★ Internal and external insights—sometimes they alternate
★ Rhythm—the writer uses it purposefully (long and short sentences)
★ Surprise! Suspense!
★ Knowledge of audience
★ It's not about big words—it's about precision and use of punctuation to make meaning
★ Musical
★ Good use of transitions to carry the reader along

This list, alongside the original pieces of writing, hung in the teachers' lounge for a week, and other staff members added comments and questions like "I love this line. It reminds me of a tree in my backyard in the house where I grew up. How can we get students to write like this?"

Ali had that same question, and she was excited to use the *Best Part of Me* project to specifically address the musicality and rhythm the teachers had noticed in their favorite pieces. Her brain infused with the thinking of her colleagues, data from a schoolwide writing sample (low scores on sentence fluency and word choice), and her own beginning-of-the-year formative assessments to guide her, she developed three learning targets for her fourth- and fifth-grade authors:

★ I can clearly communicate important aspects of my life through my description of the "best part of me."

★ I can use precise words that add detail to enhance my piece.

★ I can use a variety of sentences (some short, some long, some descriptive, some to the point) to make my piece capture the reader's attention and create a "musical" rhythm.

After thinking through her learning targets, Ali was ready to share them with students and dive into writing *with* them. Her first concern was for students to get a vision for the project and a picture in their minds of a high-quality essay. So, Ali began by writing her own essay and sharing it with students.

My Eyes
by Ali

Waves roll in and gently crash on the rocky shore. As the gulls soar overhead, my eyes carefully capture this image. Over and over, waves crash. The sun hovers just above the horizon.

We've rushed to the beach, hoping to take in this sight in time. We don't want to miss it.

Many chapters in this book highlight the use of learning targets to prioritize curricular direction and share with students the goals of projects and products. Learning targets differ from goals and objectives because their purpose is not only assessment of learning but assessment for learning along the way.

Ali and her colleagues are finding that writing learning targets helps them set priorities and target instruction throughout a unit. It helps them stay true to their original purposes and continue to spiral back to what matters most in their assignment design, minilessons, and debriefs.

Ali and her colleagues are noticing that for students, learning targets help them own their learning. They help students see the connection between assignments and the learning outcomes and help them have a vision to demonstrate their understanding.

The sun melts into the horizon. My eyes squint as the rays reflect brightly from the surface of the ocean. Colors multiply. Yellows turn to oranges, reds mix with the darkness of the ocean. Pink spreads overhead, the white of the clouds breaking the color into pieces. My eyes take it all in.

I've raced to the lighthouse hundreds of times, chasing the lowering sun, trying to make it in time for the sunset. Each time it's slightly new, but also so familiar that my eyes almost know it by heart. I close my eyes and can predict the colors, the shades of light on Ipswich bay. Sunset at the beach feels like home to me.

Dogs run in long strides as they chase the cresting waves. Mom and I whisper in quiet conversation as the chill wind bristles around us. My eyes memorize this picture. They save it and store it for when I'm in the mountains.

We turn to leave, as darkness sets in around us. We call to the dogs, who run ahead. I glance over my shoulder, taking one more gulp of the salt air as my eyes scan the remaining colors.

It's a long way back to Colorado.

Teachers use their creative juices to design engaging assignments all the time. Ali chose to use her creative energy to *do* her own assignment so she could examine her process and better anticipate what her writers might need as they went through the process of writing their "Best Part of Me" pieces.

Ali reflected on the process:

I love the process of using my work as a model. I put my piece on the overhead as I created my first draft, thinking aloud as I wrote. I think it was hugely influential to my students who needed more explicit direction at the beginning of the year. After I had completed a draft, I put it up again and asked the students for some feedback. I noticed a huge jump in engagement the day they got to critique my piece! I think kids need to see me puzzle, process and work, just as they do.

The Diet of a Writer

Personally, I don't think that you can teach people to write. I think you can teach people to read in a more nuanced way.

For instance, to look at one of Toni Morrison's books as a writer, say, and not as a cultural critic. To look and see how you can manipulate the body and objects and devices in ways you wouldn't have thought about. . . . It's about taking the book apart and looking at the characters and seeing how it is built. (Abani in Vendela 2005, 17–18)

Reading and writing are inextricably linked. The musical rhythm that Ali describes as sentence fluency can best be gained from reading musical writing. This is where the importance of having daily, ongoing readers and writers workshop and a daily read-aloud time comes in. Students need to hear musical, fluid, fluent language for it to seep into their brains and hearts and for it to come out of their pencils. Students need to be swimming in printed and oral language in order to be able to write well. Ali's favorite author, Cynthia Rylant, has much to say about this topic. She implores teachers to

Read to them. Take their breath away. Read with the same feeling in your throat as when you first see the ocean after driving hours and hours to get there. Close the final page of the book with the same reverence you feel when you kiss your sleeping child at night. Be quiet. Don't talk the experience to death. Shut up and let these kids feel and think. Teach your children to be moved. (Calkins 2001, 53)

If you want your students to write, read to them. A lot. Show them great models. A lot. Model reading like a writer. A lot. Critique published pieces by your favorite authors. A lot.

In order to get a picture of quality writing in students' heads, Ali spent three full writers workshops modeling with her piece and giving students time to read and critique models from the *Best Part of Me* book. Each writers workshop, before releasing the students to write, Ali used the minilesson to pull out and critique phrases and sentences that represented examples of precise word choice and fluid sentences from the mentor texts that helped students learn more about the authors of the pieces (see Figure 5.1).

Each day, after spending time with the models, students talked as a group in the debrief to label and define good writing in the mentor *Best Part of Me (BPOM)* pieces. Over three days of careful reading, writing, and talking about the *BPOM* mentor texts (see Figure 5.1), they created an anchor chart explicitly labeling how their mentor authors demonstrated strong writing (see Figure 5.2). This chart lived at the front of the

Figure 5.1 Models from Other BPOM Projects

Name_____   Date_____

⬭ Showing What Really Matters ⬭
In our BPOM

- Look at these sentences from our mentor texts. Do any stand out to you? Why?
- Which ones do the best job of "Showing What Really Matters"

1. Sometimes I like to squint my eyes when I am in the sun. My mom says I have nice eyes.

2. My soul knows who I truly am better than anyone or anything. My soul runs free with the breeze.

3. My arms hug my mother when I am sad. My arms feel the water and earth. My arms show love while the world passes by.

4. Mosquitoes like my legs. I take after my dad because they like his blood.

5. I love my neck because it holds the beautiful necklaces that I wear. I love my neck because it is not too big or too small.

6. My eyes read the pages of books. They see birds flying past the horizon. They see the magic and happiness of the world. They see the sadness and sorrow.

7. When I pray my hands overlap. In the sun they shine, their color is toasty brown.

8. My eyes sparkle in the sun. They see the reflection of the light off the surface of the ocean. The blue color reaches out to the hearts of everyone who sees them.

9. My eyes are brown and black. Big and round. I see lots of colors around.

10. My eyes are twins with the rolling sea. They have movement and are deep full of blue and greens. My eyes help me see the world.

> By spending lots of time looking at mentor texts (Figure 5.1), students were able to brainstorm the characteristics of strong writing for this project (Figure 5.2).

> The thinking and labeling on this anchor chart came directly from the students, so they had more ownership in trying to make it happen in their own writing. Students determined what quality writing sounded like; Ali showed them how by providing quality models for them to read and talk about.

Figure 5.2 Mentor Text Anchor Chart

Mentor Texts → a model, base or example that we use to guide our writing.

Our mentor authors demonstrated Strong writing by:

- having Words that made you think / feel
- grabbing our attention by → creating images
  → Choosing strong words
- staying on topic
- writing sentences that fit together.
- Using a lot of description
-
- Giving information about the author's life
  · what's important to him/her
  · what really matters
- Giving examples & details that matter
- Using poetic language
  description   creating images
- Picking perfect words

classroom throughout the project as a constant visual reminder as they launched their own writing about their best parts. After three days of looking at models and writing for chunks of time, Ali was ready to explicitly talk with her students about the process of revision within the crafting process. Let's listen in. . . .

The Minilesson (Catch): Building a Culture of Revision

Figure 5.3 Sentence Fluency Anchor Chart

Ali begins, "Today we are going to practice thinking about another feature of great writing. This may be a new concept for some of you. Take a look at the new anchor chart up here. It says, 'What does sentence fluency mean?' Does anybody have any ideas?"

> **Patrick:** Fluency means you understand something. You know how it works together.
>
> **Ali:** Wow, Patrick. Yeah—how all the pieces fit together. Thanks for that great start. This is what I know about sentence fluency. I know that writers work really hard to combine their words and sentences in powerful ways. What does the phrase *powerful* mean to you?
>
> **Serenah:** It means like words that stick and you hang on to them.
>
> **Dylan:** Yeah, like they capture your interest.
>
> **Ali:** Good. You guys are building from our conversation yesterday. Powerful words that capture your interest are very important, but today, we are going to think about how the combination of sentences go together to make a whole piece of writing stick in our heads. I'm going to hand out our mentor texts again. This time, I

Great Writers concentrate on Sentence Fluency.

This means that as writers work on a piece they:

☐ **Combine words in powerful ways.**
↳ effective interesting images "sticks out"

☐ **Use a variety of sentences.**
↳ Short, long, descriptive, pattern, to the point, etc...

☐ **Create sentences that sound musical to the reader.**
↳ variety, pattern, rhythm, melody, poetic, etc...

We are working on our sentence fluency in our BPOM.

ALi'S MINILESSON

Structure and Content

Instruction:
★ 20 minutes with a 10-minute release to read in the middle.
★ *Teacher sets content purpose:* To define sentence fluency by looking at models and labeling where it is used to enhance the quality of a piece of writing.
★ *Teacher sets process purpose:* To use what class figured out about sentence fluency to improve their own writing.

Teaching Cycle Implications

Assessment and Planning:
★ While conferring during the worktime, Ali will be able to remind students of the goal of revision with sentence fluency in mind and ask targeted questions to push their thinking about how writers use sentence fluency to enhance meaning and interest for the reader.
★ Reading student writing throughout the worktime allows Ali to pay careful attention to student revision processes, how they are helping improve the pieces, and clues for what students need next. Ali will have read every piece several times by the end of the writing process—a practice that makes the final assessment easier and less time-consuming.

want you to look carefully for how the sentences flow together to create a rhythm or a song that helps the piece stick in your head. Take a few minutes and underline any combinations of sentences, a repeating phrase, or anything that helps the whole piece stick in your mind. Go to your tables with a partner. In ten minutes I will ask you to return to the circle and share what you figured out.

Worktime #1 (Release): Read and Label

The students return to their tables and hungrily chew up the mentor texts (Figure 5.1), looking for good examples of sentence fluency. Some students are reading the examples aloud to one

another, others are busy underlining matching phrases or repeating lines. After ten minutes, Ali calls the class back to the rug.

Debrief #1 (Catch): Name What Students Noticed and Create Anchor Chart

Ali: Wow, I noticed you guys were really active looking at the mentor texts. Who has something to share?

Avalon: In the piece Lindsey and I read, the writer has a short sentence about her eyes, like "My eyes sparkle in the sun," and then a longer sentence about what they see, like "They see the reflection of light off the surface of the ocean."

Ali: Thanks, Avalon. Let's add that to our chart. [See Figure 5.3.] Sentence fluency means using a variety of sentence lengths, like a

short pattern sentence and then a long descriptive one. Any other things you noticed?

Robert: Well, mine used a pattern, but I thought it was boring. It was just my heart, my heart, my heart.

Ali: OK, so here is an example where a pattern didn't help make it more interesting. Why do you think?

Libby: I think it's because there weren't enough interesting descriptions. There is no picture in my mind from that one.

Ali: OK, let's add that to our chart. I want to make sure you have enough time to write today. When you go to your tables, I want you to look at your pieces with new eyes. Look at them with sentence fluency in mind and try to make the overall piece more musical to the reader's ears and eyes. What tools should you have out at your tables? What might I see as I look around the room?

Taylor: We should have the models.

Ali: Great idea. I'm also thinking your photographs for inspiration and maybe a dictionary and thesaurus. I'll be coming around to talk to you about your changes. OK, find a good work space and go to it.

Worktime #2 (Release): Write, Revise, Write, Confer

Ali's writers get to work and she begins to confer to see the effects the minilesson had on students' ability to make some substantial revisions to their "Best Part of Me" projects. Let's listen in. . . .

Ali: So, Molly, tell me what you're thinking.

Molly: I want to add some parts to my first line, "They help me grab the bar in gym."

Ali: Were there any lines in the mentor texts that you liked?

Molly: Yeah, like the one where her eyes see the ocean.

Ali: Oh, good choice. I can tell from that line, "They see the reflection off the surface of the ocean," that the seashore is something that is important to that writer. What else can you tell me about your hands grabbing the bar that might give the reader more information about something that is important to you?

Molly: I do flips and turns around and around again.

Ali: Wow! That sounds very musical and gives me more information about the kind of bar you are grabbing. Now I get the gymnastics part. Great addition. Keep going; I'll check back with you in a few minutes to see what else you've decided to revise.

Ali made a consistent effort throughout the project to make sure that the writers didn't lose sight of the overall effect of their piece on the reader. The first day of the project when the class discussed "Why do a project like BPOM?" they brainstormed "To learn something new about the author" and "To share new thinking with an audience." Many of Ali's writing conferences centered on the big question "What can I learn about you through the description of your part?" This question resurfaced in the many rounds of critique to powerful (and hilarious) effect when students discussed Ali's "My Eyes" essay. [See Fgure 5.1 and 5.8]

Debrief #2 (Catch)

After a few more writing conferences, Ali calls her writers back to the rug to have them share the revision they did during the worktime.

Ali: OK, writers. I had some great conferences with Molly, and Nadia, and Serenah today. Would any of you like to share changes or additions you made to your pieces based on our conversation about sentence fluency?

Serenah: I want to share! I had "My ears, they help me hear the sweet sound of the lullaby my mom sings," and I added, "And the whispering voices like secrets."

Ali: Great, Serenah. Thank you. Anyone else?

Lorenzo: I decided to use better words at the beginning. Instead of "I love my legs" every time, I changed to "I adore," "I enjoy," "I cherish." I think that makes it more interesting.

Ali: Thanks, Lorenzo. I'm interested to see what that does to the rhythm of your piece.

Ok, it is time for lunch. Please put all of your drafts and any other papers you have out into your writing folders and line up. Great work today.

Conferring as Art and Science

Ali responded to the coaching email that opens this chapter later that same day. I asked her:

Can you write to me a little bit about your philosophy/

thinking about conferring? How do you know if a writing conference has been successful?

She responded,

Hi Sam,

Wow, thanks for the observations. So, let's see. I'm so glad that you asked about conferring, because it's a big question for me right now. I want to see other teachers confer, because I feel like I can hardly meet with any students during the workshop. Also, I don't know that I am particularly good at it. I guess I use it in a few ways:

1. *To KNOW better what is going on with my kids as they are working on tasks.*
2. *To inform me about what's not sticking with kids, and therefore what future lessons I need to tackle.*
3. *To identify what is working in lessons, and what might need to be reinforced.*
4. *To just get to know my kids.*

I also have a few ways that I structure conferring in my workshops. Often, it looks like [what] you saw . . . me visiting and working with students, trying to gain as much knowledge about their processes, thinking, and skills as I can. Other times, I will ask a small group to stay at the green table with me, and I target certain concepts with this group. Is this still conferring? I think so, and sometimes it seems more effective to me than only working with a few kids.

I've had a variety of structures in the past for "tracking" my conferring with kids. Clipboards, binders, etc. . . . All of them work, but none of them seem to be ideal. Right now, I'm trying to visit each child frequently, in various subjects to get to know him/her.

Thanks for coming in. Have a spectacular weekend.

Thanks,
Ali

Conferring guru Carl Anderson (2000) defines conferences as *conversations* and I think his definition helps create a vivid picture of an ideal writer's conference. The word *conversation* takes the pressure off using the conference to capitalize on the teachable moment—the "What would I say?" concern—but puts the pressure *on* as far as listening closely and developing deep, sophisticated relationships with students. You have to give as much as you get. When I confer with students I imagine that I am sitting having tea with my best friend, Colleen. If we are having a conversation at my dining room table, I don't answer the phone when it rings and I barely hear the teapot when it is time for round two. I am locked eye-to-eye and fully engaged with her delightful storytelling, asking her questions to prompt her to tell me more. Eleanor Duckworth writes,

> *I learned to talk with children in a way that kept them interested*
> *in the discussion and invited them to say what they thought*
> *about the topic. And I learned the importance and the challenge*
> *of listening well enough to understand what they were saying. . . .*
> *My ways of trying to follow their thoughts turned out to be*
> *excellent ways to excite their learning. (2001, xiii)*

If you look back at Ali's conferences, you can tell that she did have a goal. She was trying to encourage Christina and Molly to tell her more about themselves, but the "part two" of the conversation was to encourage them to take additional steps as writers. You can tell that she was really listening, not just making blanket suggestions. That is exciting to a writer (believe *me*)! She based her responses on what they said about their writing, not some preconceived idea of what their writing should be. Lucy Calkins said it best, "Teach the writer, not the writing" (1994, 228).

Ali refers to her conferences as a ritual to get to know her students, and these conversations have implications for both planning and assessment. Ali knows that she wants to get better at conferring. She has lots of questions about the most effective ways to meet all of the writers' needs and also about how to document the conversations that she has. The beauty is that she stays true to conferring as a system, structure, routine, and ritual of her classroom because although she doesn't have it all figured out, she knows they are the best way for her to figure out who her students are, what they know, and what they need.

We fail the learners in our classroom when we *assume* what students know and what they need. We need to talk to them to know for sure.

Molly's Drafting Process

Schools can sometimes take on the feel of a production shop,
students cranking out an endless flow of final products with-

out much personal investment or care. The emphasis is on keeping up with production, on not falling behind in class work or homework, rather than on producing something of lasting value. As in a fast-food restaurant, the products are neither creative nor memorable. Turning in final draft work every day, often many times in one day, forces even the most ambitious of students to compromise standards continually, simply to keep up the pace. (Berger 1996, 24)

Ali intentionally planned on spending three weeks on this writing project, knowing that the final piece would be less than a page with an accompanying photograph. Ali believes that good writing requires time and intentional instruction to show students *how* writers revise their work. The New Standards Primary Literacy Committee agrees with Ali. They write:

Students must write regularly, often generating topics in which they can invest their energies. They must view writing as hard work and adjust to the fact that getting ideas down on paper is only a first step. They must be willing to rethink (often, literally, to re-vision) how these ideas are organized and expressed—and examine a draft in light of how well it communicates. They must make needed changes willingly, perhaps handing the document off for a trusted "other" to read. . . . They must assume responsibility for various rounds of changes until, finally, the document communicates—and is as good as they can make it, including precise word choice and correct spelling, grammar and punctuation. (2004, 31)

Did Molly get it? How does Ali know? She listened closely to Molly in her writer's conferences and she has the evidence of changes Molly made in multiple drafts over three weeks. Let's take a closer look (see Figures 5.4 through 5.6).

Using Ali's Own Writing as a Model for Critique

Once the students wrote their first few drafts, many of them were feeling "done" and Ali knew it was time to take the heat up a few degrees—a perfect teachable moment. The minilessons would need to switch focus from the creation and revision of text along the way to "Does my reader get

Molly's first draft has one surprising line, "They work together as a team," and a few interesting words to describe her baby kitten. The ending is fairly cliché (even though she might get points on the state assessment for bringing the topic back around). Let's see where Ali's explicit instruction and attention help Molly go as a writer.

Molly's next draft shows some evidence of thinking about organization: stanzas are separated and there is an extension of the line about her hands holding the pencil, but that is about it. I wonder . . . did Ali not get to confer with her this day? Did the minilesson go long this day and cut out time for Molly to write? It could be one of any number of reasons. I have bad writing days, too. What is important is that the process doesn't stop here. This project is not about cranking out extensive amounts of text. The focus is on quality and communication. Let's keep looking.

Figure 5.4 Molly's First Draft

DRAFT #1   My Hands

My Hands,
They Help me grab the bar in gym,
My Hands,
They hold the pencil when I write,

My Hands,
They work together as a team,
My Hands,
They feel the fuzzy, soft, comfortable
Midnight fur on my new baby
kitten Louie.
My Hands,
My Hands are my Hands and
they are the best part of
me.

Figure 5.5 Molly's Second Draft

DRAFT 2   My Hands

My Hands,
they help me grab the bar in gym,

My Hands,
they hold the pencil when I write the
outstanding storys and poems that I create
in my mind.

My Hands,
they think together as a team,

My Hands
they feel the fuzzy, soft, comfortable
Midnight fur on my new baby
kitten Louie.

My Hands are my Hands
and
they are the best
part of me.

Figure 5.6 Molly's Third Draft

> *Ahhh . . . here is evidence of Molly's revisions from the minilesson on sentence fluency. Molly adds the line "as I do flips and turns around and around again" and also adds extensively to the hands-pencil connection. Now we're getting somewhere! Yeah, Molly! Yeah, Ali!*

it?"—explicit critique to drive the revision. Critique is a tricky process. You don't want to shut writers down, but you *do* want to push them to create their best work. Ali knew she would have to take a risk and put her writing out there to be a model for students of how to ask for and get constructive feedback.

Let's listen in on the day Ali presented her model for critique.

The Critique-Focused Minilesson

Ali begins, "Yesterday, at the end of our writing time, we just started talking about the question 'How do you know when you are done as a writer?' Brainstorm with a neighbor for about thirty seconds. What are some clues that help you know you are finished?"

Nadia: You have to go get a rubric and see if it is accomplished or exemplary, to see if we have everything on there.

Ali: Thanks, Nadia. Who can tell me more about that? When is it time to get out the rubric? Lorenzo?

Lorenzo: I think when you are planning. Like the draft right before

Figure 5.7 "Finished" Anchor Chart

> ## How do you know when a piece is finished?
>
> - it's <u>neat</u> and carefully crafted
>
> - you've <u>"fixed it up"</u>
>   grammar   word choice
>   spelling
>   punctuation
>   capitalization
>
> - you've <u>read it aloud</u>
>
> - you have your <u>best ideas</u> on the page!
>
> - you've used <u>tools</u>:
>   dictionary   thesaurus
>   experts   mentor text
>
> - you've <u>stayed on topic</u>
>
> - you've used a rubric to check your work

your final so you know your final is really final.

Ali: Yeah, you are both right. I can use a rubric while I am still working on a piece or as a last step. Emma?

Emma: I know my piece is done because it just feels done.

Ali: Can you be more specific?

Emma: Like when you read it out loud to yourself and you think it just can't get any better. It just sounds right.

Ali: Yeah, that specific one really helps. Reading it out loud to yourself or to someone else. Let's add that to our list. What else?

Dylan: When you have your point down. You get rid of the gibber jabber and you've stayed on topic.

Ali: Great, Dylan. And what would you have to do after you have your best ideas down? Can you give me a couple ideas about what might be next?

Dylan: Like punctuation, capitals, and spelling?

Students continue to share ideas and Ali records them all on an anchor chart (see Figure 5.7). Then she asks students to pull out her essay, "My Eyes."

Worktime #1 (Release): Reading Models

Ali gives the students a purpose for rereading her essay: "OK, today we are going to spend some time giving each other feedback about this list we've just created. Let's start with my

piece. As a writer, the best way for me to get better is to have feedback that is *kind, specific, and helpful*. Take a few minutes to reread my essay. Looking at my piece, what might some kind, specific, and helpful feedback sound like? Am I done? What might I need to do today to improve my essay? Are there places I could put stronger or more important things about myself?

"Read for about six minutes and then let's do a quick check-in. Please write one idea on a sticky note to help me improve my essay. Thank you so much for your careful attention to my writing. I can't wait to hear what you have to say. We'll share in about six minutes."

The students, with serious looks on their faces, begin to furiously write on their sticky notes.

Debrief #1 (Catch)

Ali has enlarged her essay and has it posted on a big piece of butcher paper (see Figure 5.8).

Ali: OK, who's ready to share some kind, specific, and helpful feedback?

Lindsey: I like the last sentence, but maybe say something like, "From Massachusetts it is a long way to Colorado."

Ali: Thanks, Lindsey. I'll think about that change. Anyone else?

Cameron: I like how you use the word *strides* but maybe change the word *run* into *dash* or another word that is more precise.

Figure 5.8 Critiques Anchor Chart

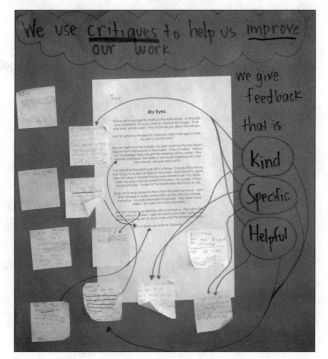

Ali: Thanks, Cameron. It was helpful that you complimented one of my words and gave me a specific example of another one to change. I think you guys really get this idea of critique.

OK, here is your job for the next thirty minutes. I want all of your essays out on your tables. Then we are all going to travel around with our sticky notes and try to give each other some kind, specific, and helpful feedback. When you are writing your feedback, think about the kind of feedback that would help you improve *your* piece. Please put your essays on top of your writing folders at your table and get started. This is a quiet activity. I should hear only pencils writing. Who is ready? OK, table one, please put out your essays and start.

Figure 5.9 A Student Critiquing Another's Piece with Kind, Specific, and Helpful Feedback

Worktime #2 and Debrief #2

As in the workshop about sentence fluency, the students are released for thirty minutes to read, write, think, and then come back to the circle to share their thinking about the process of giving feedback to their classmates. The writers in Ali's classroom understand their responsibility to do the work because they are asked to do it every day. It is a way of *being* for them.

This explicit focus on feedback and critique also has other benefits for students—the benefits that come from believing you are part of a community of writers.

Creating a Community of Writers

I am fascinated but not surprised by the feedback students gave Ali about her "My Eyes" piece. My favorite by far is the sticky note that said, "Where are you in the poem? Tell me" (see Figure 5.10). For three weeks, Ali conferred with students, asking them over and over, "What can I learn about you from your description?" This question back to her, "Where are you in the poem?" is terrific evidence of the impact Ali's questions had on her students. I love the "Tell me" part most of all. This student demands much of Ali, trusting that Ali will respond.

Carl Anderson writes,

Another way we help students become better writers is by teaching them to be reflective about their writing. . . . Good writers use strategies and techniques thoughtfully because they've learned to step back from their writing and reflect on

what they're doing. They ask themselves questions such as "How's this going?" and "What am I trying to do here?" . . . When we ask students, "How's it going?" or "What work are you doing as a writer today?" . . . we are scaffolding their growth into reflective writers. When we ask these same questions in conference after conference, students begin to ask these questions themselves—independent of us. (2000, 9)

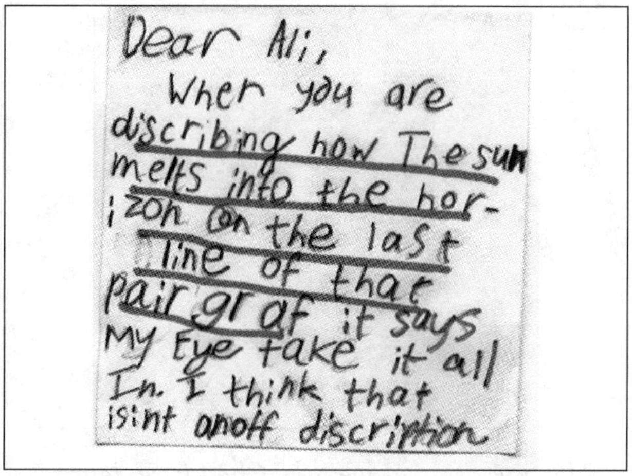

By doing her own assignment, and putting herself through the process of critique, Ali has created a community of writers in her classroom—*every* person in this room is a writer, the teacher included. With her efforts she has shown "We need each other to get better. I need you, you need me—we all need each other."

The routine of teachers doing their own assignments is an essential part of creating that community. Taking risks in front of students is the best way to model that meaning does not just arrive for readers, writers, and thinkers. If we replicate the habits and processes of writers, then we become writers.

Another essential element of Ali's community of writers is that she is not the only one who assesses writing in the room. Students assess each other's work, taking on the authentic role of reader—"Does this make sense?" "Is it clear?" "Does it communicate what you hoped?" again mimicking the questions they hear from Ali in writing conferences every day. Ali helps scaffold these feedback sessions with questions and criteria lists that focus on her learning targets: communicating about one's life, word choice, and sentence fluency. See Figures 5.11 and 5.12 for a few examples of some feedback Chad received before his final draft.

The environment that Ali creates on a daily basis in her writers workshop is one where all children expect to succeed, expect to think hard, expect to write for a purpose—and expect to carefully craft that writing in order to communicate their thinking *clearly* to a reader. Ali reflected,

I don't think of myself as an artist, but I do think of myself as someone who needs to create in order to thrive and grow and be happy. I'm constantly making things. I have since I was a kid. It's how I learn new things.

Figure 5.10 Sticky Note Feedback

Although it would be great if Augie's and Cameron's feedback to Chad were more substantive, I don't think it is all that important. Here, it is the process of reading someone else's writing and trying to help that I think will help all three of them become better writers in the future. When we replicate the habits and processes of writers over and over, we make them our own. Have you ever heard the saying "Fake it 'til you make it?" It's a cliché for a reason!

The questions Augie asks Chad here, later in the project, seem more interesting to me. Augie is looking for more narrative from Chad, and I think Chad is likely to respond to his friend and answer his questions by adding more detail to his piece. Again, the process is as important as the content in this case.

Figure 5.11 Chad's First Feedback Sheet

Name Chad   Date 10-5

BPOM
Draft #2

As you get ready to start draft #2 of your BPOM, please think about the following criteria:

- Choosing strong verbs
- Adding details
- Showing what's important about your life

When you have checked to make sure you are doing this, have two friends read your piece, get feedback, make any last changes, and then write your second draft on the back.

friend #1

Augie ___ Checked my work.
Here is their feedback: I liked when you said "My tounge can do things other toungs can't" I think you should say something extrodinary about your tounge

friend #2

Cameron ___ Checked my work.
Here is their feedback: Beter hand wrighting Say what is Rilly is important to you

Figure 5.12 Chad's Second Feedback Sheet

Name Augie   Date 10-23
Partner Chad

BPOM
Read your piece to your partner. Then answer these questions:

What did you learn about your partner?
His mom's a good cook
He shares stories at the dinner table!

What are you still wondering?
What cool shapes can your tounge make?

What else could he/she add to make this piece more informative?
Who shares his stories?

For me, crafting things is what learning is all about because it creates an automatic need to know some content to be able to make something of quality. I'm constantly trying to help students understand the importance of crafting something from beginning to end. I hope they see the importance of the process as well as the content. I hope they consider themselves real scientists, writers, etc., because I have given them the opportunity to inquire, explore, and dig deep into a crafting process.

Figure 5.13 Christina's Essay

My hands

My hands
they let me capture a juicy ripe tomato thats gargantuan in my mom garden while her zucchini is growing and flowers are blooming at the same time.

My hands
help me pick up a bright red ping-pong paddle, so I can play as good as my mom and let me hug my family and shake hands with the new people I meet

No wonder they can let me pick up a fork I can stick it in the succulent sesamae chicken, as I pick more and more.

My hands
let me cast shadow puppets against the wall while my little brother looks and laughs when I do them.

By christina

10-27

that is
The Best Part of Me

Christina's final piece speaks to the power of Ali's intentional focus on word choice, sentence fluency, and the idea that the reader should learn something important about the writer through her description.

Capture, gargantuan—writers like to have fun with words, and I can picture Christina giggling with her table partner while brainstorming these precise words together.

In the conferring script that opens this chapter, Christina said, "I chose my hands because they help me grab what I want." She wrote, "They help me eat. I would go hungry without them." Now we know through Christina's descriptive writing that her mom is a great gardener and an important part of her everyday life. What a difference a few weeks of writing with targeted minilessons, conferences, debrief, and critique makes! Ron Berger would be proud! Christina not only has created a beautifully crafted piece of writing but has also written a piece that her family will treasure forever.

Chad's piece is quintessential fifth grade to me. There are a few spots that show his attention to word choice and musicality, but this piece is more interesting for his original topic and his attempts to expand the idea of expressing what matters most to him through his tongue!

I can tell from this piece that his friends are a big part of his life and he's figured out the importance of being a good storyteller to those friendships. During one of Ali's minilessons, Chad shared that Cameron helped him add the words have conversations *because as Chad so eloquently said, "I think it tells how I like to talk to people instead of just talk, talk, talk to myself."*

The end of that stanza, "and learn about my friends and family," shows that he gets that conversations have two parts—talking and listening. Bravo, Chad!

Figure 5.14 Chad's Essay

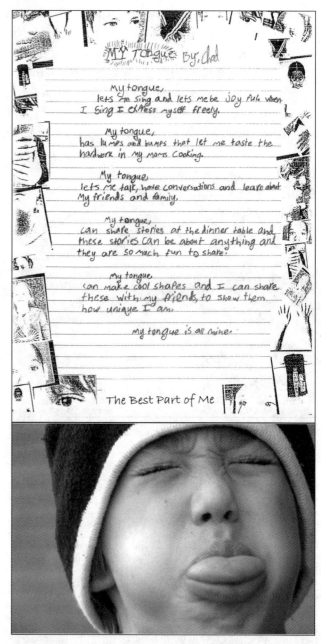

How did Ali's students respond to her focus on the careful, clear crafting of their "Best Part of Me" pieces? How did they respond to her deliberate focus on process *and* product? Take a look at their final drafts (see Figures 5.13, 5.14, and 5.15). What do you think?

At the Heart of Writing

For adults and students alike, putting letters and words on paper is almost magical. Writing seems to unlock the mind, to

Figure 5.15 Lorenzo's Essay

> One of my favorite quotes about education is "The best that education can give [is] the notion that responsibility and delight can coexist" (Pullman in Miller 2006, 58).
>
> The delight that Lorenzo takes in his legs is electric! As I read his piece, my exhaustion melts away and I want to run, jump, and play.
>
> As he shared with his class in a debrief session, he changed the "I love my legs" opening to the words adore, enjoy, and cherish. I have to believe that Lorenzo's careful attention to detailed word choice will continue in future pieces.

My legs

10-27

I love my legs, they help me complete my task in running, as I pump my legs around the park so I can build my strangth as a runner!

I adore my legs, they let me play gym games so I can sprint past people and win again! Speed pushes me along as I succeed in my passion of Hogball, a scampering and kicking game!

I enjoy my legs, they cheer me up when I'm sad, so I can defend my self!

I cherish my legs, they are able to boot a soccer ball for miles, so my teamates are able to smack the ball into the goal!

I love my legs, they carry me on in life!

by
Lorenzo Harris

The Best Part of Me

organize and synthesize thinking, to excite the intelligence. By weaving together bits of information that may never have been joined before, writers discover new meaning. The way writers ultimately convey this meaning to readers pushes writers to make a variety of very sophisticated choices. (New Standards Primary Literacy Committee 2004, 31)

To see Ali's students living the lives of writers on a daily basis fills me with a sense of awe and a lot of jealousy. I was an adult before I had the chance to write for a real purpose and audience. In my life at school, writing was about regurgitating others' ideas, never "weaving together bits of information that may never have been joined before."

Every day Ali's students have chunks of time to weave together these bits to discover new meaning. It is this thinking that excites me most of all. Ali said to Christina in a writing conference, "Everybody needs food to survive. . . . See if you can tell me something about yourself that would be unique to you." What an opportunity for Christina to feel important, powerful, skilled, and proud. And, because she's in a writers workshop every day, Christina gets to feel that way a lot. Ali makes sure she does.

As teachers, we have to ask ourselves, "How do we intentionally plan for writing experiences that cultivate the type of writers we want our students to be?" That entails many of the steps that Ali showed us how to take:

★ Think about what *you* think makes great writing. Read. A lot.
★ Write yourself.
★ Constantly feed your writers with great models of fluid writing.
★ Study the craft as much as the content.
★ Meet with writers individually and ask them, "How's it going?"
★ Teach the writer, not the writing.
★ Ask students to revise, critique, and revise some more.
★ Leverage all of the writers in your classroom to give feedback and get smarter together.
★ Listen closely and *show them how*.

Ali spent three weeks of writers workshops for a one-page piece of writing. Because she gave students lots of time with this project, she'll be able to pick up the pace a bit in future projects. The walls of her classroom are covered with anchor charts that are filled with student thinking about what makes great writing. She can continue to use these as springboards for future writing projects. Poet Seamus Heaney says,

> In fact, the ability to start out upon your own impulse is fundamental to the gift of keeping going upon your own terms, not to mention the further and more fulfilling gift of getting started all over again—never resting upon the oars of success or in the doldrums of disappointment. . . . Getting started, keeping going, getting started again—in art and in life, it seems to me this is the essential rhythm. (1996)

Ali's students feel this essential rhythm. As readers, as writers, as thinkers, we are never done. There is always time to get started, keep going, and get started again. Ali's daily writers workshop makes it so.

Ali's Systems, Structures, Routines, and Rituals

Following is scaffolding for the story of teaching and learning in Ali's classroom. Remember, whole-scale replication is not the point. What practices were intriguing to you? What practices match your beliefs about the agency and capacity of children to think and learn? The beauty is, there are dozens of entry points. Pick one that matches what you believe and the rest will come. Do you want to start by doing your own assignment? Using a mentor text to study the craft of writing? Practicing peer revision in your classroom? Here are a few ideas for places to start:

Systems, Structures, Routines, and Rituals Highlighted in Chapter 5	Narrative description found on page	Ideas to help you get started	For more information check out these resources
Using a mentor text for writer's craft and project design	113, 117–118, 128–130, 131	Ask yourself, "How does a [insert real-world job title here] demonstrate his understanding of a topic?" Find that demonstration of understanding at a library, online, or from a colleague's bookshelf. Or write one yourself.	*Understanding by Design* (Wiggins and McTighe 2005) *About the Authors* (Ray and Cleaveland 2004) *Study Driven* (Ray 2006)
Teacher write-aloud	115–116, 128-130, 131	Write/think it through the night before. What writing moves or thinking might you want students to explicitly see you make? Replicate that thinking and writing with students the next day. Write for a few minutes in front of students. Let them ask you questions.	*I Read It But I Don't Get It* (Tovani 2000) *Do I Really Have to Teach Reading* (Tovani 2004) *Strategies That Work* (Harvey and Goudvis 2000)

Systems, Structures, Routines, and Rituals Highlighted in Chapter 5	Narrative description found on page	Ideas to help you get started	For more information check out these resources
Anchor charts	111, 118, 119, 128, 129	Buy a giant sticky note pad. Each day/week, think about the key idea/skill you want students to take away—it usually is a good topic for an anchor chart. Ask students to read great writing and then label their thinking about what makes it great on an anchor chart. Think about topics/ideas you want students to have access to throughout a topic that they can come back to again and again. Think about how the walls of your classroom can speak volumes about what happens inside—what matters most? When you figure that out, ask students about it and hold their thinking on an anchor chart!	*Strategies That Work* (Harvey and Goudvis 2000) *Reading with Meaning* (Miller 2002)
Conferring	112–112, 121, 122–124, 136	Get eye-to-eye with students and ask them, "How's it going?" Teach the writer, not the writing. Listen.	*How's It Going?* (Anderson 2000) *In the Middle* (Atwell 1998) *About the Authors* (Ray and Cleaveland 2004)
Peer feedback	129–133	Have students read good models and each other's writing often. Show students how writers need kind, specific, and helpful feedback to improve. Show students how to ask each other questions about their writing instead of judging it. Model receiving feedback as a writer and how it helps you get better.	

CHAPTER SIX

Josh's Memorialists

The workshop you'll see this time:

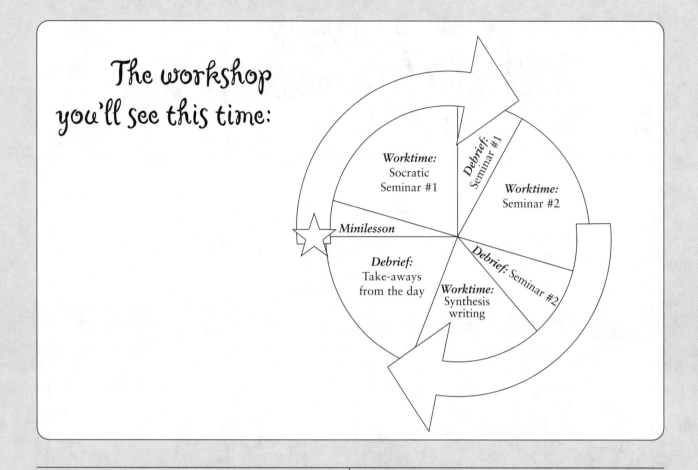

Worktime: Socratic Seminar #1

Debrief: Seminar #1

Worktime: Seminar #2

Minilesson

Debrief: Seminar #2

Debrief: Take-aways from the day

Worktime: Synthesis writing

Workshop duration: 90 minutes (5 minutes accounted for by transitions)

Minilesson (Catch) (10 minutes):
- ★ Teacher shares the purpose of the Socratic seminar:
    - ★ To grow and revise student thinking about three big guiding questions of the unit.
    - ★ To use thinking to write essays about a memorial design.
- ★ Teacher models use of a graphic organizer designed to hold student thinking and revision of thinking.

Worktime (Release) (20 minutes):
- ★ Twelve students in inner circle discuss big questions in Socratic seminar format.
- ★ Twelve students in outer circle chart the flow of the conversation and hold their thinking on the graphic organizer.

Debrief of Socratic Seminar #1 (Catch) (5 minutes):
- ★ Outer circle critiques the conversation it heard—both content and process—and gives suggestions for improvement.

Worktime #2 (Release) (20 minutes):
- ★ Inner circle and outer circle of students switch and repeat process.

Debrief of Socratic Seminar #2 (Catch) (5 minutes):
- ★ Outer circle critiques the conversation it heard—both content and process—and gives suggestions for improvement.

Worktime (Release) (12 minutes):
- ★ Students write paragraphs to synthesize and revise their thinking after discussion and debate with their classmates.

Debrief of whole process (Catch) (13 minutes)
- ★ Students share take-aways from the Socratic seminar and their current thinking about the guiding questions.

Hi Josh,

Thanks for your brilliant, inspirational teaching once again today. Your spiral structure, long view, and focus on what is most important is phenomenal. I can't wait to see how these Sand Creek memorial designs and essays turn out.

Things I saw today that struck me:

- use of your own memorial essay as a model to kick off the project
- use of a real-world structure: an essay with two drawings (using Maya Lin's essay and drawings for the Vietnam Memorial as a model) for students to "pitch" their Sand Creek Memorial designs

Something you mentioned today:

- the importance of continuing to spiral the important questions to help students continue to deepen their knowledge in order to answer these questions:
  1. What is the significance of the Sand Creek Massacre?
  2. How do memorials happen?
  3. Who owns history? Who owns memory?

What intrigues me:

- How will you assess the depth of student understanding of these big questions through the memorial design and essays? What do you hope students remember about this topic in ten years?

Much as you use email check-ins with your students to add layers of understanding of them as readers, writers, thinkers, and learners, I need to know what is going on in your brain to help you help your students. Please write to me for ten minutes and push Send. Thanks.

See you tomorrow,
Sam

An Environment Setup for Flexible Thinkers

In the book *Intellectual Character*, Ron Ritchhart writes,

> *When students first step into a classroom, they receive a series of messages about the teacher's aesthetic, organizational abilities, interests, and attitudes toward teaching and learning. To discern [these messages], we look as much for what is present as what is not. We look at the content of what is up on the wall, not just its arrangement. We also look at how the physical environment of the classroom gets used and integrated into the instructional day. We [must] look more closely at these components of the environment to better understand what a classroom that conveys an attitude and expectation of thinking actually looks like. (2002, 57–58)*

To truly appreciate Josh's learning environment, we must spend some time studying the walls and the flexible physical setup of his classroom. The walls are covered with quotes and questions and anchor charts and student work. Over the board in giant letters is posted:

fREADom

As your eyes travel clockwise around the room, you read in foot-high print:

"You can't do your own thing unless your own thing is the right thing for the struggle." —Malcolm X

In the corner is a cozy nook with shag carpet and beanbags, sheltered by three bookshelves organized by genre—nonfiction, science fiction, history and historical fiction, reference, poetry, classics, self-help—with a few surprises thrown in, such as the "All About Aliens" section, the "Teen Angst" section, and my personal favorite, the "I Forgot My Book—Cool Things to Read" section.

Along the back wall is an anchor chart with the question, What is Terrorism? and student responses (see Figure 6.1).

And next to this chart are two related quotes (see Figure 6.2).

Josh's room is a showcase of student and teacher thinking. I can walk

What can you infer about Josh's beliefs about access to power, choice, and voice in our world from looking around his room?

Figure 6.1 Terrorism Achor Chart

> ### WHAT IS TERRORISM?
>
> ★ Someone who attacks someone or something
>
> ★ Act of terror
>
> ★ Destruction
>
> ★ When someone makes someone else do something else by threatening them
>
> ★ Someone who harms another to spread fear
>
> ★ An act or comment that hurts someone either physically or emotionally
>
> ★ When a person commits a violent act that affects many people

Figure 6.2 Terrorism Quotes

> ### TERRORISM
> *(as defined by the CIA)*
>
> The term *terrorism* means premeditated, politically motivated violence perpetrated against noncombatant targets by subnational groups or clandestine agents, usually intended to influence an audience.
>
> ### TERRORISM
> *(as defined by Ayatullah Shaykh Muhammad 'Ali Taskhiri)*
>
> Terrorism is an act carried out to achieve an inhuman and corrupt objective and involving threat to security of any kind, and violation of rights acknowledged by religion and mankind.

Anchor charts with student-generated responses are a great way to hold thinking day to day and to chart growth in student thinking over time.

A Socratic seminar is a structured discussion around a common text or question. Socrates believed that the best way to gain knowledge was through disciplined conversation. The day before the Socratic seminar, students are asked to prepare by reading a common text and responding to an essential question. During the seminar, students sit in a circle, a central question is posed, and the dialogue begins! Let's see how Josh prepares his students for the Socratic seminar.

in on any day and look around the room to see the big ideas they are wrestling with, learn what they read, wrote, and talked about yesterday, and make inferences about the direction they'll be going in tomorrow. The walls of his classroom hold a wealth of information about Josh's planning, instruction, and assessment. Let's listen to the voices of his students to learn a little more as they participate in a Socratic seminar.

The Minilesson (Catch)

Understanding is the ability to think and act flexibly with what one knows. In keeping with this, learning for understanding is like learning a flexible performance—more like learning to improvise jazz or hold a good conversation or rock climb than learning the multiplication table or the dates of the presidents or that F = MA. Learning facts can be a crucial backdrop to learning for understanding, but learning facts is not learning for understanding. (David Perkins in Wiske 1998, 40)

Josh's middle school students have been *reading, writing, talking, and thinking* about the Sand Creek Massacre for the past three weeks. (The Sand Creek Massacre was an infamous incident in Colorado history when the local militia led by Colonel Chivington attacked a village of Cheyenne and Arapaho Indians encamped on the Eastern plains.) In the center of the classroom there is a circle of chairs, surrounded by tables creating an outer horseshoe. Twelve students sit in the inner circle, holding index cards with their thinking. The rest of the class sits behind the tables with a graphic organizer (see below):

Sand Creek Socratic Seminar

Based on the short articles we've read over the past few weeks, please be prepared to share your thinking about these three questions:

1. Were the Dog Soldier attacks just?
2. Is terrorism ever an appropriate response?
3. Is there such a thing as "right" or "true" justice?

Points with Which I Agree/Disagree:	Now I'm Thinking . . .

Once the students are settled, Josh begins his minilesson.

Josh: Our learning about the Sand Creek Massacre this fall is like climbing up a mountain. Every day we are reading, holding our thinking, learning a little bit more, and building our background knowledge. Today we are going to participate in a Socratic seminar. I'm interested in this idea that the Socratic seminar is a revision tool for you guys. Instead of *only* discussing today, I want you to hold on to your ahas in writing during the seminar so you can evolve your own thinking through writing and figure out how it applies to the description of the Sand Creek memorial project you are developing.

The twelve students in the *inside* circle will be debating the questions on the board. While they are discussing the questions, the twelve students in the *outside* circle will be holding the thinking that strikes them. On the left-hand column they will write comments that make them go "Yes!" or "Hmph!" or "Hmmm . . . ," and then on the other side I want you to add "Now what I'm thinking . . ." Think rock in the puddle—how is your thinking growing when you hear the opinions and supporting reasoning of your classmates? Think about expanding the circles of your knowledge today. OK, who's got one point that you are dying to make today? Tommy?

Tommy: The Dog Soldier attacks *were* an example of justice because they tried to negotiate peacefully first and it didn't work. The government wouldn't listen.

Josh adds to the graphic organizer on the overhead:

Points with Which I Agree/Disagree:	*Now I'm Thinking . . .*
Dog Soldier attacks were an example of justice because they tried to negotiate first and it didn't work. (Tommy)	

Josh continues, "And Trevor, how might that opinion affect your thinking?"

"I agree. Killing *is* justice if they are taking your land or refusing to listen to your ideas for more peaceful ways to live," Trevor replies.

Josh continues his modeling, "OK, so if I'm Trevor, I write over on this side of the chart just what he said." Josh adds to the overhead model:

Points with Which I Agree/Disagree:	*Now I'm Thinking . . .*
Dog Soldier attacks were an example of justice because they tried to negotiate first and it didn't work. (Tommy)	I agree! Killing *is* justice if someone is taking your land or refusing to listen to your ideas for more peaceful ways to live. (Trevor)

Josh: This is just an example of one way for you to hold your thinking about the discussion today. I want this stapled into your Sand Creek Journal. So a quick reminder of the guidelines we discussed

JOSH'S MINILESSON
Structure and Content

Instruction:

★ 10 minutes long

★ *Teacher sets immediate purpose:* To grow student understanding through a discussion in a Socratic seminar format about three big questions:
1. Were the Dog Soldier attacks just?
2. Is terrorism ever an appropriate response?
3. Is there such a thing as "right" or "true" justice?

★ *Teacher sets long-term purpose:* To inform student thinking about the Sand Creek memorial design and essays.

★ Teacher models use of graphic organizer to hold thinking (see page 144–145).

Teaching Cycle Implications

Assessment:

★ Prior to the Socratic seminar, look through students' responses to entrance tickets (initial responses to seminar questions) to place students into balanced discussion groups.

Planning:

★ Knowing the end—how students will demonstrate their understanding of the guiding questions with a Sand Creek memorial design and essay

★ Making sure questions posed in Socratic seminar tie to the bigger ideas/guiding questions in the unit and will help students think through the rationale for their Sand Creek memorial design and essay

★ Creating the graphic organizer and planning time to model the use of the graphic organizer for students to hold and revise their thinking

For those of you not intimately familiar with Colorado history, the Dog Soldiers were an elite band of warriors from the Cheyenne tribe. In the 1860s they were attacking white convoys attempting to settle former tribal lands.

yesterday: Only the inside circle should be speaking. If you are on the outside circle, bite your tongue and write your thinking on your chart. Inner circle, feel free to write too if you want to capture a thought that you don't feel like sharing out loud.

We are going to start with the first question, "Were the Dog Soldier attacks just?" If you feel like you've exhausted the discussion on a question, feel free to move on to "Is terrorism ever an appropriate response?" and/or "Is there such a thing as 'right' or 'true' justice?" OK, ready? Begin.

The Worktime (Release #1)

Walker, a seventh grader, gets things started:

Walker: What do people here think justice is? I'm thinking that justice is not the same as revenge, so I don't think the Dog Soldiers' attacks were justice. I guess there is a very fine line. A lot of times when people say they are getting justice, it is just for revenge.

Priscilla: Dragging the bodies through the streets?! That was not justice. That was definitely revenge. The Dog Soldiers were just trying to retaliate for the American soldiers killing all the women and children in the Sand Creek Massacre. So it was terrorism for terrorism. Is that justice?

Nate: If their message was "leave us alone," then the Dog Soldiers' attacks sent the completely wrong message.

Tommy: I disagree. If you have been the victim of a terrorist attack, like the Dog Soldiers felt about the Sand Creek Massacre, then why can't you go back and terrorize?

Ruby: I'm wondering why the terrorists, both sides, always go for the innocent. Why do they go for the weaker victims? The American soldiers went for the women and children in Sand Creek and so the Dog Soldiers did the same thing.

Jason: Do you think revenge is an OK thing?

Priscilla: When is killing ever OK?

Terrence: They had a reason to do it; maybe it isn't the best thing to do, but it doesn't make it unjust.

Oliver: Terrorists always go for the weak spot or the hard spot to hit it harder to make the people who want to destroy them give up.

Micah: I don't blame the Dog Soldiers, but they are somewhat responsible. If they hadn't done some of the raids, maybe the Sand Creek Massacre wouldn't have happened. That is one of the reasons Colonel Chivington attacked at Sand Creek, so the people of Denver would feel safe and vote for him.

Jason: No, I think Chivington had a personal thing. It wasn't about the Dog Soldiers. He just used that as an excuse.

Priscilla: It is an endless chain that never ends! Everything is revenge. Killing is never justice.

Micah: So, that brings us to the big question, "Is terrorism ever the appropriate response?"

The Debrief (Catch)

(Note: This debrief script is a condensed synthesis of the debrief of Socratic seminar #1, the synthesis writing worktime, and the final take-away debrief. See the workshop description that opens this chapter for more details.)

The students continue their rollicking Socratic seminar discussion for twenty minutes, and then Josh asks each student to share his current thinking.

Tommy: I do think that terrorism is an appropriate response. Sometimes it is the only way to get people to hear you. It might not be a great thing to do, but it gets the message out.

Walker: I believe that you have to turn the other cheek. I know it is a metaphor, but people say it for a reason. It is the only way to stop the violence.

> **Tess:** I don't think there is "right" or "true" justice because everybody believes something different. What is right for one group is not right for another.
> **Chelsea:** It is not OK to kill their innocents because they killed yours.
> **Holly:** I don't think you can just kill them—it only breeds more hate and revenge. Terrorism is never appropriate.
> **Caroline:** I think that terrorism is never an appropriate response. True justice is the ideal, but I'm not sure if there is ever justice that will satisfy everyone.
> **Ruby:** I believe there is true justice even when people believe in different things.
> **Micah:** Trying to get justice through violence always gets out of hand and you don't know why you are terrorizing them and then you don't know why you are fighting. It all gets lost.
> **Priscilla:** I think it is really hard to define right and wrong.

After this brief share-out, Josh wraps up the class.

> **Josh:** While it is fresh in your head, I want you to highlight any thinking you wrote in your chart that you might want to include as part of your essay. [He pauses and allows students to highlight their thinking with yellow markers.]
>
> Now, while this discussion is fresh in your head, at the bottom of your chart, please add any new thinking you have. How has your thinking changed in the past forty minutes? Maybe you have a question, or new supporting evidence, or maybe your opinion has not changed, but you have strengthened your argument. Maybe you have some new evidence to add to support your ideas. [Again, Josh pauses and allows students to write.]
>
> We are going to start back up tomorrow by taking a look at the thinking you recorded today and start thinking about how to integrate those thoughts into an essay to inform and support the design of your Sand Creek memorial. Thanks for your thinking today. See you tomorrow.

What Is Worth Students Knowing?

These eleven- to thirteen-year olds are discussing the similarities and differences between justice and revenge, using a historical case study, the Sand Creek Massacre of 1864, to support their opinions. As we try to figure out the guiding question of this book, "How do we know what students know and are able to do?" we cannot overlook the importance of the question "What is worth students knowing?"

Jerome Bruner (1960) says it best. "For any subject taught, we might ask [is it] worth an adult's knowing, and whether having known it as a child makes a person a better adult" (52).

So, will determining their opinions on the shades of gray between justice and revenge help these students be better adults in our current world? Josh, with every teaching move he makes—in his planning, in his instruction, and in his assessment, says, "Yes! It *will* make them better adults—the kinds of adults I want to share the world with."

Planning for Instruction and Assessment

As Josh's students' Socratic seminar discussion cycles through justice and revenge, violence begetting violence, and what is right versus what is an appropriate response, they are replicating what they hear their teacher model for them every day: what it means to be a thinking person in our world.

Before the students were introduced to the unit, Josh thought through the big questions and issues he wanted them to wrestle with. He collected a variety of texts (varied in content and reading level) for students to read and figured out how students would demonstrate their understanding of these complex issues at the end. See Figure 6.3 for some excerpts from the planning document Josh shared with students before the unit began.

Figure 6.3a Josh's Unit Write-Up

MONSTERS IN HISTORY— THE SAND CREEK MASSACRE

"the savages fought like devils to the end"
—*1864 Rocky Mountain News editorial*

Guiding Questions:
- What happened at Sand Creek and why did it matter?
- How should Sand Creek be remembered?
- Who are the monsters? Who are the heroes? To whom?
- What makes a powerful memorial?

With a grounded understanding of the role that fear and monsters play in our mythology, we'll turn our attention toward history and the role that fear has played within our own state. We'll

---

Being able to answer the question "Why do we need to know this?" is essential to motivation and engagement as well as keeping the teacher honest as far as planning, instruction, and assessment goes. If you are trying to know the story of students as thinkers and learners, they need something important to learn and think about.

State standard alert! "Gather information from multiple sources, to understand events from multiple perspectives; determine if the information gathered is sufficient to answer historical questions."

Josh explicitly planned backward—first, he figured out the guiding questions of the unit:

- *What happened at Sand Creek and why did it matter?*
- *How should Sand Creek be remembered?*
- *Who are the monsters? Who are the heroes? To whom?*
- *What makes a powerful memorial?*

And then he asked himself, "What would it look like at the end if students get it? What do historians and memorialists do in the real world?"

With a little research, he found Maya Lin's proposal for the Vietnam Veterans Memorial and used it to show his students how an expert in the real world presented her ideas on how to memorialize history.

No fake school diorama projects allowed here! The world is too filled with amazingness to ignore it.

Figure 6.3b Josh's Unit Write-Up (continued)

explore the factors that led Colonel John Chivington and a volunteer Colorado Calvary to attack and murder 200+ Cheyenne men, women, and children in a remote area of Colorado. We'll try to understand the political reasons behind the attack and the threat that the Cheyenne people posed to white settlers.

Students will be asked to consider multiple perspectives as we investigate not only how fear has driven historical actions, but also the way that fearful events are remembered differently by both the "winners" and "losers" in history. Exploring the politics of memory will enable us to tackle such questions as "Who owns history?" "How should Sand Creek be memorialized?" and most importantly, "How do our stories shape our culture?"

Throughout this phase of the expedition, students will be keeping a thought journal to hold their thinking as their understanding unfolds. We'll also be conducting a number of Socratic seminars as students construct their own meaning of these complex historical issues. Our final project will be to actually create memorial proposals for the Sand Creek Massacre.

In the 1980s, a young, unknown architecture student by the name of Maya Lin entered a competition to design a Vietnam War Memorial in Washington DC. There were over 1,400 entries from all over the world, including by many of the most prestigious architectural firms in the country. Maya Lin won the competition, setting off a firestorm within many different communities both on Capitol Hill and among Vietnam vets. Not only was she only 20 years old, but she was of Asian descent and her design—a black gash stretched out along the Washington Mall—and determined by some as merely "a pit"—was unlike any memorial ever built. Many questioned Lin's credentials and her idea—could it really honor the legacy of Vietnam?

Ultimately, her idea prevailed and the monument was built. It is now considered not only brilliant, but also the measuring stick for the design of all future memorials. The story is recorded in a remarkable Academy Award winning documentary entitled, "Maya Lin: A Strong

Figure 6.3c Josh's Unit Write-Up (continued)

Clear Vision." Using Maya Lin's process as a model, and together with Anna, our fantastic art teacher, students will propose and design a memorial to honor the Sand Creek Massacre. During this project, we'll also have the opportunity to speak with the Sand Creek Site Superintendent, one of the descendants of George Bent (one of the principal players in the massacre), as well as Pat Mendoza, a Sand Creek historian.

Similar to the Vietnam memorial competition, we will be having a competition of our own as students will be asked to submit two-part memorial proposals. The first will involve an artistic interpretation/memorial design. And the second will be a written reflection about the design elements and the politics of memory.

Projects: Email Check-Ins, Thought Journal, Socratic Seminars, Memorial Research Outline, Sketches, and Essay

Colorado State Standards

History/Reading and Writing
- Reconstruct the time structure and identify connections found in historical narratives;
- Formulate historical questions based on examination of primary and secondary sources including documents, eyewitness accounts, letters and diaries, artifacts, real or simulated historical sites, charts, graphs, diagrams, and written texts;
- Gather information from multiple sources, including electronic databases, to understand events from multiple perspectives; determine if the information gathered is sufficient to answer historical questions;
- Interpret the data in historical maps, photographs, art works, and other artifacts;
- Examine data for point of view, historical context, bias, distortion, or propaganda;
- Examine current concepts, issues, events, and themes from multiple, historical perspectives;
- Describe how attributes of various people have affected their individual political rights;
- Use a full range of strategies to comprehend non-fiction, technical writing, newspapers,

Collaboration with the art teacher helps increase the amount of time students have to create a quality product as well as increase the expertise to help show them how to work with pastels, the medium Maya Lin used to present her ideas to the committee.

Ways for Josh to know what his students know and are able to do all along the way—not just at the end of the unit

This list presents evidence of Josh setting priorities within the Colorado state standards and aligning his assessment with the wisdom of our "foremothers and forefathers," who have determined what students should know and be able to do! Far from a checklist, Josh uses these standards to guide him and his students thoughtfully and with intent. This list says, "I will purposefully design my instruction and assessment to ensure that my students know and do these things really well. I will intentionally design my instruction so that students do these things over and over and over again and show growth in their knowledge, skills and understanding."

Figure 6.3d Josh's Unit Write-Up (continued)

> magazines, poetry, short stories, plays, and novels;
> - Extend thinking and understanding while reading stories about people from similar and different backgrounds;
> - Recognize an author's or speaker's point of view and purpose, separating fact from opinion;
> - Use reading, writing, speaking, listening, and viewing skills to solve problems and answer questions;
> - Make predictions, draw conclusions, and analyze what is read, heard, and viewed;
> - Locate and select relevant information.

Figure 6.4 Josh's Socratic Seminar Assessment Sheet

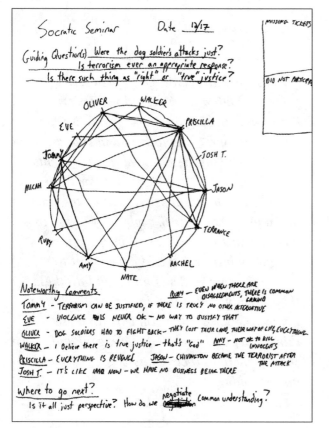

You've seen the plan and long-term view with the end in mind. Now let's see what Josh heard his students saying and writing and how he used that information to guide his next steps . . .

What Josh Learned About His Students During the Socratic Seminar

As his students are doing the work—discussing big ideas in a Socratic seminar format—Josh was listening and learning about what they know and *what they need to know* to demonstrate deep, flexible understanding in the design of a memorial to the Sand Creek Massacre.

As the students discuss the questions of justice and revenge, Josh is busy teaching. While the students talk, Josh listens and records things that are important to him using a handmade recording sheet (see Figure 6.4). The circle with names around it records the flow of the conversation. As if a piece of string were connecting each speaker as she added a comment, the threads of conversation are tracked by the crisscrossing lines. That information is important to Josh because he wants to know when a student isn't participating or to gauge if a few voices are dominating the discussion. Most times, he assigns a student in the outer circle to help gauge the airtime of students and give the inner circle a heads-up if a few people are dominating the conversation. By handing off this task to a student, Josh can spend the majority of his time recording the "Noteworthy Comments" section that will help him guide individual students in his writing conferences with them later in the week as they continue to craft their memorial designs and essays. Josh is struck by many student comments revolving around students' "lines in the sand" around terrorism. From these responses, Josh's wheels are spinning about how to push their thinking further. He writes in the "Where to go next?" section: "Is it all just perspective? How do we negotiate common understanding?"

Why a Handwritten Recording Sheet Matters So Much

I am struck by Josh's recording sheet for many reasons. First, it shows that *he knows what he wants to know* about his students—the intentionality of it is what makes it so important. From this sheet, I can tell a lot about Josh as a thinker and a learner and a teacher. He wants a majority of students to participate and get their voices heard. He wants to collect evidence of student understanding, not just so he knows where to go next (which is a laudable goal in itself), but also to replay their thinking to them in writing conferences so the students can design a thoughtful memorial and write a powerful essay.

In this era of high-stakes accountability, teachers often defer to textbook publishers (and book authors!) to show them the best graphic organizer or worksheet that will help. Josh knew what he wanted and he made a template to match his needs. It isn't pretty. It doesn't need to be. It reminds him what he is looking for and is a quick and dirty way to hold his own thinking in order to help him teach better so that his students can learn more, do more, be more and perform better.

After the Socratic seminar, Josh reflected,

> *I noticed that the kids ended up in two camps—either "it is all perspective/it is all point of view" or "terrorism breeds terrorism and you can't help it." I noticed them beginning to wrestle with reality. They are starting to realize that winning and losing are relative. I am comfortable with whatever reasoning they go with, but I am more interested in the evidence they use for their argument and getting to know what that looks like. I want them to show their understanding of the complexity of the issue and formulate a compelling line of reasoning.*
>
> *As far as individual students, Nathan really surprised me today—his role in the crew was really different than usual. I*

KEYS TO A SUCCESSFUL SOCRATIC SEMINAR

- Choose a big question with no right answer for students to discuss (think about questions you would want to discuss around your dinner table on New Year's Eve with twelve of your best friends).

- Have students read a rich text with the big question or idea in mind and hold their thinking on the text.

- Have students create an entrance ticket to the seminar that shows they have opinions *based on textual or factual evidence* and can refer to that support for their arguments during the discussion (this helps avoid the "Just because I said so," get-nowhere types of discussions).

- Have an end in mind. How will students need to use their thinking in the future? Toward what end are they trying to figure out what they think about the big ideas?

heard passion from him, which was inspiring. Eve and Jackson need to work on the confidence and courage front. It was new for Joseph to be more of a facilitator. Pricilla needed to do more reading; she had no evidence for her arguments. It was pure emotion, which we worked hard for two days prior to the seminar to avoid.

I was really proud of Chelsea for speaking up. I know that is hard for her. Oliver continues to wow me; he was more reclusive than I was expecting, but he was working hard writing and adding thinking to his chart. I'm worried about Holly's confidence. She couldn't look at the group when she was making her final comments. I'm going to talk to her about that tomorrow.

I'm also very intrigued by Barbara's written responses. She was in the outer circle, but her chart was filled with outrage! When some of the students said things like, "You have to fight back!" She wrote, "That isn't the way things are supposed to go!" She was so fired up about this Socratic seminar. She wrote four pages last night in her journal based on a two-minute conversation with me in the hall about justice—I need to find out more about how that happened. I'm not sure what triggered the passion for this topic with her. I'm just thrilled about it!

By listening to teach, Josh added a layer of understanding about his students he wouldn't have had if he had been leading the discussion or, as in some classrooms, *dominating* the discussion. And now, by listening to his students' thinking, both written and verbal, he knew what he wanted to do next. Josh shared,

I need to let them write for a few days about this through the lens of their memorial design, and then I think we need another Socratic seminar with some more provocative text. They are so stuck on the "perspective" thing that it is allowing them to not take a stand. They just say, "Well, it depends what side you are on." I want them to see that they do *know right from wrong, regardless of perspective, and be vehicles for change. I want them to be literate and be confident about right and wrong and do things to advocate and promote what is right. They aren't quite at the critical analysis stage. I don't just want students to be consumers of culture—they have to be producers of culture as well. We need to do this again to push their thinking further.*

Instruction, assessment, planning. The listening to teach cycle played out several times in one workshop, for individuals and for a group. Let's go in for a closer look.

What Planning to Know Looks Like

Written into Josh's unit plan was a list of projects designed to help students deepen their understanding while giving Josh a window into their brains to see how their thinking would grow over time and, ultimately, what understanding of the guiding questions they would come to. This list included email check-ins, thought journals, Socratic seminars, memorial research outlines, sketches, and essays. It is important that this list includes both *process,* in the forms of email check-ins, thought journal, Socratic seminars, memorial research outlines, and *product,* the memorial sketches and essays. It is essential that we know along the way how students are thinking, making meaning, and growing their understanding so that we can figure out who and where they are as learners and why. In the real world we know there are consequences for not completing projects, like getting fired. If we can help scaffold experiences for students, we can also serve as the bridge to teaching them why the ends of things are so important, but also that projects can't just be whipped out.

When I was in middle and high school, I completed most projects and essays the night before they were due. If my teachers had asked to see my thinking along the way, providing texts that helped inform and change my thinking over time, there would have been no way I could have waited until the last minute to demonstrate my understanding. In many classrooms this is where the great divide of those that can do school and those that cannot lies. There was only one time that I was unable to complete a paper (on King Lear—sorry, Mrs. Condray), but my consequence was a B for the semester, which at the time was a consequence I was willing to accept in exchange for fun with my friends and completing assignments in other classes. For many students, the end is too late. The project is too big and too daunting—with no scaffolding nor small steps along the way, school seems impossible, and they fail, and fail, and fail. Josh's focus on the *process* of developing thinking about a topic and the synthesis of that thinking along the way and at the end ensures that no students fail.

My ability to whip projects out at the last minute certainly did not help me in the first few years of my teaching career. In my first few years, I was up until midnight every night designing cool activities for my middle schoolers to do, teaching all day, and then staying up late the next night to do it all over again. Very few of my own school experiences helped me build stamina for a long-term project or to think, rethink, revise, and rethink again, which is what long-term planning for student learning looks like. I repeat, *process and product are essential.*

In his reflection, Josh was intrigued by Barbara's passionate response to the questions of justice and revenge. Let's look at some of Barbara's process before we take a look at her product: the final memorial design and essay.

Barbara's Initial Thinking

Barbara was in the outer circle during the Socratic seminar. Some of her notes are shown in Figure 6.5.

Skill-wise, Barbara is doing what good note takers do—writing down just enough to jog her memory about what spurred her thinking.

When Barbara asks, "Is terrorism always revenge?" and "9/11: is the U.S. innocent"? she is getting to the big ideas and using her background knowledge of current events to try to make sense of it all—a huge step in the right direction to create a lifelong, engaged citizen. Nothing like harnessing adolescent outrage to drive engagement in the project!

She's wrestling with her thinking here, trying to make sense of it. Who's land is it and why? A big, meaty question.

Figure 6.5 Barbara's Socratic Seminar Notes

Remember back to the Socratic seminar. At the end, Josh asked the students to answer the question "How has your opinion or thinking changed in the past ninety minutes?" Figure 6.6 shows what Barbara wrote.

What do you notice? What do you wonder? What do you see as implications for instruction? If you were going to confer with Barbara tomorrow, what would you talk to her about? *There is no one right thing to say to her.* How would you engage her in a conversation to help her make more meaning and create an incredible memorial of the Sand Creek Massacre?

Here is what you know for sure: Tomorrow, you will have workshop time for her to read back through her notes and begin to create her memorial design and essay. So, you know that you might want to use your *minilesson* to model the process of how *your* notes and thinking from the Socratic seminar might influence your memorial design. During the

Figure 6.6 Barbara's Reflection on the Seminar

Reflection-
How has your opinion/thinking changed in the past 90 minutes.

I don't think it has. I'm thinking more in-depth now, and I can have more back-up for my opinion, but I still think that the day soldier's attack weren't just and that terrorism isn't an appropriate response. I still think there is a "right" and a "justice" and if I were to write it again I would add more evidence. But more that I think about it, the right and justice are related to perspective. In our country, defined by the government - it is "right" to follow the law, but who defined that, right is perspective - so I guess my opinion has changed a tiny bit.

> Aha! Evidence of her thinking like a historian! She knows she needs evidence to support her opinions!

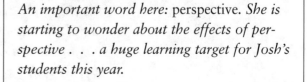

> An important word here: perspective. *She is starting to wonder about the effects of perspective . . . a huge learning target for Josh's students this year.*

worktime, you would circulate to as many students as possible to talk to them about their design process and product, and then in the *debrief*, you would have students share pieces of their writing from the worktime and give all students time to add some thinking to their work. When you know that the workshop is your structure every day, it makes the connection between student work and the assessment of that work for planning and instruction clear.

Memorial Design and Essay: The Importance of a Real-World Model

> *When I speak of modeling, it is more in the context of the teacher acting as a role model, someone worth emulating, than as a demonstrator. When you are in the presence of such models, you get the sense of the teacher as a thinker and not as a teacher of thinking. (Ritchhart 2002, 162)*

Josh scaffolded six weeks of instruction, in a daily classroom workshop, asking students to *read* a variety of texts and *write* to hold their thinking along the way, pausing occasionally to *debate* important questions in a Socratic seminar format, all with the end goal of designing a memorial for the Sand Creek Massacre. No such memorial exists in Denver; this was not a fake, just-for-school project. It was real and there were a lot of local politics surrounding it.

Before the students began their writing, Josh, through several mini-lessons, showed students his own essay submission as well as Maya Lin's design sketch and essay for the Vietnam Memorial. Josh and his students, using a formalized critique process, defined a series of characteristics that helped or hurt the designers' chances of getting their memorial accepted.

Maya Lin submitted sketches in pastel accompanied by a one-page essay, so Josh challenged his middle schoolers to make an impact within the same parameters. Most students wrote four- to eight-page first drafts and then had to cut, and refine, and revise, and cut, and refine, and revise. Just like real authors.

Here are the first two paragraphs from Josh's essay:

> *As the visitor descends into the site, the first experience is an aural one. Approaching the memorial, the ground slopes gently downward, and the noise from downtown, I-25, and city byway traffic recedes into the background. Taking its place, the natural babble and chatter spring from the river conflu-*

ence. Still further, a large circular platform appears at the center of the Platte, connected by two bridges to the grassy shores. One bridge begins upstream and crosses down to the platform; the other originates from the platform and extends downstream to the lower shore, echoing the flow of the river.

These bridges spark the beginning of the memorial experience of Sand Creek. For historical events lie midway between the past which stumbles upon them, and the future which decides the importance of remembering them. The approach to the center platform can be made from either perspective, offering visitors foresight or hindsight into the complexity of the historical event itself.

Figure 6.7 Barbara Notices Maya Lin's Craft as a Writer

Name Barbara

"Reading like a writer," this makes me think... (What do you notice about the craft of her writing?)	Maya Lin's Design Submission to the Vietnam Veterans Memorial Competition
• 1st sentence captures everything - introduced us to the "rift", the wall, earth and park. • How will the visitor experience the memorial? • This is a memorial that demands close examination • Strong verbs - word choice that really accentuates the Portrayal of her memorial. • "Unchanging" - metaphors? • a sense of togetherness • a brief significance of wall, size, shape, location, metaphor... • 2nd ¶ is a good discription of wall and its purpose. •	[Walking through this park-like area, the memorial appears as a rift in the earth - a long, polished black stone wall, emerging from and receding into the earth.] - the wall is breath Approaching the memorial, the ground slopes gently downward, and the low walls emerging on either side, growing out of the earth, extend and converge at a point below and ahead. Walking into the grassy site contained by the walls of the memorial we can barely make out the carved names upon the memorial's walls. [These names, seemingly infinite in number, convey the sense of overwhelming numbers, while unifying those individuals into a whole. For this memorial is meant not as a monument to the individual but rather, as a memorial to the men and women who died during this war, as a whole.] The memorial is composed not as an unchanging monument, but as a moving composition, to be understood as we move into and out of it; the passage itself is gradual, the descent to the origin slow, but it is at the origin that the meaning of the memorial is to be fully understood. At the intersection of these walls, on the right side, at the wall's top, is carved the date of the first death. It is followed by the names of those who have died in the war, in

It is important to note that Josh used his own essay as well as Maya Lin's as models. Maya Lin's essay offered a model of a *what*—an end product. That was an essential piece to help students have both *the desire* and *the will* to complete the project. Using Maya Lin's winning sketches and essay as a model showed students that this was a process that exists in the real world and that Josh was asking them to do important work. The sheet in Figure 6.7 is an example of how Josh asked Barbara and the rest of his class to analyze both the writer's craft and the message of Maya Lin's essay.

However, using Maya Lin's essay alone, Josh would not have been able to help his students with the *how*—the dispositions of thinking needed to craft the essay. That is why it was a crucial step for him to create his own design and write his own essay.

An adage attributed to Maya Angelou says, "We all do the best we can until we know better and then we do better." I believe that all students *want* to succeed—they want to do better—but many of them need us to show them how. By doing his own assignment and going through the steps he was asking students go through, Josh was able to model how he was thinking as he was writing. He was able to share with students what mattered most to him in the physical structure and how he would translate that into narrative. He was able to model his process for generating ideas, word choice, and revision and how writing informed his design and the design helped him with the flow of the writing.

Sometimes when teachers first consider the idea of modeling writing for their students, many dismiss the idea with "If I showed them my work they would just copy it." Yes, hopefully. That is the point. Writers learn to write, painters learn to paint, and tennis players learn to serve by watching and imitating experts who know how to do things well. The first few times you model, some students *will* copy you. But if you continue to model day after day in minilessons, and confer with them one-on-one during the worktime, helping them navigate the rough waters of authorship, and provide a real purpose and audience to write for, they will begin to have more faith in *their own* words than in yours. You may have heard this labeled as a gradual release of responsibility or the belief that success breeds success or the journey of a thousand miles begins with one step. Students need multiple entry points and multiple examples of how to write. Modeling helps students see a way into a writer's knowledge, craft, and skill.

Josh first showed students his memorial essay in the very beginning of the Sand Creek unit. He wanted them to see the end so that the students had a *reason to know* the facts about the Sand Creek Massacre. He set them off on a voyage of discovery instead of on a task to memorize facts. They needed to use their skill at writing and holding their thinking in order to know the facts. They had to know the facts so that they could demonstrate their understanding to a panel of judges about why their memorial design should be chosen. They had to determine for themselves the answer to the question "What is the significance of the Sand Creek Massacre?" Peace activist Judith Groch once said, "Those who have been required to memorize the world as it is will never create the world as it might be" (1969). Josh, through the memorial design project, asked students to create the world around them.

If you aim for the goal of understanding, you will have to help students gain knowledge and skills to demonstrate that understanding. And everyone (you included) will have fun doing it. In *Pathways: Charting a Course for Professional Learning*, Marjorie Larner states the case, "If we are teaching for true deep learning based on student need, we do not need to lure students into learning with teacher-intensive activities so they think they're having fun. Learning is the most fun. It makes a person feel bigger, competent, and powerful" (2004, 9). I agree. Learning is the most fun.

Josh made it fun by diving into the process with his students, not prescribing a step-by-step process. Each day for his minilesson, throughout the weeks that students had to craft their essays, Josh put his essay on the overhead projector and took students through his thinking on a section before they dove into their own writing during the worktime. If, during the worktime, he came across student writing that was exemplary or helped illustrate a powerful teaching point, he shared that piece of writing on the overhead during the debrief or (with permission) used that student's writing as the model to launch the workshop the next day.

The Role of Fieldwork and Experts

Figure 6.8 Barbara's Sand Creek Memorial Design

Josh not only used writing experts to show students how but also brought in content experts to help his students make deeper connections in their brains. One of the first experts Josh brought in was Pat Mendoza, a historian and filmmaker who wrote a historical novel about the Sand Creek Massacre. Students read passages from his book to prepare for his visit and had lists of questions for him when he arrived.

Once students had a strong base of content knowledge about the event and the historical context, they dove into the study of memorials. To set the context for their memorial site plan proposals, the students had a day of visiting memorials around Denver. Before they left, the Sand Creek site superintendent visited and shared the steps of the memorial process and the politics involved in commemorating this event. The school's art teacher also paid a visit and gave students a lesson about drawing landscapes so they could capture the natural surroundings at each memorial visit.

So, how do we know? Did any of this assessment, planning, and instruction impact Barbara's memorial design and essay? Did she get it? There is only one way to find out—by listening closely to her work. Take a look at Barbara's final design (Figure 6.8) and essay (Figure 6.9).

What content knowledge do you see in Barbara's essay? What writer's craft? Where would you push her to go next as a writer? What books or authors would you encourage her to read? What would you want to talk about with her in her next readers or writers conference during workshop worktime? How would you meet her needs as a reader, writer, and thinker in the next unit? How would you capitalize on her new passion for societal justice in your next unit? Just a few small questions to ponder.

I love the dramatic, flowery language. I see Barbara attempting to emulate writerly writing. She is using sensory images to paint a picture in the reader's head, and as all middleschoolers know, more is better.

In the first paragraph there is a distinct echo of Josh's memorial essay language—entering the memorial from the visitor's point of view and the importance of the site as the "confluence" of the two rivers. Yet, the composition is still entirely her own.

"Water never stops moving, just like we need to continue into the future" serves as evidence for why memorials are important—one of Josh's learning goals. Also, Barbara speaks to the lessons learned from this history.

Figure 6.9a Barbara's Memorial Design Essay

DESIGN SUBMISSION TO THE SAND CREEK MEMORIAL COMPETITION

Surrounded by buildings yearning for the sky and the chaos of life, yet protected from sound, the visitor experiences a sense of peace while descending down the gently sloping black granite steps onto the chalky pavement below. The murky blue river is directly ahead, just below the confluence of the Platte River and the Cherry Creek—the confluence of two very opposite cultures coming together. As the visitor continues their journey down the pavement, something creeps into their peripheral vision, a sculptural creek with both guns and arrows, a painful recognition of both the Indians and the soldiers who died during the Sand Creek Massacre. The memorial represents two very different sides of an argument, blended into a whole composition.

A small creek trickles along a brick wall made up of hundreds of rust-colored bricks. To the far right side of the wall, a small waterfall falls gently down into the bronze sculptural creek, like tears dropping quietly down a face. Water never stops moving, just like the need to continue into the future, carrying with us the knowledge we have gained from past mistakes and conflicts. There are lessons that can be learned from the Sand Creek massacre. Hate and revenge don't heal, killing other men doesn't solve anything, except for maybe a personal craving for revenge. We can take these lessons to journey swiftly to the future, even around obstacles planted in our midst.

The engraved arrows, like obstacles, embedded in the creek are like an unwanted splinter, representing a sadness for the Indians who were showed no mercy at Sand Creek. The

A "Final" Assessment

A photo album typically contains a number of pictures taken over time in different contexts. When viewed as a whole, the album presents a more accurate and revealing "portrait" of an individual than does any single snapshot within. It is the same

Figure 6.9b Barbara's Memorial Design Essay

arrows then show such opposition to the broken guns, scattered about, embedded so deep in the creek like something buried under so may layers that it's hard to see the real thing, the truth. Yet, the truth is found in the thoughts. It is each person's perspective on it, and their beliefs. It's who they think the heroes and the villains are. Which is why, when the visitor stares at the sculptural creek with arrows and guns and blood revealing the pain and loss, they will see a number of plaques above it, multiple feelings already knotted inside.

A simple stone plaque of black granite and simple block-style lettering helps to unfold the story of the massacre at Sand Creek and all of those figures who played a significant role in the massacre, yet it's all up to each individual person to decide who the heroes and villains are as they ponder all those burning questions the memorial won't always give answers to. The creek ignites the Sand Creek experience with its subtle beauty, revealing the truth that something with a terrible history can still have overwhelming beauty. Red glass shards, sharing the blood spent, energy from the creek, help to contribute to the realness of the creek and person's need to embrace it, to learn from it, and help reduce the fear one man can inflict on another man. A man different from himself.

The memorial emerges from the soft earth and recedes back into it, representing the natural world and creative beauty. The creek extends the full length of the wall, from where the granite steps end to where the concrete slabs form the bridge found already in Confluence Park over the Platte River, near to the confluence of two rivers.

Barbara uses simile and visualization to help her reader get a picture in his head. This makes me wonder about what helped her write like this. Was it the scaffolding of drawing the memorial? Josh's use of models? Barbara writing like a reader? Probably a combination of all three!

"Yet it's all up to each individual person to decide." She refers to the power of the individual here. Another one of Josh's learning goals!

"The arrows then show such opposition to the broken guns, scattered about, embedded so deep." This shows evidence of content knowledge and her earlier thinking about perspective, empathy, and who owns history.

with classroom assessment—a single test at the end of instruction is less likely to provide a complete picture of a student's learning than a collection of diverse sources of evidence is. (Tomlinson and McTighe 2006, 60)

From mid-November through December, Josh's students read a variety of texts about the Sand Creek Massacre—texts that addressed the question of who owns history, violent and nonviolent responses to conflict, the history of Denver, and historical and present-day responses to terrorism. From mid-November through their final products in February, students were asked to hold their thinking in the margins of different readings, in their Sand Creek journals, in weekly email check-ins to Josh, in entrance and exit tickets to Socratic seminars, and in multiple drafts of their Sand Creek memorial outlines, designs, and final essays. The classroom workshops morphed from reading-based workshops, to discussion-based workshops, to writing-based workshops, but the structure was the same. Minilesson, worktime, debrief. Minilesson, worktime, debrief. All with the purpose of helping students make meaning and grow their thinking around big, important ideas that would help students be better, more thoughtful, more thought-filled people.

As with the Socratic seminar assessment sheet Josh developed, he had a variety of ways to know what students knew and were able to do all along the way. After he had written his own essay, but before the student essays were under way, Josh developed a criteria list to help students meet the multiple goals he had for this project. In Josh's class, in order for student essays to reach the level of "accomplished," they had to meet the following descriptors:

★ Author's understanding of the history around Sand Creek is solid, convincing, and detailed.

★ Author's thinking shows thoughtful and rich consideration of the many perspectives of Sand Creek.

★ Author has given rich consideration to all of the physical elements of the memorial including intent, context, and feeling.

★ Author demonstrates understanding and sensitivity toward the historical issues around Sand Creek and powerfully realized them within a memorial form.

★ Author's tone is formal and appropriate for the audience.

★ Phrasing is original, even memorable. It's clear the writer was inspired by Maya Lin.

★ Writing is organized clearly, balanced, and persuasive.

★ Content evolves throughout the draft process. Author shows he or she can use critique to rewrite in order to better meet the expectations of the assignment.

What is fascinating to me about these descriptors is that they tell us as much about Josh and what he cares about as they do about Barbara's essay being accomplished. There are many camps of thought around the development of criteria lists and whole books devoted to the subject of rubrics. My point in sharing Josh's list with you is the *intentionality* behind it. There are some specific goals for the development of student thinking and the skills of student writing that Josh cares about. What matters is that Josh *and his students* understand what they are going for. To communicate their thinking and understanding in writing is no easy task, and there is no single correct way to do it.

Josh's list was informed by state writing standards, six-trait guidelines, the Rubric for the Six Facets of Understanding from *Understanding by Design* (Wiggins and McTighe 2005, 178), his guiding questions, and what he knows about writing as a writer himself. He was not only explicit with students in his criteria list but also explicit with them in his daily instruction, assessment, and planning. You may or may not believe that Barbara's essay met the standards of accomplished middle school essay writing. There are parts that are unclear, a few run-on sentences, and images that fall flat. Josh, after seeing several drafts and listening closely to Barbara all year long, deemed her essay accomplished. She met *his* standards, which were informed by a variety of other standards, deemed appropriate by "experts" in the field.

Josh had to use a variety of sources to develop this rubric and to make sure that his teaching allowed students to meet these goals. Have you ever assessed student writing around word choice without ever having explicitly taught word choice during the time students were writing? Criteria lists and rubrics are important for a variety of reasons, for teachers and for students. They keep us honest as teachers, because we have to explicitly *teach* what we are assessing. Mike Schmoker writes, "Students need to be consulting their criteria throughout the writing process; they need samples—exemplars—of student and professional written work that illuminate these criteria as nothing else can" (2006, 168).

Criteria lists and rubrics are a great way for teachers to match goals to assessments, and to assess students uniformly, but they are also a great way for *students* to know what they are

Using rubrics and criteria lists routinely *in your classroom is intimately tied to your teaching beliefs. The teachers I know who use rubrics consistently believe to their core that if students knew better, they'd do better and that students would if they could. My colleague Cris Tovani says, "When my students don't do what I've asked them to do, it is because I haven't modeled enough." Rubrics matched to models are one way to show students how.*

going to be assessed on. Rubrics help students only if they are handed out *before* students finish final drafts, and matched to examples and models. If students know what they are being assessed on, what it explicitly looks like, and what the teacher (informed by guiding questions, state standards, and personal teaching beliefs) cares most about, then they can attempt to meet those standards. When assessment becomes "guess what is in the teacher's head," it is entirely unfair, no fun, and it doesn't help learners learn more, learn better, or perform to our exacting standards.

How Barbara Knows What She Knows and Is Able to Do

What did Barbara think about her essay? What did she think about herself as a reader and a writer? Luckily for us, Josh uses a portfolio system of assessment that relies heavily on student metacogntion as part of assessment. It is *as important* to know what Barbara thinks of her own strengths and weaknesses as a reader, writer, thinker, and learner to see if she is ready to progress to the next grade as what Josh thinks. Here is an excerpt from Barbara's reflection on her Sand Creek Memorial essay.

> *[Throughout the creation of my memorial design and essay] I was amazed at how my writing and ideas grew from my outline to my essay. This was a very challenging process for me because my outline was very long and I didn't synthesize enough to create a one-page essay. This was where my reading strategies came in handy. I determined importance and made connections to help me define what I should include in my essay. I had a lot of inspiration as well. I used Maya Lin's design submission to the Vietnam memorial competition as well as my peers' essays and my teacher, Josh's. These essay examples helped me reflect on my own essay as well as my own process as a creative thinker and how I communicate my knowledge of a certain subject to somebody else.*

Performing this act of metacognition deepened Barbara's desire *and* ability to learn more. She saw writing as thinking, as a flexible process that changes over time. She also saw the value of having models to both inspire and improve her own writing. These are lessons that are best learned through the experience of writing for a real purpose and a real audience.

Putting It All Together: The Flexibility of a Classroom Workshop

Knowledge, skill and understanding are the stock in trade of education. . . . Knowledge is information on tap. We feel assured a student has knowledge when the student can repro-duce it when asked. The students can tell us what Magellan did, where Pakistan lies, what the Magna Carta was for. . . . [S]kills are routine performances on tap. . . . To know whether a student writes with good grammar and spelling, sample the student's writing . . . but understanding proves more subtle. . . . Understanding is the ability to think and act flexibly with what one knows. (David Perkins in Wiske 1998, 39–40)

Knowledge. Skills. Understanding. I think one of our shortcomings as educators is a failure of vision. Many times, we stop short at knowledge and skills as our end-all and be-all. The problem with this is that without the goal of *understanding*, there is no *reason* to know facts and to have skills. Understanding is the part about being a better adult. You can think and act flexibly only if there is something to think and act flexibly about, but if you are never asked to think and act flexibly, you have no motiva-tion to know.

For many young people, their in-school world is just a series of unconnected, unrelated, uninteresting facts. I hear teachers say all the time, "Yeah, that may work with your kids, but my students have no background knowledge, so they can't do what your kids do." Hey, guess what? THAT IS YOUR JOB—to build their background knowledge! But you can't build students' background knowledge unless you know what conceptions and misconceptions are already inside students' brains. Learning is connecting the new to the known. If you want new stuff to go in, you have to find something to connect it to. The National Research Council states it this way: "All new learning involves transfer based on previous learning. . . . Teachers who are learner centered recognize the importance of building on the conceptual and cultural knowledge that students bring with them to the classroom" (2000, 53, 134).

Teaching for understanding helps you give students the *why* and the *how* this will make them better adults. All students can think. Entice them with something juicy to think about.

If I were a student in Josh's middle school classroom and he said, "Now, class, we are going to study the Sand Creek Massacre," I would immediately start writing a note to my best friend about our plans for the weekend.

Ahhh, but he didn't start that way. He started by saying, "Who are the heroes? Who are the monsters? To whom?" and "Why do terrorists do the things they do?" These are questions I have some opinions about. These are questions adolescents *and* adults can and should care about. If you are bored as a teacher, that's your first clue that you need to do something differently. If you already know the answer to all the questions you are asking, something is very, very wrong.

Steph Harvey says it best: "You can't think about nothing." That is why the question "What is worth understanding?" is an essential piece in creating a classroom where thinking is the thing.

As you've read in example after example, the workshop is a very flexible structure. Especially in content-driven classrooms, the workshop morphs through phases of building background knowledge and then using that background knowledge to develop communication (writing and speaking) skills to be able to "think and act flexibly"—that is, demonstrate understanding.

The first four weeks of Josh's unit functioned as a readers workshop, where students were reading a variety of texts, holding their thinking in the margins of that text, and reflecting in their Sand Creek journals answers to the big guiding questions week after week:

1. What is the significance of the Sand Creek Massacre?
2. How do memorials happen?
3. Who owns history? Who owns memory?

Each week, students' thinking grew and changed based on the short texts they read, their discussions in small groups, their discussions with Josh in individual reading conferences, and the conversations in the whole-group/debrief time at the end of every day. After four weeks of reading workshops and Socratic seminars, the class morphed into a writers workshop. Josh used the readers workshop to build the need to know and after four weeks of reading and talking, the students were chomping at the bit to design their Sand Creek memorials and write their essays to demonstrate their understanding of the politics of memory and the significance of the Sand Creek Massacre.

The students were incredibly focused on their essays, writing multiple drafts, not because they were required to for some predetermined sequence of steps in a writing process, but because Josh had made it so with his careful scaffolding of building students' knowledge and skill. He took four weeks to build their knowledge from a variety of perspectives and gave them chunks of time to read, write, and talk. He helped them have confidence in their skill by the using models and explicitly teaching the craft of writing through looking closely at his own memorial design essay and Maya Lin's design and essay.

I don't believe the old adage "You can lead a horse to water, but you can't make him drink." If you lead the horse to water, you are probably pretty thirsty yourself. A horse is way too strong for you to force his head down, but if you kneel down, cup your hands, and sigh with relief as the cool, crystal water trickles down your throat, I bet that with a snort and a whinny you'll have a big old head slurping right next to you.

If you are bored, so are your students. If you already know all the answers, why bother? There is a lot of work to be done in this big, wonderful, dangerous, compelling world. Ask students to help. Give students an important, real-world reason to read, write, and talk—and show them *how*.

Josh's Systems, Structures, Routines, and Rituals

Following is some scaffolding for the story of teaching and learning in Josh's classroom. Remember, whole-scale replication is not the point. What practices were intriguing to you? What practices match your beliefs about the agency and capacity of children to think and learn? The beauty is, there are dozens of entry points. Pick one that matches what you believe and the rest will come. Do you want to start with planning a Socratic seminar? Finding a variety of texts about a compelling topic? Here are a few ideas for places to start:

Systems, Structures, Routines, and Rituals Highlighted in Chapter 6	Narrative description found on page	Ideas to help you get started	For more information check out these resources
Doing your own assignments	141, 158–161	It will help you break down process and product. It will help you plan targeted, effective minilessons. It will help you see holes in your assignment design and think of alternate ways students may need to demonstrate their understanding of essential content and skills. It will make you humble. It will help you be compassionate. It will help you develop empathy. It will make you a better teacher.	*Understanding by Design* (Wiggins and McTighe 2005) *Best Practice* (Zemelman, Daniels, and Hyde 1998) *The Students Are Watching* (Sizer and Sizer 1999)
Using a real-world model/mentor text for writer's craft and project design	141, 150–151, 158–161	Ask yourself, "How does a memorialist/ historian/biologist/reader/ writer/city planner/journalist/essayist/mathematician demonstrate her knowledge and skill in the real world?" Find a model on the Internet, at a library, or from an expert in the field. Don't ask students to do fake assignments. Only museum curators make dioramas, and usually only to demonstrate complex contextual narratives. If that is your goal, go for it and build in four weeks of workshops for your students to create a high-quality diorama complete with historical/scientific content displays that describe all the features.	*Understanding by Design* (Wiggins and McTighe 2005) *Best Practice* (Zemelman, Daniels, and Hyde 1998) *Results Now* (Schmoker 2006)
Using an academic journal to track changes in student thinking over time	145, 148, 150	Put composition books on your school supply list. Anytime you hand out a text, a graphic organizer, a chart, and so on, have students staple it into their journal. Ask students to leave the journals in the classroom. Periodically, have the students go back through their journals and highlight important thinking that shows how they have grown. Use the journals as your evidence to prepare progress reports, grades, or parent-teacher conferences.	*Best Practice* (Zemelman, Daniels, and Hyde 1998)

Systems, Structures, Routines, and Rituals Highlighted in Chapter 6	Narrative description found on page	Ideas to help you get started	For more information check out these resources
Socratic seminar	143–148, 150, 152–155	Think of a big, meaty question that doesn't have a right answer. Find a compelling text (or two). Give students a day (or two) to read and hold their thinking about the text. Ask students to prepare an entrance ticket—their initial thinking about the question. Review the criteria for a productive conversation. Model the process first. Divide the class in half. Give the observers a job. Debrief the process and the conversation afterward.	Type "Socratic seminar" into your web browser's search engine
Criteria lists and rubrics	162–166	Brainstorm a list of essential content knowledge and skills from your current unit. Try writing the criteria in student-friendly language: "I can write a paragraph with one main idea that makes sense to a reader." Give it to students *before* they begin writing.	*Classroom Assessment for Student Learning* (Stiggins et al. 2002) Type "rubric" into your web browser's search engine Collaborate with colleagues; see what rubrics others in your school are using

CHAPTER SEVEN

Jenn's Citizens

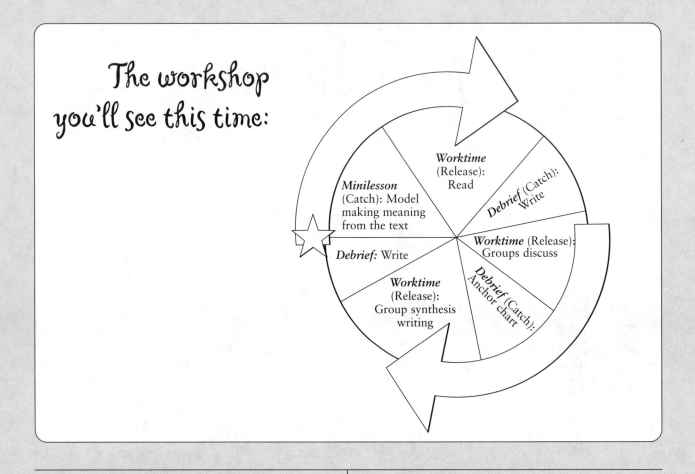

The workshop you'll see this time:

Workshop duration: 90 minutes

Minilesson (Catch) (22 minutes):
- ★ *Teacher sets process purpose:* To show students how she makes meaning of a difficult text (the Fourth Amendment) using questions, connections, and background knowledge and to model what holding thinking on the text looks like.
- ★ *Teacher sets content purpose:* To use the thinking strategies to build background knowledge on the *New Jersey* v. *TLO* court case and answer the question "Was the search legal?"

Worktime (Release) (20 minutes):
- ★ Students reading background information on Supreme Court case *New Jersey* v. *TLO*.
- ★ Teacher confers with students.

Debrief (Catch) (5 minutes):
- ★ Students write current understanding of text ("Was the search legal?") to capture their thinking before they talk in small groups.

Worktime (Release) (20 minutes):
- ★ Students discuss Supreme Court opinions in small groups.
- ★ Teacher listens, labels thinking, and targets students to share during debrief.

Debrief (Catch) (10 minutes)

Worktime (Release) (10 minutes):
- ★ Students prepare overhead transparencies for presentations to the class about the Supreme Court opinion according to the Reasonable Clause and the Warrant Clause of the Fourth Amendment.

Debrief (Catch) (3 minutes):
- ★ Students write current thinking about the question of the day, "Was the search legal?"

Hi Jenn,

It was great to be in your classroom today to see your planning ideas come to life. Already, I saw evidence of students grappling with the big guiding question, "How do I access power in our democracy?" I can't wait to see how the essay plays out as a demonstration of student understanding.

Here is what I noticed and wondered today:

What I noticed:

- Guiding questions for the unit are posted over the board:
  - How can I access power in our democracy?
  - Who has the power?
  - What is our democracy?
- I noticed that you are a master questioner these days. Every time a student asked you a question, you responded with: "Wow, great question, what do you think?" Another time I heard you say, "My question back to you is should power be shared? What do you think?"
- I noticed you labeling student thinking and behaviors that help them make meaning.
  - You said to Cosmo, "You have some real-world information to bring to this discussion. That will help you as this gets more complex. Keep talking."
  - As you were conferring with a small group, you said, "I love how Alon said, 'To be secure is to have your privacy.' Lan, what is secure to you?"
  - And to Josh, "Will you write some of that down in your academic journal? That is the thinking I am looking for. Is it a good use of power? How do you know?"
- When you were debriefing with the whole class, you said, "Zak, what a powerful question: 'What if there is no time to get a warrant?' Let's hold that question over here and see if we can get more information from the text to help us answer that."

What I wonder:

- What did you learn about your students as thinkers today? How did they move along the continuum of understanding about the Fourth Amendment?
- What propels students to work during the worktime of a workshop structure?

Thanks for including me in your "power"-full classroom today. Write to me for ten minutes and push Send.

Talk soon,
Sam

The Setup

Jenn begins her middle school humanities class thanking the students who are ready to begin. "Thank you, Jackson. Thank you, Emma. Thank you, Dana. Thank you, Cam." The rest of the students settle in and Jenn starts, "We are going to shift our focus a bit from our discussions about who has the power and . . ."

Just then, the door blasts open and Alon, an eighth grader, noisily enters the classroom. Jenn says calmly, "Alon, you are late. Come in and have a seat. *Quietly*." As she approaches him, she says, in a too-loud voice, "You smell like smoke. Where have you been? What have you been doing?"

"Nothing."

"I don't think so. Come out into the hall with me for a minute."

But the pair stops abruptly in the doorway, and with every student's eyes riveted to them, Jenn says, "Are you sure you weren't smoking? Empty your pockets. Hand me your backpack."

Then Jenn, with a dramatic flair, yanks the backpack open and a pack of cigarettes leaps out of the bag. "What's this?" Jenn exclaims with (not so) genuine surprise. "Go straight to the office. *Now*."

As Alon exits the classroom, Jenn, with a sad sigh, walks slowly to her desk and smacks the package of cigarettes down with a "Thwap!"

As she looks up, she attempts to hold her best mean-teacher straight face, but after three seconds she breaks into a smile just as Alon bounds back into the classroom, beaming.

Cries of protest and relief rise up from the students. There are some cries of "No way!" and a "Jenn, that's not fair!" as Alon makes his way to his table. Jenn stands in the center of her students and says, "So, did I have the right to search Alon's bag? What does the Constitution say?"

What Good Citizens Do

Jenn's classroom walls speak fluently about her beliefs and practices as a teacher. A particular strand of questions over her whiteboard catches my eye. From right to left, they read:

★ Are you a good community member?
★ What is your social responsibility?
★ Do you treat others with respect and equality?
★ Do you obey the laws?
★ Do you question unjust laws and policies?

★ Do you engage in discourse with others about important issues?

★ Are you critical, looking for multiple perspectives on issues and events and history?

★ Are you kind to your neighbors?

This is Jenn's list of what it means to be a good citizen. I would argue this list helps define what it means to be a better adult. Many of these questions come from another one of my *landmark* educational texts, a book on classroom management called *Being Good: Rethinking Classroom Management and Student Discipline,* by Steven Wolk. He writes,

> At its best the classroom becomes life itself. We no longer teach about democracy and community, but live democracy and community. . . . Perhaps the central issue of a democracy is the behavior of its people. This means we must ask questions of our citizens and our students that go far beyond whether they know when to be quiet and if they follow the rules. (2002, 10)

Jenn's passion for creating citizens of her middle school students is more than an instructional goal. For her, it speaks to the core of the purpose of education. In a reflection about a teacher who influenced *her* life, she wrote,

People become teachers for all different reasons, but usually those reasons show up in powerful ways in their practice. Let's see if we can track this thread of a "life of service through active citizenship" in Jenn's teaching.

My favorite teacher was Robin Rhodes, my mentor in college. She was an Adjunct Professor of Anthropology and Women's Studies at Florida State University who saw learning as part of everything we do. Since she believed learning took place beyond the ivory towers, she encouraged me to do a multiple-year independent study on a topic I was highly interested in. I spent almost two years under her guidance learning about the 1994 welfare reforms being legislated through the Contract for America. This self-driven opportunity inspired me to a life of service through active citizenship. It also allowed me to discover discourse. Robin and I would meet for dinner or lunch to really examine the historical, cultural, economic

*and political issues surrounding this legislation. I thank Robin
for developing my curiosity of both humanities and politics.*

For Jenn, the questions of "Who has the power?" and "How do we
use the power we have for the good of others?" sit at the center of every
unit she teaches—whether it is a study of American government, a study
of civil rights, or a study of how to write a great persuasive essay. Because
her teaching beliefs so strongly permeate her practice, the students who
emerge from a three-year middle school loop with her cannot help but
constructively participate in the world around them. Let's take a peek
inside the walls of this laboratory for the development of citizens. . . .

The Minilesson (Catch)

Upon Alon's triumphant return to the classroom,
the students' heart rates return to normal and
Jenn starts her minilesson:

"A backpack search just like you witnessed
today really happened in a school. And the parents *really* sued the school district for a violation
of their daughter's privacy and it *really* went all
the way to the highest court in the land, the
Supreme Court of the United States. We are going to read about this case
today and try to figure out how the Supreme Court decided if the backpack search was legal or not."

She continues, "But first, we need to know a little bit about the
Fourth Amendment to the Constitution of the United States. Take out
your academic journals, and tape in the slip of paper that is in the center
of your table. That is the exact wording of the Fourth Amendment. Let's
try to make some meaning of it together."

On the overhead is written the text of the Fourth Amendment:

*The right of the people to be secure in their persons, houses,
papers, and effects, against unreasonable searches and
seizures, shall not be violated, and no Warrants shall issue,
but upon probable cause, supported by Oath or affirmation,
and particularly describing the place to be searched, and the
persons or things to be seized.*

Jenn continues, "I'm going to walk you through my thinking on the
first part of this by showing you how my brain works when I read—what
connections I make, what questions I have, what background knowledge I

Figure 7.1 Minilesson Think-Aloud—Making Meaning from the Actual Text of the Fourth Amendment

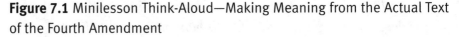

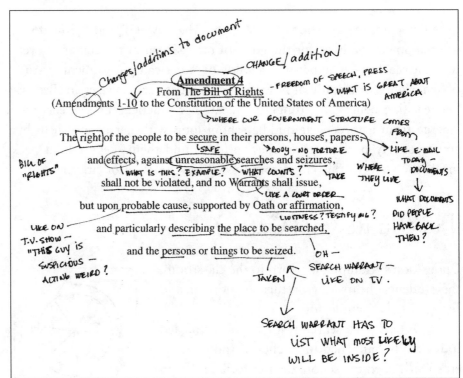

Jenn thinks aloud while she underlines, circles, and writes phrases on the text on the overhead to model for students how she makes meaning as she reads. By using her own background knowledge to make connections, ask questions, and make inferences, she provides students with concrete strategies to make meaning from the complex language of the Fourth Amendment (see Chapter 4 for more information on what good readers do).

have. So after the first part, if you have a connection or a question, raise your hand and let's make meaning of this text together" (see Figure 7.1).

Jenn begins the think-aloud:

So, "Amendment 4" . . . I know that the word amendment means a change or an addition [she adds the words changes/additions to document]. "From the Bill of Rights" . . . oh, I know the Bill of Rights it is like freedom of speech, press, and things like that. It is one of the reasons America is so great. I can write my opinion of the government without getting thrown in jail [adds this thinking next to "Bill of Rights"].

OK, so here I see Amendments 1–10 of the Constitution is called the Bill of Rights and the amendment we are reading about is number 4. Aha. The Constitution. I know that the Constitution is the document that outlines the structure of what our government looks like. When a government is trying to form, it is the first document they write. The Iraqis are try-

ing to write a new Constitution now to outline how their government works.

"OK, now you dive in. Read the first line quietly to yourself, and someone share their thinking with me," Jenn says.

The students read the first line of the text, "The right of the people to be secure in their persons, papers, houses, and effects." Sophie raises her hand.

> **Sophie:** Well, it starts off with *right* because this is in the Bill of Rights.
>
> **Jenn:** Great, Sophie. I'll add that here on the overhead. What else does that first line make you think?
>
> **Sophie:** Well *secure* means safe. *Person* means like their body, so that is like, safe in your body, like you can't be tortured.
>
> **Jenn:** Great, Sophie. Great use of your background knowledge. How did you make the connection to torture?
>
> **Sophie:** Well, it is like with Saddam Hussein. He could take people out of their houses and just torture and kill them. I know that from the news.
>
> **Jenn:** Interesting connection. OK, anyone else? Alex?
>
> **Alex:** *Houses* and *papers* are like the places people live and their documents. Like email today. Or maybe like driver's licenses. I don't know what *effects* means.

Jenn continues prompting students to share their thinking and records their background knowledge, connections, and questions on the overhead (see Figure 7.1). A big connection comes up with the word *warrant*. Many students know that word from detective shows on television.

> **Zak:** What if the police don't have time to get a warrant? What happens then?
>
> **Jenn:** Great question. Let's hold that over here on our anchor chart to come back to it later.

Then the students start a raucous conversation about the phrase *probable cause.*

> **Josh:** What does that mean exactly?
>
> **Dana:** I think it means a means like a *really good reason* that someone broke the law. They *probably* did it.
>
> **Josh:** Probably isn't enough! They need real proof!
>
> **Jenn:** OK, great thinking everyone. . . . I'm going to stop you right there and let you read a little bit to build your background knowl-

JENN'S MINILESSON

Structure and Content

Instruction:

★ 22 minutes long

★ *Teacher sets process purpose:* To show students how she makes meaning of a difficult text (the Fourth Amendment) using questions, connections, and background knowledge and to model what holding thinking on the text looks like.

★ *Teacher sets content purpose:* To use the thinking strategies to build background knowledge on the *New Jersey* v. *TLO* court case and answer the question "Was the search legal?"

Teaching Cycle Implications

Assessment:

★ Students' thinking held on the text of the *New Jersey* v. *TLO* case will help Jenn know if and how her students are making meaning as they read and how they are building background knowledge on the important points in the case.

★ Conferring during the worktime, Jenn will be able to listen carefully to individuals to see how they are making meaning of the case and do some immediate instruction to answer any questions and clear up any misconceptions.

Planning:

★ Jenn will use what she learns during conferring to figure out how she should focus the minilesson tomorrow. What do students need most to understand the facts presented *in New Jersey* v. *TLO?*

edge. Josh and Dana, I'll be anxious to see if your thinking changes after you read today.

Jenn has them right where she wants them to begin digging into the background of the court case that spelled out the rights of students in schools regarding search and seizure. She has effectively built a need to know, which translates into a need to read. She continues,

The reenactment that Alon and I did for you today is based on a real case called New Jersey *versus* TLO.[1] *So during the worktime today, you are going to read a short background of this case and try to answer the question "According to the Fourth Amendment, was the search legal?" That is the same question that the Supreme Court Justices wrestled with in 1985.*

While you are reading, I want you to hold your thinking in the margins, just like we did with the Fourth Amendment.

At the end of reading time, I want you to share your thinking with your small groups about "Was the search legal?" Write that question at the top of your paper, and be ready to share what you think. You have about twenty minutes to read.

At the end of the twenty minutes, we are going to move into small groups to talk and I will ask you to share your understanding of the case and the Supreme Court's decision.

While you read, I'll be coming around to talk to you about your thinking, so make sure you have lots of questions and connections held in the margins, so we have lots to talk about. Get started.

---

1. *New Jersey* v. *TLO* (1985) was the Supreme Court case that set the precedent for the rights of students in cases of search and seizure in schools. TLO was a student whose purse was searched by the assistant principal after she was caught smoking in a school bathroom. The purse contained a small amount of marijuana and other drug paraphernalia. Was the search legal? Rejoin the students to find out (www.landmarkcases.org)!

Worktime #1 (Release): Read

As students read, Jenn circulates and confers with individual students about the background of the case and the Supreme Court's decision. She ends up conferring with six students, roughly one at each table in the twenty minutes.

After twenty minutes, she asks students to give her their attention.

Debrief #1 (Catch): Quick-Write

Jen asks for the students' attention.

> *It is important to remember that Jenn's students have been with her for a semester already and have built their reading stamina up to twenty minutes. In the beginning of the year, Jenn would release them for five to seven minutes and then pull them back to share their thinking before releasing them again for five to seven minutes. Think of that fly fisherman again . . . catching the fish, holding it out of the water just long enough to admire its beauty and unhook its lip, but not long enough to suffocate it, then toss it back in the water to swim again. In the beginning a workshop looks like that: catch and release, catch and release, so that by January (sometimes sooner) students can work for up to forty-five minutes on a rich reading or writing task! In the beginning of the year, Jenn was explicit with her students in setting stamina goals for the worktime so she could build time to confer with individuals and listen to teach.*

> *OK, I know you need a lot more time with this text, but I want you to give you some time to talk about it.*
>
> *Before you start talking, I want you to write what you're thinking right now. Based on your current understanding of the Fourth Amendment, was the search legal? What do YOU think?*

The students take out their journals and write their current understanding of the case. Jen gives them about five minutes to write and then asks them to begin a discussion with the small group at their table.

Worktime #2 (Release): Small-Group Discussion

Jenn assigns each group to one of three opinions published by the Supreme Court. Two groups focus their attention on the majority opin-

Figure 7.2 Sixth Graders Discussing *New Jersey* v. *TLO*

Each person adds powerfully to the group's construction of understanding. Dana consistently brings the group back to the text; James starts with the big idea, but his questions propel the group to go deeper. Cameron follows Dana's lead by adding textual evidence, but he also adds confirmation of other thinking. Although Josh doesn't speak up until the end of the script, he's the one that nails it! He gets that schools take on the role of the parent. That is the crux of the majority opinion! Hooray for Josh!

ion, two on the concurring opinion, and two on the dissenting opinion. Let's listen in on the group discussing the majority opinion. This discussion was based on the text "*New Jersey* v. *TLO* (1985): Key Excerpts from the Majority Opinion" (www.landmarkcases.org).

James: OK, so according to the majority opinion of the Supreme Court, I think it says that the assistant principal's search [of the student's purse] was legal.

Dana: This part here [pointing to text] tells you why you would need or not need the warrant. . . . The assistant principal didn't need a warrant because he had a probable cause. He found her smoking in the bathroom.

James: But here it says, "A warrant must be given." How come schools can get away with it without a warrant?

Dana: Because you have the safety of the kids . . . You are the first one that is in charge of the kids . . . during school time. That is your main responsibility.

Cameron: On the first page it says "public school officials assume the rights of their students' legal guardians," so that means that the school has kind of the same rights of your parents. . . . They have to have probable cause, but they do not have to have a warrant.

Dana: Can you say no?

Cameron: You can say no, but you'll get in more trouble.

Dana: Right here it says [pointing to the text], "We have respected the value of preserving the informality of the student-teacher relationship. . . ."

James: I don't get that. What does that mean? What is the "informality of the student-teacher relationship"?

Dana: I think it means like when we get in trouble with Jenn. We take care of it ourselves, we don't go to jail.

Cameron: Oh, like the teacher and the student deal with it right then and there. . . . If it was serious . . . like a fight, then there are bigger consequences, like we have to go to the office.

Josh: I want to share this . . . this connects: "Maintaining order in the classroom has never been easy, but in recent years, school disorder has taken particularly ugly forms: drug use and violent crime in the schools have become major social problems."

Cameron: What does that quote have to do with it?

Josh: Like, if it is a big deal and students are in danger, they can't wait for a warrant.

Dana: Yeah, like a gun is a violation and they have to keep us safe.

Jenn [approached the group when Josh was sharing]: It sounds like you guys are having a great conversation. So tell me, why is it that schools don't have to have a warrant but everybody else does?

Josh: Because their first job is to keep us safe. Like our parents.

Jenn: Interesting point, Josh. Will you share what you just said about schools not waiting for a warrant when we debrief in a few minutes? The warrant part is one of the keys to this. Thanks. That would be great.

Debrief #2 (Catch): Groups Share Their Thinking

As Jenn was walking around listening in to the group discussions, she noticed that students in every group had brought up the two key clauses of the Fourth Amendment: the Warrant Clause and the Reasonable Clause. Perfect! As she did with Josh, whenever she heard students mention warrant or probable cause or reasonable she asked those particular students if they would share their thinking when she brought the group together. Let's listen.

Jenn: I was really impressed with the thinking I heard when I was walking around. As I was walking around, I asked a few of you to share your ideas. Josh, will you start us off? What is your thinking about "Was the search legal?"

Josh: Yeah. I think it was, because schools don't need a warrant. They have to keep kids safe and they don't have time to get a warrant.

Jenn: OK, so I am going to start an anchor chart up here. On one side,

I am going to write, "Warrant Clause," and under that I am going to write Josh's point, "Schools have to keep kids safe and they don't have time to get a warrant." Who else has some thinking?

Cosmo: The search was totally legal because she was breaking a rule by smoking in the bathroom. She provided the assistant principal with a reason, which makes the search *reasonable.*

Jenn: Thanks, Cosmo. OK, on the other side of this chart I'm going to write "Reasonable Clause" and underneath write Cosmo's thinking. Wow. Do you see what you guys have just done? You figured out the two biggest parts of this case. The Fourth Amendment is all about these two things. The need for a warrant in school and reasonable suspicion. OK. Now I want you to go back into the text with your groups and see if you can hold your thinking about these two clauses.

We only have about ten minutes but I want you to get a good start on this. Tomorrow, each group is going to teach the class about the Supreme Court decision you read today. What are the main points in your decision? You are going to need to determine importance here. Please organize your paper like this anchor chart: on one side, write, "Warrant Clause" and on the other, write, "Reasonable Clause."

Who can tell me your group's job in the next ten minutes? Rico?

Rico: We need to put our ideas about the decision in two columns like you did.

Jenn: OK, great. And why am I asking you to do this? Becca?

Becca: Because we are going to teach our decision to the rest of the class tomorrow.

Jenn: Excellent. OK groups, I will pass out overhead transparencies for you to write your ideas on for your presentations tomorrow. In ten minutes we'll come back together. Get as many ideas down from your text as you can. Go!

Worktime #3 (Release): Small Groups Synthesize Their Thinking

Jenn releases the groups to hold their thinking under new categories, the Warrant Clause and the Reasonable Clause, with an important end in mind: to teach what they figured out to the rest of the class the next day. Let's take a look at a few examples of the students' synthesis of the majority (Dana, James, Josh, and Cameron) (Figure 7.3), concurring (Figure

Figure 7.3 Group Synthesis of the Majority Opinion

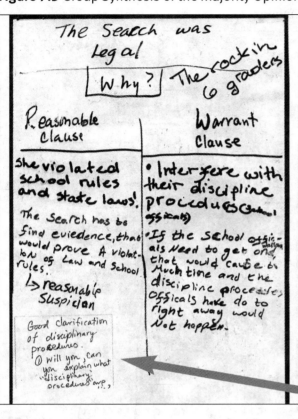

Figure 7.4 Group Synthesis of the Concurring Opinion

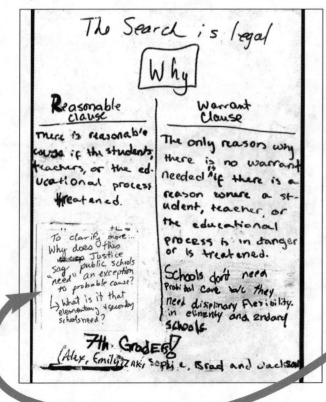

Written under "Warrant Clause": "If the school officials need to get one [a warrant] that would cause too much time and the discipline procedures officials have to do right away would not happen." Shows the group understands that there are time constraints in schools that affect the ability and efficacy of getting a warrant. In this case the needs of the whole outweigh the rights of the individual. Jenn asks the group to clarify their use of the phrase disciplinary procedures from the text to make sure they really get it.

Jenn added a comment to push the group's thinking.

Jenn asks for clarification from this group to make sure there are no misconceptions about the need for a warrant in schools. She writes, "To clarify more, Why does this Justice say public schools 'need' an exception to probable cause? What is it that elementary and secondary schools need?"

She is paying careful attention to their writing and asking them to be precise in their explanation—giving immediate feedback to help them get better.

This Dissenting Opinion group is crucial to helping students see that even Supreme Court justices have big questions that they don't know the answers to *and* that they don't agree on!

There is great evidence here that students are getting it. The students are able to determine importance in the text and flush out the main points of the argument.

They are starting to mirror Jenn's use of language about "preventing abuse of power." The group summarizes the dissenting opinion and writes, "Schools should not be exempt from probable cause and the process of attaining a warrant because it prevents abuse of power." Jenn wants to know more, so she writes in response, "Is it important to make sure a person of power has probable cause? Why? How do we (USA) ensure probable cause? What's our check system?" She also challenges them to make a connection between the two clauses.

Do you think these students know their teacher is listening?

Figure 7.5 Group Synthesis of the Dissenting Opinion

7.4), and dissenting (Figure 7.5) opinions of the Supreme Court in *New Jersey* v. *TLO*.

Final Debrief (Catch)

After ten minutes, Jenn realizes that students will need more time to work on their overhead presentations for the class. She calls the students back together and says,

> *Great work today. I saw lots of great thinking on your charts and I'm excited to hear your presentations tomorrow. How many groups feel like they need a little more time to get their thoughts and evidence together? OK, that looks like almost everybody. Tomorrow at the start of class, we'll dive right into finishing up your charts on the different opinions and then we'll move into the presentations. Before we go today, I want to see how your thinking has changed since the beginning of class. Please take the next three minutes and write what you think now. . . . Was the search legal? As soon as you are finished writing, put your journals in the bin. Please hand me your group's overhead on your way out the door so I can add some questions to it for tomorrow. Have a great day.*

Structures for Individual and Group Accountability

The use of the workshop model to structure class time helps Jenn listen to teach. Asking each group to present their thinking and share with the other students what they figured out helped keep the groups on track during the group discussion time. But it wasn't just on this one day that students were accountable to share what they read, wrote, and talked about during the worktime. It is every day. Every day, Jenn makes sure to save time at the end of the class for students to share their writing and thinking. It is that consistency over time that helps students stay focused during the worktime. She then adds a layer of individual accountability by having each student hold his individual thoughts on the text and also asks each student to reflect in his journal as his exit ticket out. In little ways every day, Jenn's practices reinforce with students the belief that we are smarter together, but we are each responsible for our own learning as well.

The Importance of Grappling

> *Increasing motivation and engagement is unlikely to be accomplished by simple policy prescriptions. . . . The fundamental challenge is to create a set of circumstances in which students take pleasure in learning and come to believe that the information and skills they are being asked to learn are important or meaningful for them and worth their effort, and that they can reasonably expect to be able to learn the material. (National Research Council 2004, 14)*

If you take a look at the website www.landmarkcases.org, there is a suggestion to begin student learning about *New Jersey* v. *TLO* with a role-play much like I just described from Jenn's classroom. The role-play itself is not remarkable, but what is important is how Jenn's planning and instruction *unfolds from the role-play*—how she decides to structure and sequence the learning from this compelling event.

If you follow the website's advice, you share readings with students (the site offers three reading levels, which is excellent because it provides opportunity and access for a wide variety of students). Unfortunately, the next suggestion is to have students answer the questions at the end of each reading. Ugh! Not so great for motivation and engagement with such a compelling topic!

Why kick off a Fourth Amendment study with an engaging role-play and then go to a ho-hum textbook activity of reading and answering the questions? How will that lead students to grapple with the compelling content of the Supreme Court decision? Short answer: it won't.

By asking the students to answer the question "Was the search legal?" Jenn is asking students to replicate the thinking process of the Supreme Court justices, not just swallow their decision. She wants students to practice the same habits of mind that the justices practice every day. Read the facts. Apply what you know about the Constitution. Jenn's instruction reminds me of one of my favorite quotes:

> *Those who have been required to memorize the world as it is will never create the world as it might be. (Judith Groch 1969, 177)*

In order to truly understand the nuances of the Constitution and attempt to answer the big guiding question "Who has the power in our society?" Jenn has to intentionally plan for students not to merely *know* the Supreme Court's decision but *wrestle* with the facts, just as the justices did in 1985. It took four courts *three years* to figure out the case. First the Juvenile Court of New Jersey, then the Appellate Division of New Jersey, then the Supreme Court of New Jersey, and then in 1985, the Supreme Court of the United States. The court presented a majority opinion, a concurring opinion, and a dissenting opinion. The case was so filled with questions that nine of the most amazing brains in our country could not agree! The Constitution is not black-and-white. Interpreting the Constitution is not black-and-white. Student learning about the Constitution and the role of the Supreme Court shouldn't be either.

Jenn shared her thinking about her Fourth Amendment study kick-off:

I decided to start our study of "How can I access power in our democracy?" with the TLO case and the Fourth Amendment because it directly relates to students' rights in school. Because it deals with schools, there is an immediate need to know why I can look in Alon's backpack if I expect he's been smoking. Working backwards from that, students need to know what the Supreme Court decided, why the Supreme Court gets to make decisions, and where the Bill of Rights comes from.

It is also a great way to enter into looking at different perspectives. When a court case has a dissenting opinion and a majority opinion, it is a great way to model different views of well-researched and backed-up opinions. Using the rhythm of the language of the court decisions, I want students to continue to develop their own opinions. Using this case as a model, they continue to go back to text to develop a consistency of perspective about the rights of people and then transition to the rights of groups of people. My goal is for them to begin to develop a philosophy about the protection of personal rights and then go out and look at the protection of groups of people and how those balance out in our democracy.

It has been an incredible few weeks listening to students debate the merits of this case and figure out what it means to them as citizens of the United States.

From the beginning of the unit, Jenn asks students to grapple with the same information that the Supreme Court justices (and their clerks) did in 1985. In their book *The Students Are Watching*, Ted and Nancy Sizer write extensively about grappling.

Most interactions in life are complex; more than talent and good habits are needed to address them well. Few are mastered by merely applying a slogan such as "Just Say No." Context is critical if not crucial. The thoughts and resultant actions of . . . a Polish-German day laborer working near Auschwitz in 1944, a person who sees the full trains come and the empty trains go, might be appreciably different from the conclusions about the Holocaust reached by an outraged American teenager sitting in an unthreatened high school classroom fifty years later. It will help the teenager to absorb complexity if he can reflect from the shoes of the laborer, not necessarily to agree but to empathize, to understand. In that Second World War moment there is powerful stuff: the particulars of a situation, in necessarily exquisite and painful detail. That stuff, if well and carefully considered, provides the perspective which is the heart of ultimately truly moral decisions. Educators call this content. (1999, 22)

In her minilesson, Jenn focuses on *how* readers interpret text and determine importance as well as *what*—the facts of the case that students need to understand in order to predict, discuss, and debate the decision of the Supreme Court. One of her guiding questions is "Who has the power?" Her instructional practices speak loudly—in our society, thinkers have power.

Jenn's Planning Process

How did Jenn plan for students to grapple? Well, first, she had to set some priorities from the standards. As a humanities teacher, Jenn is responsible not only for social studies standards but for language arts standards as well. Planning explicitly for both is essential. She had to consider two big questions:

★ How do I know that students are growing in their knowledge of content?

★ How are they growing in their skill at making meaning from text? (Especially important since for an entire semester, they would be reading the complexly written decisions of the Supreme Court.)

A research study on citizen participation released by Common Cause, a nonpartisan governmental watchdog organization, found that contrary to common belief, low citizen participation in the United States is *not* due to apathy but rather due to *a lack of strong reading, writing, and speaking skills* (Goldin-Dubois 2002, 3). That study has very important ramifications for every teacher in America, but it is a louder cry for our teachers of American history and American government. Like it or not, they are teachers of reading and writing.

With this and a schoolwide study of learning targets in mind, Jenn experimented with writing learning targets to help guide her instruction and help students track their own progress toward learning. Here are the learning targets she drafted:

1. I know and can apply the basic principles of government (such as the social compact, balance of powers, separation of powers, natural rights, and higher law).
2. I know how power is shared in our democracy among the three branches of government and I know my role as a citizen within the three branches.
3. I can exercise my rights and responsibilities as a citizen through participation in civic life.
4. I can read to locate and make use of relevant information from a variety of media, reference, and technological sources to exercise my rights and responsibilities as a citizen.

It is interesting to look at these learning targets in light of Jenn's big guiding questions:

★ How can I access power in our democracy?
★ Who has the power?
★ What is our democracy?

In the beginning of this chapter, the Fairy commented on Jenn's beliefs about a "life of service through active citizenship." Hmmm . . . notice any connections?

As a third-year teacher, Jenn was still working out the systems and structures that worked for her as a planner of multilayered instruction. Her beliefs about how people learn were intricately tied to how she went about planning the unfolding of her instruction. Jenn reflected,

> *Overall, I know that I seek to develop units that have a compelling topic, that create a need to know for students, that connect to students' personal lives, and that have a fun,*

The shift in language from goals and objectives to learning targets is an important one. A learning target is meant not only for teachers but ultimately for students. The article "Inside the Black Box: Raising Standards Through Classroom Assessment" by Black and William (1998) was an opening salvo of research about the importance of formative assessment and assessment for learning. Rick Stiggins is the other guru in the field of assessment for learning. My understanding of the full implications of assessment for learning is infantile, which is why our school is undertaking a schoolwide study on the effects of writing learning targets on our planning processes and the effect that making learning targets explicit to students has on students' ability to meet them! For a more thorough explanation I suggest reading Classroom Assessment for Student Learning *(Stiggins et al. 2002) published by the Assessment Training Institute. Doesn't this remind you of* Miracle on 34th Street *when the Macy's Santa tells the frantic mother to go to Gimbels to get the toy her child wants? Funny.*

authentic, active project designed at the end. I believe that students need to have an important anchor experience or anchor text that is relative and accessible. I think a parallel historical and current study helps with this.

I know for me this means that I have to dedicate a lot of time to "mucking about" in the content when I am planning. . . . I need to read about it, talk about it with my friends . . . sometimes I write extensively in my journal, and then read some more, ask questions, talk some more, etc. This is how I learn, so I need to create the same experiences for the students in my classroom.

Jenn knew she needs to muck about to make meaning and built in time for her students to do the same. Jenn spent several workshops digging into the majority, concurring, and dissenting opinions of the Supreme Court in *New Jersey* v. *TLO*. Jenn's minilessons, all connected to the purpose "Was the search legal?" were also informed by students' ability to determine importance and make meaning from the text over two weeks. Because of the complexity of the text, the complexity of the case, and the complexity of the Fourth Amendment, Jenn had to toggle back and forth between attending to content and attending to the processes of making meaning. After each minilesson, the students continued to read, write to hold their thinking, and talk to deepen their understanding of the Fourth Amendment, the court case, and the Supreme Court decisions. The minilesson topics included:

★ Making Meaning from Supreme Court Decisions
  • Content goal: Warrant Clause and Reasonable Clause of the Fourth Amendment
  • Process goal: How to break down complex text. Jenn did a think-aloud with the Supreme Court decisions using one color highlighter for information that applied to the Reasonable Clause and another color for information that applied to the Warrant Clause. She showed students how for a few paragraphs and then asked students to do it on their own. At the end, she asked students to synthesize what they had highlighted in their own words.

★ Reasonable Clause
  • Content goal: What counts as a reasonable search? What counts as an unreasonable search?
  • Process goal: Jenn modeled how she determines importance in text to get to the content.

★ Citizen Rights

- Content goal: Do kids and adults have the same rights?
- Process goal: Activating background knowledge

★ Reasonable Suspicion and Probable Cause
  - Content goal: Reasonable suspicion and probable cause
  - Process goal: Apply and extend understanding by role-playing different reasonable suspicion and probable cause scenarios

The reflective quick-writes morphed over time, too. Two big questions she asked students to reflect on over and over were

★ Should there be a set standard for searches that people in power must follow?

★ Should the standard be the same for kids and for adults?

These questions were directly tied to Jenn's big guiding questions and also related to her reflection about students taking action as citizens. She wanted them to understand that although their rights were limited, TLO fought the powers that be and students *do* have power in our society *if* they engage by reading, writing, thinking, and talking.

Writing to Demonstrate Understanding Versus Writing to Build Understanding

> *I write entirely to find out what I'm thinking, what I'm looking at, what I see and what it means. What I want and what I fear. (Didion 1976, 50)*

Jenn intended this Fourth Amendment study to be an immersion into a semester-long study of American government and a prelude to a longer, more in-depth citizen action project. Since this study was the first swipe at building student understanding of the learning targets, Jenn decided to do a "quick and dirty" assessment of student understanding. Students would *demonstrate* their understanding by writing a one-page essay on the Fourth Amendment in schools. She wrote her own essay as a model and taught several minilessons that were targeted to the craft of writing an essay filled with strong evidence.

Throughout the study, Jenn asked students to reflect about specific topics in order to scaffold and *build their understanding* of the content and also to *build their skill* of writing an essay filled with support for their opinion. This was writing to build understanding. I think it is an important distinction to make because too often we ask students to write only to demonstrate understanding. In order for students to understand how writing *is* thinking, we need to allow them to muck around in writing to come to know. Many famous quotes by famous authors say the same. Joan Didion opens this section with one of my favorites. E. M. Forster says, "How do I know what I think until I see what I say?" (1956, 101).

Jenn asked students to write to *build understanding* usually during quick-writes in the debrief time of the classroom workshop. Writing to build understanding topics included

★ How do the ideas/questions of power relate to my life?
★ Should there be a set procedure for searches that people in power must follow? Is it the same for kids and adults?
★ What are the most important issues to consider in deciding *New Jersey* v. *TLO*?
★ What evidence/support will help me show deep knowledge of the Fourth Amendment?

At the end of the study, Jenn asked students to go back and read their responses to these questions in order to craft an essay that would demonstrate their understanding of the Fourth Amendment in schools (specifically), and some big ideas of government (generally), before they began their citizen action project.

When Jenn felt like she needed to check for understanding, to decide if students needed an additional reading or minilesson on a specific topic, she asked students to write to *demonstrate their understanding*. Writing to demonstrate understanding topics included

★ Was the search of Alon's backpack legal according to the Constitution?
★ What is the difference between reasonable suspicion and probable cause?
★ The "Fourth Amendment in Schools" essay (final assessment)

Let's see how the students responded . . .

Did Students Get It? How Do We Know?

Over two class periods, Jenn asked students to craft their essays on the Fourth Amendment in schools. They were to answer two questions: "Why are schools governed by reasonable suspicion and not probable cause?" and "Is this right? Why or why not?" While students wrote, Jenn was busy

Figure 7.6 Emma's Essay

MY ESSAY ON THE FOURTH AMENDMENT IN SCHOOLS
By Emma

Why are schools governed by reasonable suspicion and not probable cause? Is this "right?" Why or why not?

Schools need reasonable suspicion instead of probable cause because if there is a big problem, they need to operate quickly. The Supreme Court decided that they don't even need a warrant, because warrants would slow down and complicate the process. Schools need to keep a certain amount of informality. I agree with the Supreme Court decision. It is right to bend the rules in the case of school searches. I say this because I feel that if my safety is in danger, I would want the threat to be uncovered as quickly as possible. I also feel that schools are different somehow. I can't quite explain it, but schools are just different. I guess it seems sort of ridiculous to require a warrant for school searches. If a teacher wants to look through a student's bag, they shouldn't need a warrant. I mean, it's just a bag, right? Not too big of a deal.

The Fourth Amendment doesn't specify the requirements for school searches, but at one stage of the T.L.O. case, they agreed the school officials don't need a warrant. I actually don't understand that too well. If there is nothing in the Fourth Amendment, how can they make that decision? Is it because we're "just students" to some people? I would really like to have that explained.

What do you notice in Emma's essay? What do you wonder?

I think it is fascinating to be able to trace the effect of explicit minilessons to Emma's writing . . . from the first discussion of the definition of probable cause to Jenn's think-aloud to the group discussion of "informality of the student-teacher relationship," we can see that Emma understands that schools are different in the first part of her essay. By the end, though, she has a big lingering question about the interpretation of the Constitution. Her question "If there is nothing in the Fourth Amendment, how can they make that decision?" is a great question for the whole class to tackle! If Emma still has that question, many others do too. That question connects directly to Jenn's goals for students to understand the role of the Supreme Court in interpreting the law of the land! Emma has left the door open for a powerful teachable moment. Three steps forward and a great clue for where to go next. Thanks, Emma!

conferring with individuals, reading their writing, and prompting them to reflect on all they knew and beef up their essays with evidence. Did they get it? Let's take a look at three samples (Figures 7.6, 7.7, and 7.8).

What strikes me most about these essays is their diversity. Each essay is filled with the voice of the student, yet their consistency in content show that Jenn hit many of her learning targets. Her narrow focus paid off in student ownership of the learning. Each student arrived at his or her understanding at a slightly different angle. These essays remind me of another of my favorite quotes from Ted and Nancy Sizer's *The Students Are Watching*:

Figure 7.7 Scott's Essay

> **ESSAY**
> *By Scott*
>
> Schools are governed by reasonable suspicion. This is because the Supreme Court decided that was the way things should be. I guess you could say protecting the life of the whole school community is worth sacrificing some liberty, privacy, and property. The purpose of the Fourth Amendment is to protect people's rights and protect people from abuse of power. The problem is that in a school community swift decisions need to be made. That is what the Supreme Court said in the T.L.O. vs. New Jersey court case. That is why schools are governed by reasonable suspicion. Say someone with an AK-47 comes barging in shooting everybody. It's a real issue to get a warrant to stop them. Warrants take a while to get. I think that problem should be fixed. It's a matter of opinion if schools relying only on reasonable suspicion. It is a trade off situation of social compact. How much power should the government be give in order to protect us? If only government didn't corrupt so easily.

Scott makes a great connection in the first part of his essay about the social compact that we make with the government to give up individual rights for the good of the whole group. I am particularly struck by his last line, "If only government didn't corrupt so easily." Out of the mouths of babes . . .

Schools exist for children, but children are often seen as the school's clients, as its powerless people. They are told that they are in school not because of what they know but because of what they don't know. All over the world, powerless people lose the instinct to help, because it is so often rebuffed in them. [Students should be allowed to] fulfill the real purpose of schooling: to equip [themselves] to be of use. (1999, 20)

I believe these essays demonstrate that Jenn's students see themselves as part of the world. These essays speak loudly about students' beliefs about power in our society and how they can play a role. If they knew better, they'd do better. Jenn's students are able to write with clarity of voice and clarity of purpose because Jenn has shown them *how*—how to access power in our society by reading carefully, by determining importance, by appreciating the complexity of the law, and by *participating* in a debate about the interpretation of the Constitution. She asked them to read for meaning, to talk to strive to understand, to write to both hold and push their own thinking, and finally to demonstrate their understanding. Her focus helped give them purpose.

Figure 7.8 Cece's Essay

ESSAY ON FOURTH AMENDMENT
By Cece

- Why did the Supreme Court decide that it was legal?
- Is this right or wrong that schools are governed by reasonable suspicion and not probable cause?

The Supreme Court decided that it was legal for schools to search people and people's things without a warrant. All you need is reasonable suspicion. I believe this is because you never know what circumstance the principal or whoever's searching is under when he wants to search someone. The situation may be that they don't have enough time to get a warrant or the suspect is about to get away. It could be the only way to protect the other students or the suspect himself. In the Supreme Court Majority Opinion of the T.L.O. vs. New Jersey court case it says, "Maintaining security and order in the schools requires a certain degree of flexibility." Also the Fourth Amendment says that people have the right to be secure from "unreasonable" searches, and due to the fact that there was a lot of reasonable suspicion, searching T.L.O's purse was "reasonable."

According to the Dissenting Opinion of the T.L.O. case, none of what is stated above matters. What does matter is that if you don't have a warrant, adults in power (principals, teachers, deans, etc.) could easily abuse this power to search with little or no suspicion.

My personal opinion dangles somewhere between the two. I can see through the eyes of both sides. People should have the right to protect their privacy (to a certain extent) and it's true that many people in power tend to abuse it, but there definitely needs to be exceptions, especially if getting a warrant interferes with the education of the children. In the case of T.L.O., I agree with the decision that was made. No warrant was needed. Cops have to act quickly to enforce the laws—teachers and principals should be able to too.

What do you notice about Cece's essay? What do you wonder? What implications for future instruction do you see?

Cece demonstrates strong knowledge of content and great skill as an essayist in this piece. She seamlessly weaves in quotes from the Supreme Court decision to back up her argument as well as presenting an opposing view, which, by the end, strengthens her opinion by showing that she understands the dangers of the abuse of power. I hope I'll be voting for this girl someday (soon!).

Earlier in this chapter I shared a quote from the National Research Council's *Engaging Schools* (2004). I think the quote bears repeating here. The National Research Council says, "The fundamental challenge is to create a set of circumstances in which students take pleasure in learning and come to believe that the information and skills they are being asked to learn are important or meaningful for them and worth their effort, and that they can reasonably expect to be able to learn the material" (2004, 14). Jenn set up this study from the beginning to be important, meaningful, and worth students' effort. Students' essays showed that her expectations were more than reasonable, because she didn't just create an assignment for students to do—she showed them *how* and *why* their thinking mattered.

This chapter opened with an e-mail to Jenn about her classroom and her kids. I asked her two questions:

★ What did you learn about your students as thinkers today? How did they move along the continuum of understanding about the Fourth Amendment?

★ What propels students to work during the worktime of a workshop structure?

A few days later she responded:

Hi Sam,

Wow what a week in the classroom. I can't tell you how many times this week I got goose bumps from listening to the powerful thinking from my students. Alon was asking why Supreme Court justices are there for life. After putting another question back to him he was like, "Wow, that's so smart to have them there for life. That's just smart." Then Zak, wow! We were discussing current events about appointing Alito. Zak just sat back with an awed look and he said, "It's really complex isn't it?"

In your e-mail you asked me, "What propels students to work during the worktime of a workshop structure?" I think it is a connection to their lives—I'm convinced that going in through the personal connection first of power and second with the court case has created an environment of curiosity and interest. Also I began by asking them to suspend their own opinion until we gathered multiple perspectives. I have talked about over and over again that critical thinking is about being able to think through different perspectives.

Other perspectives can help deepen one's own opinion or can change their opinion, but either way, knowing all sides of an issue helps you think and helps you take action, and that this is what we want to see happen!

How do I know they are propelled? In every writing reflection time, I have the majority of the class writing non-stop for 5–10 minutes. On Friday, they were given a choice to read the Supreme Court decision or to dialogue more—they said, "We need to talk more about it!" So they did! One large class, having dialogue, self-regulating the conversation so everyone had a chance to speak. It was a spontaneous Socratic Seminar! I wish I had it on video.

I tell you, it has been a great week! Thanks for your feedback. I'll see you tomorrow.

Cheers,
Jenn

Cheers to you, Jenn, and to your students. Thank you for believing that they can and showing them how to be reading, writing, thinking, engaged citizens.

Jenn's Systems, Structures, Routines, and Rituals

Following is scaffolding for the story of teaching and learning in Jenn's classroom. Remember, whole-scale replication is not the point. What practices were intriguing to you? What practices match your beliefs about the agency and capacity of children to think and learn? The beauty is, there are dozens of entry points. Pick one that matches what you believe and the rest will come. Do you want to start with planning with guiding questions or learning targets? Using academic journals? Asking students to respond to a question each day before they leave your room? Putting students in small groups to discuss a compelling text? Here are a few places to start:

Systems, Structures, Routines, and Rituals Highlighted in Chapter 7	Narrative description found on page	Ideas to help you get started	For more information check out these resources
Small-group discussions	183–185, 200–201	Prepare students to talk about text by giving them a juicy, important question with no right answer to develop an opinion about, and use a text as support.	*Best Practice* (Zemelman, Daniels, and Hyde 1998)
		Have an end in mind—for example, for students to teach others what they figured out.	*Results Now* (Schmoker 2006)
		Explicitly label what a good conversation looks like and sounds like with students.	
		Try a fishbowl conversation with a few students in the center of the circle to show students what it looks like.	
Teacher think-aloud	179–182	Read the piece slowly the night before and pay attention to your background knowledge, connections, questions, and inferences; re-create the experience for students the next day with the text on the overhead.	*Mosaic of Thought* (Keene and Zimmermann 1997)
		Think aloud with the first paragraph, then have students work with the second paragraph. Then bring them back together to share their understanding.	*Reading with Meaning* (Miller 2002)
		Label the thinking strategies students use to make meaning so they can do it again!	*I Read It but I Don't Get It* (Tovani 2000)
			Do I Really Have to Teach Reading? (Tovani 2004)
Writing to build understanding	181–182, 187–188, 193–196	Ask students all along the way to record their thinking in a variety of ways as their thinking grows and their understanding deepens (typically pretty short): • exit tickets related to the purpose of the day/week/quarter • holding thinking on a text • quick-writes to the guiding questions • opinion paragraphs to access background knowledge • responses to a quote	*Understanding by Design* (Wiggins and McTighe 2005) *How People Learn* (National Research Council 2000) *Best Practice* (Zemelman, Daniels, and Hyde 1998)

Systems, Structures, Routines, and Rituals Highlighted in Chapter 7	Narrative description found on page	Ideas to help you get started	For more information check out these resources
Writing to demonstrate understanding	195–199	At the end of a unit, or after a section of content has been uncovered Anytime you need to determine if students get it before you move on and connect more information to known information	*Understanding by Design* (Wiggins and McTighe 2005) *How People Learn* (National Research Council 2000) *Best Practice* (Zemelman, Daniels, and Hyde 1998)

CHAPTER EIGHT

Take Flight

Lyra began to talk of the world she knew. . . . As she spoke playing on all their senses, [they] crowded closer, feeding on her words . . . and willing her never to stop.

[Tialys called out], "When she spoke just now, you all listened, every one of you, and you kept silent and still . . . why was that?"

"Because she spoke the truth. Because it was nourishing. Because it was feeding us. Because we couldn't help it. Because it was true . . . Because it brought us news of the world and the sun and the wind and the rain. Because it was true." (Pullman 2002, 317)

After completing each chapter in this book, I shared it with the teacher to make sure I got things right. To make sure it was the truth. Jenn happened to be at school late one afternoon, and I asked her to read her chapter with me in the room so I could hear when she laughed. As she finished the last page, she looked up with faraway eyes and said, "Wow! I have a lot to learn from myself!"

Yeah. She does. So do you.

Where Do I Start?

When it comes to teaching . . . my purpose can be informed by legitimate research and best instructional practices. Or it can be defined by other people's agendas. I can serve my students well only by reading, writing, and talking with colleagues. And most of all, I can never forget that in the midst of classroom upheaval, someone like Evan is always waiting to learn from me, and to teach me. (Tovani 2004, 119)

Transforming your classroom into a workshop doesn't have to be a radical step. Remember, it is the small things you do each day that make the biggest difference. Let's think about a few things we learned from the teachers *inside*:

★ the importance of giving students chunks of time to read, write, and talk with *explicit instruction before* they read, write, and talk and *time to share, debrief, and build collective understanding after* they read, write, and talk.

★ the importance of showcasing yourself as a reader, writer, and thinker and showing students *how*

★ the importance of doing your own assignments

★ the importance of making time to confer one-on-one with students to know them deeply, put books in their hands, and differentiate instruction

★ the importance of collecting and saving student work over time (in writing folders, reading notebooks, academic journals, and/or portfolios) so teachers, students, and parents can see growth and mastery of knowledge and skills

★ the importance of the use of mentor texts and real-world models to put a vision of high-quality work in the heads of students

★ the importance of the use of mentor texts and real-world models to study the *craft* of writers

★ the importance of the use of anchor charts to focus planning and work and record student thinking over time

★ the importance of asking students to *replicate the processes and products* of readers, writers, editors, ornithologists, humanitarians, advocates, citizens, memorialists, and so on

★ the importance of knowing what you want students to know and be able to do

So, where should you start? Pick *one* important thing from this list. Because assessment, planning, and instruction are a cycle, anywhere you start will impact the rest of what you do. Trust yourself. Trust your students. You can do it.

WWFS?

Everybody has a Teaching Fairy. She (or he) is the one who makes you feel a little lightheaded after a particularly inspiring day with kids. She's in there. When you are going through the recap of each day, say to yourself, "What would Fairy say (WWFS)?" Make more days predictable, and the unpredictable will happen more.

So, What Matters Most?

Learning is messy. When teachers dive in as learners *of* their students, things get muddled. Sequences for reading, writing, and content that once seemed clear now seem more like sticking your hand into a mud bank and grasping for an oyster with a pearl. We have to *embrace* the muddiness of our chosen profession. It is one of the things that makes it so amazing and so fun, and it is the main reason that only the best and the brightest can handle the important work of helping students find their way. The paradigm of teacher as control freak needs to disappear, and soon. Our new mantra should be: Embrace the muddiness! Dive in! Get dirty!

Listening to teach and the classroom workshop are basic nonnegotiables for this type of work. It really isn't all that radical. Choose one thing to do differently, and see what you get. The beauty of learning is that everything is interconnected, so no matter where you start, it will affect a whole bunch of other things. There is really only one thing to do: dive in and persist in the pursuit of understanding these *really* important things. Children need us.

> *For millions of children, we can change the world. Let's start this school year. (Schmoker 2006, 164)*

Snip, snap, snout. This tale's told out!

References

Allington, Richard L. 2001. *What Really Matters for Struggling Readers: Designing Research-Based Interventions*. New York: Longman.

Alsop III, Fred J. 2001. *Smithsonian Handbook Birds of North America: Western Region*. New York: DK Publishing.

Anderson, Carl. 2000. *How's It Going?: A Practical Guide to Conferring with Student Writers*. Portsmouth, NH: Heinemann.

Angelillo, Janet. 2003. *Writing About Reading: From Book Talk to Literary Essays, Grades 3–8*. Portsmouth, NH: Heinemann.

Atwell, Nancie. 1998. *In the Middle: New Understandings About Writing, Reading, and Learning*. Portsmouth, NH: Heinemann.

Berger, Ron. 1996. *A Culture of Quality: A Reflection on Practice*. Providence, RI: Annenberg Institute for School Reform.

Black, Paul, and Dylan William. 1998, October. "Inside the Black Box: Raising Standards Through Classroom Assessment." Phi Delta Kappan, 139–48.

Calkins, Lucy. 1983. *Lessons from a Child*. Portsmouth, NH: Heinemann.

———. 1994. *The Art of Teaching Writing*. Portsmouth, NH: Heinemann.

———. 2001. *The Art of Teaching Reading*. Longman, NY: Addison-Wesley.

Chalofsky, Margie, Glen Finland, and Judy Wallace. 1992. *Changing Places: A Kid's View of Shelter Living*. Mt. Rainier, MD: Gryphon House.

Daniels, Harvey, and Nancy Steineke. 2004. *Mini-Lessons for Literature Circles*. Portsmouth, NH: Heinemann.

Didion, Joan. 1976, December 5. "Why I Write." *New York Times Magazine*, xx–xx.

Duckworth, Eleanor. 2001. *Tell Me More: Listening to Learners Explain*. New York: Teachers College Press.

Ewald, Wendy. 2002. *The Best Part of Me: Children Talk About Their Bodies in Pictures and Words*. New York: Little, Brown and Company.

Expeditionary Learning Schools. 2003. "Core Practice Benchmarks." *www.elschools.org/publications/books.html*

Forster, E. M. 1956. *Aspects of the Novel*. New York: Harvest Books.

Frank, Laurie. 2004. *Journey Towards the Caring Classroom: Using Adventure to Create Community in the Classroom and Beyond*. Oklahoma City: Wood 'N' Barnes.

Gladwell, Malcolm. 2006. "Million Dollar Murray: Why Problems of Homelessness May Be Easier to Solve than to Manage." *The New Yorker* February 13 and 20, 96–107.

Goldin-Dubois, Jonathan D. "Increasing Participation in American Politics." Common Cause, 2002.

Graves, Donald. 1983. *Writing: Teachers and Children at Work*. Portsmouth, NH: Heinemann.

Groch, Judith. 1969. *The Right to Create*. Boston: Little, Brown and Company.

Guning, Monica, and Elaine Pedlar. 2004. *A Shelter in Our Car*. San Francisco, CA: Children's Book Press.

Hansen, Jane. 1987. *When Writers Read*. Portsmouth, NH: Heinemann.

Harvey, Stephanie. 1998. *Nonfiction Matters: Reading, Writing, and Research in Grades 3–8*. York, ME: Stenhouse.

Harvey, Stephanie, and Anne Goudvis. 2000. *Strategies That Work: Teaching Comprehension to Enhance Understanding*. York, ME: Stenhouse.

Heaney, Seamus. 1996. Commencement Speech at the University of North Carolina at Chapel Hill. *http://www.ibiblio.org/ipa/poems/heaney/unc-commencement.php*. Retrieved May 14, 2007.

Hindley, Joanne. 1996. *In the Company of Children*. Portland, ME: Stenhouse.

Keene, Ellin O., and Susan Zimmerman. 1997. *Mosaic of Thought*. Portsmouth, NH: Heinemann.

"Key Excerpts from the Majority Opinion of the Supreme Court of the United States of America: New Jersey v. TLO." 1985. *www.landmarkcases.org*

Larner, Marjorie. 2004. *Pathways: Charting a Course for Professional Learning*. Portsmouth, NH: Heinemann.

Lopez, Barry. 1998. *Crow and Weasel*. New York: Farrar, Straus and Giroux.

Merriam-Webster's Collegiate Dictionary. 2001. (10th ed.) Springfield, MA: Merriam-Webster.

Miller, Debbie. 2002. *Reading with Meaning: Teaching Comprehension in the Primary Grades*. Portland, ME: Stenhouse.

Miller, Laura. 2005–2006. "Far from Narnia: Philip Pullman's Secular Fantasy for Children." *The New Yorker* December 26 and January 2, 52–75.

National Commission on Teaching and America's Future. 1996. *What Matters Most: Teaching for America's Future*. New York: National Commission on Teaching and America's Future.

National Research Council. 2000. *How People Learn: Brain, Mind, Experience and School*. Washington, DC: National Academy Press.

———. 2004. *Engaging Schools: Fostering High School Students' Motivation to Learn*. Washington, DC: National Academies Press.

Newkirk, Thomas. 2002. *Misreading Masculinity: Boys, Literacy, and Popular Culture*. Portsmouth, NH: Heinemann.

New Standards®. 2004. *Reading and Writing Grade by Grade*. Washington, DC: National Center on Education and the Economy.

Northwest Regional Educational Laboratory. "6 + 1 Trait Writing Rubric." Retrieved July 2006. *www.nwrel.org/assessment/dfRubrics/6plus1traits.pdf*.

Pearson, P. David, L. R. Roehler, J. A. Dole, and G. G. Duffy. 1992. "Developing Expertise in Reading Comprehension." In S. Jay Samuels and Alan E. Farstrup, eds., *What Research Has to Say About Reading Instruction*, 2d ed. Newark, DE: International Reading Association.

Perkins, David. 1992. *Smart Schools: Better Thinking and Learning for Every Child*. New York: Free.

Pullman, Philip. 1995. *The Golden Compass*. New York: Alfred A. Knopf.

———. 2000. *The Amber Spyglass*. New York: Alfred A. Knopf.

Ray, Katie Wood. 2006. *Study Driven*. Portmsouth, NH: Heinemann.

Ray, Katie Wood and Cleaveland, Lisa. 2004. *About the Authors: Writing Workshop with Our Youngest Writers*. Portsmouth, NH: Heinemann.

Ritchhart, Ron. 2002. *Intellectual Character: What It Is, Why It Matters, and How to Get It*. San Francisco: Jossey-Bass.

Schmoker, Mike. 2006. *Results Now*. Alexandria, VA: ASCD.

Schultz, Katherine. 2003. *Listening: A Framework for Teaching Across Differences*. New York: Teachers College Press.

Sedaris, David. 2000. *Me Talk Pretty One Day*. Boston: Little, Brown.

Sis, Peter. 2003. *The Tree of Life: Charles Darwin*. New York: Farrar, Straus and Giroux.

Sizer, Theodore, and Nancy Sizer. 1999. *The Students Are Watching*. Boston: Beacon.

Spandel, Vicki. 2006, Summer. "Assessing with Heart." *Journal of Staff Development* 27:3, 14–21.

———. 2006. Journal of Staff Development Press.

Stein, Gertrude. 1993. *The Autobiography of Alice B. Toklas*. New York: Modern Library.

Stiggins, R., Judith Arter, Jan Chappuis, and Steve Chappuis. 2002. *Classroom Assessment for Student Learning: Doing It Right—Using It Well*. Portland, OR: Assessment Training Institute.

Strunk, William Jr., and E. B. White. 2005. *The Elements of Style*. New York: Penguin.

Teste, Maria, and Karen Ritz. 1996. *Someplace to Go*. Morton Grove, IL: Albert Whitman.

Tomlinson, Carol Ann, and Jay McTighe. 2006. *Integrating Differentiated Instruction and Understanding by Design: Connecting Content and Kids*. Alexandria, VA: ASCD.

Tovani, Cris. 2000. *I Read It but I Don't Get It: Comprehension Strategies for Adolescent Readers*. Portland, ME: Stenhouse.

———. 2004. *Do I Really Have to Teach Reading? Content Comprehension Grades 6–12*. Portland, ME: Stenhouse.

Updike, John. 1955. *Assorted Prose*. Greenwich, CT: Fawcett Publications.

Vendela, Vida, ed. 2005. *The Believer Book of Writers Talking to Writers*. New York: McSweeney's Believer Books.

Wiggins, Grant, and Jay McTighe. 2005. *Understanding by Design: The Expanded 2nd Edition*. Alexandria, VA: ASCD.

Wiske, Martha S. 1998. *Teaching for Understanding: Linking Research with Practice*. San Francisco: Jossey-Bass.

Wolk, Steven. 2002. *Being Good: Rethinking Classroom Management and Student Discipline*. Portsmouth, NH: Heinemann.

Zemelman, Steven, Harvey Daniels, and Arthur Hyde. 1998. *Best Practice: New Standards for Teaching and Learning in America's Schools*. Portsmouth, NH: Heinemann.

Index